A Relationship Restored
Trends in U.S.-China Educational Exchanges, 1978-1984

David M. Lampton
with
Joyce A. Madancy and Kristen M. Williams
for
The Committee on Scholarly Communication
with the People's Republic of China

NATIONAL ACADEMY PRESS
Washington, D.C.   1986

National Academy Press   2101 Constitution Ave., NW   Washington, DC 20418

NOTICE: The project that is the subject of this report was sponsored by the Committee on Scholarly Communication with the People's Republic of China. Those responsible for the report were chosen for their special competences and with regard for appropriate balance. The report has been reviewed by a group other than the authors.

This study was made possible by funds provided by the Bureau of Educational and Cultural Affairs of the United States Information Agency under the authority of the Fulbright-Hays Act of 1961 and by the Ford Foundation.

The Committee on Scholarly Communication with the People's Republic of China (CSCPRC) is jointly sponsored by the American Council of Learned Societies, the Social Science Research Council, and the National Academy of Sciences. The Academy provides an administrative base for the CSCPRC.

Since the normalization of diplomatic relations between the United States and China in 1979, the CSCPRC has developed programs with the Chinese Academy of Sciences (CAS), the Chinese Academy of Social Sciences (CASS), and the State Education Commission, in addition to those with the China Association for Science and Technology (CAST), with whom CSCPRC began exchanges in 1972. Current activities include a program for American graduate students and postdoctoral scholars to carry out long-term study or research in affiliation with Chinese universities and research institutes; a short-term reciprocal exchange of senior-level Chinese and American scholars; a bilateral conference program; and an exchange of joint working groups in selected fields.

CSCPRC programs are funded by the National Science Foundation, the U.S. Information Agency, the National Endowment for the Humanities, the U.S. Department of Education, the Ford Foundation, the Henry Luce Foundation, the John D. and Catherine T. MacArthur Foundation, the Andrew W. Mellon Foundation, the Starr Foundation, and select corporations.

Library of Congress Catalog Card Number 86-61028

ISBN 0-309-03678-X

Printed in the United States of America

Steering Committee

Chairman
GEORGE BECKMANN, Provost, University of Washington

Members
CLARENCE ALLEN, Professor of Geology and Geophysics, California Institute of Technology

PETER D. BELL, President, Edna McConnell Clark Foundation

ROBERT BOCK, Dean of Graduate Studies, University of Wisconsin, Madison

JEFFREY B. GAYNER, Counselor for International Affairs, The Heritage Foundation

DAVID N. KEIGHTLEY, Professor of History, University of California, Berkeley

YUAN LEE, Professor of Chemistry, Lawrence Berkeley Laboratory, University of California, Berkeley

ROBERT MARSHAK, University Distinguished Professor, Physics, Virginia Polytechnic Institute and State University

DOUGLAS P. MURRAY, Executive Director, Trustees of Lingnan University; Executive Secretary, Committee on International Relations Studies with the PRC

SUSAN NAQUIN, Professor of History, University of Pennsylvania

WALTER A. ROSENBLITH, Foreign Secretary, National Academy of Sciences

ROBERT SCALAPINO, Director, Institute of East Asian Studies, University of California, Berkeley

iii

Research Team

Project Director
DAVID M. LAMPTON

Research and Editorial Consultants
PEGGY BLUMENTHAL
JOYCE A. MADANCY
SUSAN WALTON
TYRENE WHITE
KRISTEN M. WILLIAMS

Senior CSCPRC Staff Person
Patricia Tsuchitani

CSCPRC Staff Researchers
Evie Lotze
Pamela Peirce
Kyna Rubin
Danny Sebright

Foreword

One result of the resumption of relations between the United States and the People's Republic of China has been the development of extensive academic exchange programs. Thousands of Chinese students and scholars are studying and pursuing research at American colleges and universities, and many of them are returning to their homeland to play important roles in China's modernization programs. American students and scholars have been going to China in increasing numbers for study and research. Their efforts are expanding our knowledge of Chinese culture and society, and contributing to the social and natural sciences more generally.

This report embraces five major aims: (1) to describe these academic exchange relationships, (2) to analyze the nature of the exchanges, (3) to assess their impact, (4) to focus attention on issues and problems, and (5) to make policy recommendations.

The Steering Committee determined the initial outline and broad directions of the report and worked closely with Dr. David M. Lampton and his capable staff, who have prepared successive drafts of the report for our review. The Steering Committee therefore assumes responsibility for the report.

The Steering Committee believes that this report will be of broad interest to Americans and Chinese and that it will enhance efforts to improve and further develop academic ties between our two countries.

George Beckmann
Chairman, Steering Committee

Acknowledgments

This study was made possible by funds provided by the United States Information Agency (USIA) and the Ford Foundation.

Scholars, college and university administrators, foundation officials, and policymakers in both the United States and China need basic information about the magnitude, character, and impact of Sino-American academic exchanges between 1978 and 1984. Equally important, the academic relationship between China and the United States is changing so rapidly that it is time to step back and address some of the basic policy issues that have arisen. Therefore, in late 1983, the Committee on Scholarly Communication with the People's Republic of China (CSCPRC) constituted a Study Steering Committee chaired by University of Washington Provost George Beckmann, with the membership listed on page iii of this volume. A team was assembled to undertake the research and writing. The following report is the fruit of that labor. The research and writing team is greatly indebted to George Beckmann and the other members of the Steering Committee for providing essential guidance.

We are indebted to the many individuals and organizations that cooperated in the preparation of this study even though it is not possible to thank each one individually here. We must, however, express our gratitude to everyone at the universities, colleges, foundations, and professional associations who responded to our questionnaires. We particularly wish to acknowledge the assistance of those universities where Kyna Rubin of the CSCPRC conducted interviews: Appalachian State

University, Hofstra University, Oberlin College, Stanford University, the University of California at Berkeley, the University of Minnesota, and the University of Pittsburgh. Halsey L. Beemer, Jr., executive director of the International Advisory Panel of the Chinese University Development Project, was of great assistance in providing information concerning World Bank activities in China. Linda Reed at the National Association for Foreign Student Affairs in Washington, D.C., provided essential lists of names and guidance as we developed our survey questionnaires. In addition, Mary Ernst at the Council for International Exchange of Scholars compiled much of the information on Fulbright participants.

Our analysis of the impacts of academic exchanges on specific fields of study would have been impossible without the commissioned papers prepared by Joseph Birman of the City College of New York, Bruce A. Bolt of the University of California at Berkeley, Ronald Glaser of Ohio State University, Terry Sicular of Stanford University, and Sylvan Wittwer of Michigan State University. We would also like to thank Mary B. Bullock, staff director of the CSCPRC, and Michel C. Oksenberg of the University of Michigan for making available to us the draft chapters in their forthcoming volume on Sino-American exchanges. We appreciate the cooperation of contributors to that volume as well.

Cooperation in this undertaking was not limited to the private sector. Many U.S. government agencies and the dedicated individuals who work for them provided essential assistance. In particular, we thank Louise Crane, James Huskey, Joseph Simpson, and Gordon Tubbs of the USIA for their efforts on our behalf. Gene B. Marshall, Lynn Noah, Leon Slawecki, and Karl Olsson of the U.S. Embassy in Beijing each greatly facilitated our work, as did Peter Chase and James Keith of the U.S. Department of State in Washington, D.C. Finally, Ann I. Schneider of the Department of Education provided invaluable statistical information on Title VI and National Defense Foreign Language fellowships.

In the course of this study, some questions arose that only Chinese authorities could answer. We wish to thank China's Ministry of Education (which became the State Education Commission in 1985) and China's representatives in Washington, D.C., for their assistance in providing specific statistical and policy information.

To the staff of the CSCPRC and the National Academy of Sciences' Office of International Affairs, who endured nearly two years of dislocation on our behalf, we express our particular appreciation. Special thanks are due Mary B. Bullock and Victor Rabinowitch for their patience, guidance, and encouragement. Patricia Tsuchitani played an especially important role in this study, and we acknowledge her help with gratitude. Peggy Blumenthal and Tyrene White both played critical roles in the early stages of the study, particularly in questionnaire design and preliminary analysis. Chuck Rexroad at the National Academy of Sciences' Office of Automation Services helped design and implement our data analysis system and our archive of statistical information on the exchanges. We wish to express particular appreciation to Susan Walton, who edited the entire manuscript superbly and with good cheer. Finally, to Dale R. Corson, President Emeritus of Cornell University, we express our thanks for his advice and wise counsel.

David M. Lampton
Project Director

Contents

Technology Transfer: Issues for the Future, 175
Future Opportunities for Cumulative and Cooperative
    Research, 177
Involvement in Scientific, Economic, and Technical Change
    in China, 177
Notes, 179

List of Tables

Chapter 4

Appendix A

A Relationship Restored

Trends in U.S.-China
Educational Exchanges, 1978-1984

Executive Summary

In the 1970s, the United States and the People's Republic of China (PRC)* began to resume the educational and scientific exchanges that had been interrupted more than two decades earlier. Private American institutions, as well as the federal government, responded quickly and enthusiastically to the renewed ties and set up many diverse programs. Among people in both public and private life in the United States, there was a conscious recognition, or in some cases an intuitive sense, that the dramatic economic, social, and foreign policy experiments occurring in China would affect Americans. This sense of the importance of the current historical juncture in China has provided much of the impetus to the rapid growth in Sino-American academic exchange.

Today, educational and scientific exchange between the two nations far exceeds anything that was foreseen in the 1970s and constitutes one of America's largest and most rapidly growing academic relationships. Multiple official, bilateral agreements link the two countries, and a complex web of public and private arrangements offers extensive opportunities for exchange. The scale of Chinese society, the rate, breadth, and direction of change there, and the inherent value of scholarly interaction here and in China all should command the continued close special attention of both the public and private sectors in the United States. Educational and scientific exchange are and probably will remain piv-

---

*In this study, the terms *China* and *People's Republic of China (PRC)* are used interchangeably.

1

otal to America's relationship with the PRC. America's ties to China assume added importance given the United States' rapidly increasing economic, intellectual, and strategic stake in the entire Pacific region.

PRINCIPAL FINDINGS

The United States has become a major partner in the PRC's educational and scientific development. In the decade following the 1979 normalization of Sino-American diplomatic relations, more students and scholars from the PRC will have studied in the United States than did so between 1860 and 1950, when approximately 30,000 came here. About 50 percent of all PRC students and scholars currently sent abroad are coming to the United States. This influx of young and increasingly well-prepared Chinese suggests that the PRC will feel the effects of today's scholarly exchange for decades to come, particularly if China succeeds in providing a suitable intellectual climate for those who return.

Part of this impact will result from the sheer number of PRC Chinese who are coming to the United States. Roughly 19,000 PRC students and scholars came to the United States in calendar years 1979 through 1983. During academic year 1983–1984, there were approximately 12,000 PRC students and scholars in America; two-thirds of them were students. This figure represents only 6 percent of the total number of students from Asia studying here, and only about 2 percent of all foreign students in America. Nonetheless, between academic years 1981–1982 and 1983–1984, the number of PRC students grew much more rapidly than did the overall foreign student population in America. This trend is likely to continue.

For the PRC, academic exchange with the United States now plays an important role in its quest for modernization. The students and scholars who have come to the United States since 1979 have worked in fields that reflect the Chinese government's emphasis on science and technology as keys to modernization. Approximately two-thirds of all PRC students and scholars who hold J-1 visas (persons generally sponsored by the Chinese government after rigorous selection procedures) were in engineering, physical sciences, computer science, health sciences, life sciences, and mathematics. A little more than one-half of these students and scholars were in the physical and life sciences alone. In comparison, in academic year 1983–1984, fewer than 8 percent of *all* foreign students in the United States were studying the physical or life sciences. Relatively few PRC Chinese, however, have come to the United States to study management, agriculture, social sciences, or the humanities. This situation reflects both the availability of American funding and Chinese priorities. Among PRC students who are F-1 visa holders (persons generally in the United States under private arrangements), a slightly higher proportion studies the humanities and management than is true for "J-1s."

The majority of PRC Chinese students and scholars who come to the United States are from urban areas along China's coast, particularly Beijing, Shanghai, and Guangdong Province. Of those who arrived in 1983, a disproportionately small number came from the four large provinces of Anhui, Henan, Shandong, and Sichuan and the five autonomous regions. These administrative units account for almost 40 percent of China's population. These and other inland areas are eagerly seeking external ties, presenting new opportunities to American institutions that want to broaden the reach of educational and scientific exchange with the PRC.

Upon arrival in the United States, the PRC students and scholars are dispersed relatively uniformly across much of the country, although there are concentrations of them in New York and California.

The rapid growth in the number of PRC students and scholars on American campuses is due in part to the willingness of American colleges and universities to assume a substantial share of the costs. These institutions, using funds from a multitude of sources, paid over 40 percent of the estimated costs for PRC students and scholars issued J-1 visas from 1979 through 1983. During this same period, the percentage contributed by the PRC government declined from about one-half the estimated cost in 1979 to about one-third in 1983. This percentage, however, is still far higher than the proportion of funding that most foreign governments provide for J-1 students and scholars.

The significant expenditures by American universities reflect several factors. PRC J-1 visa holders have proved academically competitive in winning financial support, particularly in the physical and life sciences, where extensive teaching and research assistance is required. Moreover, in the United States, some of the technical fields of high priority to the PRC have adequate funding but an inadequate number of qualified American students. Thus, many American institutions have welcomed the opportunity to support highly competent and highly motivated students from the PRC in these fields.

About 100 American colleges and universities have formal exchange agreements with Chinese institutions, many of which were signed in the initial postnormalization rush to establish linkages of all descriptions. The proliferation of agreements also reflects the decentralized nature of American higher education and of American university administration, the entrepreneurial character of American academics, and the divergent motives of various constituencies within these institutions. For Chinese university and research institute leaders, these agreements offered a way to circumvent the slow central bureaucracy in Beijing, to overcome the hard-currency shortage, and to gain visibility for their institutions. Many of these agreements are inactive or moribund. Nonetheless, many agreements have worked very well, and these relationships should be strengthened. The advantages of some interinstitutional ties should be recognized: they give Americans entry into many different areas and types of institutions in China, they are flexible, and their reciprocal nature creates incentives for the Chinese to respond to American academic needs and desires.

Together with interinstitutional agreements, the many national-level exchange programs provide the flexibility to meet the needs of diverse constituencies. Sponsors of these programs include the federal government, private organizations, and scholarly and professional societies. Pluralism is one of the greatest strengths of the Sino-American educational and scientific relationship.

According to rough estimates by official Chinese sources, more than 3,500 American students and scholars went to the PRC to study or conduct research from 1979 through 1983, the majority for short-term language study. Of those who have conducted research in China, about two-thirds have been in the social sciences and humanities. Because American scholars' interests have been concentrated in these fields, access to Chinese society, as well as to archives, research institutes, and museums has been critical in the exchange relationship—and not without problems. There has been improvement since 1982, as scholars have been given somewhat greater access to archives and permitted to conduct limited survey research and interviewing. Nevertheless, many American scholars who might otherwise have gone to the PRC to undertake research have been discouraged by restrictions and difficulties. Natural scientists have encountered similar problems in securing access to field sites, particularly when they sought to collect and remove specimens.

Academic exchanges with China have affected fields of study within the two nations differently. In the United States, exchanges have had the greatest effect on Chinese studies. In China, the impact has been most apparent in scientific and technical fields. This simple dichotomy, however, obscures significant American contributions to economics, law, and, increasingly, the other social sciences in China, and also masks the contributions of China to the natural sciences in the United States (e.g., agriculture and cancer epidemiology). Even in fields such as physics, where most technical information flows from the United States to China, American programs have benefited from the infusion of exceptionally talented PRC students and scholars.

There is every reason to believe that the overwhelming majority of PRC students and scholars holding J-1 visas have thus far returned to their homeland upon completion of their work in the United States. Their successors probably will continue to do so as well, provided job opportunities in China remain attractive and the current "open" policy continues. These students and scholars generally are older, married, and either employed or enjoying secure employment prospects in China. An unknown, but undoubtedly much smaller, percentage of PRC students who are in the United States on F-1 visas will return home. These students—younger, less advanced in their careers, and frequently unmarried—may lack the bonds that tie the J-1 visa holders to their homeland. Whether these trends will continue depends on economic conditions in the United States and in China, on the types of visas issued to PRC students and scholars, and on feedback about how well the skills of returnees are being used.

For the PRC, the effects of academic exchange extend beyond training some of its most promising students and scholars. Over the last decade, exchanges have exposed China's educational, scientific, and political leaders to Western and American institutions. As reform has proceeded, the Chinese have considered an increasing range of institutional possibilities in the educational and scientific realms, although the leadership is aware of the dangers of indiscriminate borrowing from abroad. Whether or not Western institutions are appropriate models for the PRC, the expanded range of choice alone seems of great significance as Beijing's leaders tackle their nation's special problems.

ISSUES AND DIRECTIONS FOR THE FUTURE

Following is a list of eight issues and trends that now are affecting Sino-American academic relations or will do so in the future.

1. Americans and Chinese should focus upon *quality* and *responsiveness* in the exchange relationship, giving each nation's best students and scholars access to programs and resources that meet their needs. Strict numerical reciprocity, once the watchword, is thus not a useful concept, since the two societies are at very different stages of economic, scientific, and technical development and do not seek the same objectives from exchange. The PRC wants to train large numbers of its citizens in the United States, while Americans' scholarly interests in China have

generally focused on language training, individual research, and teaching. Nonetheless, a relationship in which the Chinese are responsive to American needs is critically important. For a more productive scholarly relationship, Americans must have greater access to China's research materials in the natural, social, and cultural environment and would benefit greatly from increased access to Chinese scholarly conferences. To make the best use of this access, Americans must also improve their Chinese language skills. As they ask for greater access to China, American institutions of higher education should continue to assure PRC students and scholars the same access to information on campus that all other members of the university community enjoy. American universities should not become instruments for the enforcement of export-control regulations. America is best served by its universities when information is exchanged freely.

2. University and college exchange activities should be encouraged and supported: they offer different but complementary advantages to national programs, such as responsiveness to local needs and flexibility. America's academic ties gain strength from their pluralism. For some American universities and colleges, interinstitutional agreements with the PRC are excellent channels through which faculty and students may gain access to China while at the same time making both American and Chinese campuses more international in character. Although many such agreements have not realized their full potential, consortia-like arrangements among American institutions with complementary needs and interests might revitalize their ties with the PRC. Funding should go to the most promising of these cooperative programs.

3. Although many images of China are held in the United States, that of the nation as a developing country is gaining increased currency. Arising naturally from this perception has been the increased involvement of American private and public educational and philanthropic institutions in economic change in China. As this report notes, applied science and agriculture are two of the areas in which Sino-American exchange should be further strengthened. Generally, the United States government supports cooperation in these fields in developing countries through its foreign-assistance programs. Which agency or agencies are most appropriate to support Sino-American cooperation in these fields is a decision fittingly left to others. Private American philanthropy has become extensively involved in providing grants to Chinese libraries and universities for faculty, disciplinary, and institutional development. This should promote increased opportunities for mutually beneficial collaborative undertakings in the future.

4. The United States must recognize that involvement in China's development effort carries certain risks. If this involvement is taken to extremes or is engaged in without great sensitivity to China's past experiences with the West, there could be a backlash. Inevitably, future internal debate concerning the course of China's development will focus on the costs and gains of foreign involvement in China and on how these relate to the social, political, and economic inequalities that arise with economic change. The issue of maintaining China's cultural identity will be ever present.

5. American funding agencies should continue to support American scholarship in China and about China, should continue to support programs to help the American public better understand China, and should increase support for Chinese language study. Past investments have proved invaluable. In the 1970s, both the U.S. government and private American institutions were able to move rapidly to establish and consolidate extensive ties with China because major human and financial investments had been made in Chinese studies during the 1960s and 1970s. Given today's rapidly expanding opportunities, there is an even greater need to enhance our capacity to understand and deal with China by maintaining the Chinese studies infrastructure of libraries, Title VI language and center grants, and opportunities for research and language study in the PRC, Hong Kong, and Taiwan.

Furthermore, American schools and funding agencies should sustain programs for Chinese language study at the undergraduate and graduate levels, target funds on students and on institutions that perform well, and encourage the promotion of disciplinary incentives that reward persons who maintain and improve language skills. Efforts also should be made to determine the utility and cost-effectiveness of Chinese language instruction at the secondary level.

6. Institutions in both the PRC and the United States should make further investments in training Chinese students in the humanities and social sciences (particularly American studies, international relations, and law), management, library sciences, and agriculture, recognizing that some of these disciplines are culture-bound. To date, only a relatively small proportion of Chinese students and scholars have come to the United States to study in these fields. Progress in these disciplines, however, will affect, in varying degrees, the success of China's economic strategy and the capacity of our two societies to interact effectively.

7. The PRC government's official stipend level should be increased to enhance the learning experience, language acquisition, and physical

well-being of PRC students and scholars in the United States. The level should approximate current figures listed in the Institute of International Education's annually updated publication, *Costs at U.S. Educational Institutions*. Parity with these levels is being required by an increasing number of American institutions. An increase in the official stipend level also is desirable to eliminate inequities now arising when universities do not enforce general foreign-student support levels for PRC students. American institutions of higher education should assure that these levels are maintained. This recommendation is aimed at both improving the experience of PRC students and scholars in America and reducing the problems on campuses that arise when foreign students and scholars have insufficient financial support.

8. Change in China is creating new possibilities for study, cooperative and multiyear research, applied-science cooperation, and American involvement in PRC education. Given the diversity of America's academic ties with the PRC, national leadership is needed in order to assess emerging exchange opportunities, to monitor trends in the relationship, to mobilize economic and intellectual resources, and to focus attention on the issue of access. Therefore, there continues to be a need for an institution such as the Committee on Scholarly Communication with the People's Republic of China (CSCPRC) that has performed these functions in the past.

1

The Sino-American Academic Relationship: Images and Interests

---

The images that Americans hold of China and their understanding of U.S. interests in the Sino-American relationship are pivotal to shaping the goals, the strategies, and the very character of academic exchanges with China. Defining American interests will always be difficult and controversial for two fundamental reasons. First, there are tensions between long-term and short-run goals of exchanges. To reap future benefits, investments must be made now—but they must be made with no guarantee that these immediate, tangible costs will be offset by long-range and less tangible future benefits. Second, China does not present a single face to the United States. Various politically potent segments of our society see different opportunities and challenges in China.

At least three general images of China are currently held in the United States, and each has its own implications for academic exchange. If China is perceived principally as a Third World nation at a comparatively low technical level, then American academic exchange policy might logically focus on building a long-term relationship by assisting China to develop economically and scientifically. With this view comes less concern about issues of strict numerical reciprocity and technology transfer. This perspective has significantly shaped this study and is exerting increasing influence on the thinking of American policy-makers.

If, however, China is viewed as a potential economic competitor, as it is by some American industries (e.g., textiles and, increasingly, agriculture), one might conclude that assisting Chinese economic and scientific development now could be detrimental to the United States later. Of course, the opposite conclusion also could be reached: that global economic competition is the engine that will drive the American economy forward. As China, or enclaves within China, develop economically, this image will exert increasing influence over the formulation of policy toward China in the United States.

Finally, if China is viewed as either a regional or a strategic military power that will, in the course of military modernization, present security problems to the United States and its allies, concerns about the transfer of technology will be heightened. To the degree that China is perceived as an ideological threat, these concerns will be still greater. Insofar as the PRC's military power is believed to offset Soviet armed might, such concerns may diminish. Since the early 1980s there has been a gradual reduction in the degree to which China is viewed primarily in strategic and military terms.

China, of course, has all of these dimensions. It is a nuclear power with at least a nascent submarine missile-launching capacity, but it is also a country with very low per capita income. It is a country where village society coexists with pockets of modernity along the coast that have the potential to become world-class economic competitors. The entrepreneurial ability of the Chinese is legendary, yet they have been enmeshed in a sociopolitical system that has frustrated this entrepreneurship. The PRC is still a self-declared Marxist–Leninist state but one in which the impulse for reform seems comparatively strong and the Confucian ethic of intellectuals serving the state reigns supreme. China has many talented scientists and scholars, and yet it is a society with a very significant degree of illiteracy. The issue is, therefore, how academic exchanges fit into this complex web of images and reality. What are *American* interests?

The next step toward understanding the dynamics of exchange lies in recognizing that the Chinese have clearly pursued their own interests in designing an official program to send students and scholars abroad. Since late 1978, Beijing has systematically followed a plan (see Chapter 3) that specifies the number of persons the Chinese government will send abroad for training, the fields in which they will study, the duration of their stay, the strategies to obtain maximal foreign funding, and the age and professional standing of these individuals. In addition, there are many "self-paying" PRC students coming to the United States who are outside this detailed plan.

The importance China's elite places on the program to send students and scholars abroad is clearly evident in the following account of the 1984 National Conference on Sending Students Abroad to Study:

The CPC [Communist Party of China] Central Committee and the State Council attach great importance to sending students to study abroad. . . . The CPC Central Committee Secretariat . . . has made it a practice to discuss this question almost every year. In 1983 Comrades Hu Yaobang, Zhao Ziyang, Peng Zhen, and Deng Yingchao personally talked to those going to study abroad. . . . Last March the CPC Central Committee and the State Council again elucidated the principles, main points, targets, and avenues of sending students to study abroad, and their guidance is an important guarantee for doing our job well.[1]

Given the purposefulness with which the Chinese have pursued these goals, American academe and policymakers must think equally clearly about American interests, both long- and short-term. Herein, however, lies a difficulty; America is a pluralistic society in which interests are defined differently by various groups. Although U.S. societal and governmental structures make it difficult to achieve consensus, unified action, and policy consistency, the United States can and should identify the range of interests to be considered.

Americans seek to meet multiple objectives in academic exchanges with China. Some want to promote charitable objectives or gain scientific and technical knowledge to advance global science and technology, while others may seek access to Chinese society and culture to better understand one of the world's oldest civilizations and to advance the understanding of fundamental social processes. Some constituencies also want to promote American commercial interests in the PRC, while others want to bring to the United States some of the world's most talented students and scholars to enrich teaching and research at American institutions.

These multiple objectives are matched by equally varied opinions about the effects of exchange. Some observers assert that what is widely regarded as the positive flow of scientific and technical information toward China has not been, or cannot be, offset by American gains. Other analysts point to the generally high quality of the Chinese coming to the United States and underscore their positive impact on American graduate programs and on the overall quality of American campus life.

Although the United States has already benefited from the academic exchange relationship by acquiring previously unavailable scientific data, greater knowledge of Chinese society, and high-quality foreign students on American campuses, the relationship should not, and probably cannot, be justified purely by short-term effects.

In the face of an unpredictable future, what long-term national interests should guide American academic ties with China? Three are of paramount importance. First, China's present "open" policies present a unique opportunity to inform the perspective of a generation of Chinese intellectual and technical leaders who will be active well into the next century. While one cannot simplistically assume that exposure to America will assure future friendly relations much less policy agreement, it is undeniable that the comparatively few students and scholars trained in the West in the pre-1949 era have played a very important role in the present opening up to the West. There is no reason to believe that their contemporary successors will be less influential.

Second, the United States, like the rest of the world, has a positive stake in the success of China's modernization effort. It would be folly to think that China's "success" or "failure" hinges on decisions made by Americans, but America's attitude toward China's development effort is important. It is hard to imagine long-term regional peace and stability if China is struggling economically and is alienated by American aloofness to the aspirations of the Chinese people.

Finally, China's land, society, and culture all are exciting areas for research, offering the prospect for significantly advancing knowledge. Whether for purposes of studying global geosphere-biosphere interactions, demographic change, social behavior, or art, access to China is valuable to both American and global scholarship. Present American investments in Chinese professional training and scientific instrumentation are laying the foundation for meaningful, future joint research and cooperation.

The short-term interests of the United States should not yield entirely to long-term considerations. Indeed, America must achieve some short-term objectives if its relationship with China is to remain strong. It is essential that the Chinese respond positively to American requests for research access to China more frequently than they have in the past. The watchword in the relationship should be responsiveness, not necessarily strict numerical reciprocity. As long as Americans know that the Chinese are making good-faith attempts to meet their requests—requests that must remain sensitive to Chinese conditions—the basis for an increasingly fruitful relationship exists. America's continued pursuit of its own short-term interests, as well as Chinese responsiveness, is a precondition for achieving the long-term objectives that are the principal raison d'être of the relationship for *both* countries. Likewise, Americans must be responsive to Chinese needs and desires.

Any assessment of American or Chinese interests in academic exchange must rest on a thorough analysis of both the scope of the relationship and its impacts to date. Thus, this study begins by analyzing heretofore unavailable quantitative data on the numbers of students and scholars from each country, their fields of study, sources of financing, sociological attributes, and length of stay. But it then probes deeper by addressing the following questions: (1) What impact has the exchange process had on selected fields of study in both countries? (2) What problems have students and scholars from each society encountered in carrying out their work? (3) How easily have students and scholars from China been "reabsorbed" on returning to their homeland? (4) What financial and institutional problems have arisen? (5) How adequate has the preparation of both American and Chinese students and scholars been for their experience, particularly in language training? (6) How have problems of access and technology transfer affected research and study in each country?

Three overriding themes emerge in the following pages. First, fundamental social, cultural, and economic forces in the two societies have produced remarkable continuity in the nature of the Sino-American academic relationship. The problems that Americans and Chinese have encountered in the academic exchange relationship in the 1970s and 1980s are similar, in general, to those confronted during scholarly interchange prior to the 1950s.

Second, the rapidity with which academic exchanges have become "normalized" is striking. American universities and colleges moved quickly to treat PRC students and scholars like other foreign students and scholars in the United States, and the PRC students and scholars adapted swiftly to the American system in terms of providing admissions offices with improved academic documentation, competing successfully for available financial resources, and performing well academically.

Finally, the rapid growth in the number of PRC students and scholars on American campuses, the comparatively few Americans who are qualified and motivated to spend long periods of study and research in China, and the PRC's status as a developing country all vitiate the concept of strict numerical reciprocity in the two nations' academic relationship. Instead, responsiveness and quality are more appropriate guiding principles for Sino-American educational ties. Chinese authorities should be increasingly responsive to American scholars' needs for access to natural, social, and cultural phenomena in the PRC. Americans should be better prepared linguistically and culturally to avail themselves of those expanding opportunities. Improving the relationship qualitatively is as important as expanding it quantitatively.

The Sino-American scientific and educational relationship is moving toward a future for which the past, with its focus on individual students and scholars, has only partially prepared both sides. China is looking to the West and the United States for alternatives to at least some of the

Soviet-style institutional structures built in the 1950s, whether in the administration of higher education, the funding of scientific research, or the provision of high-quality scientific and technical advice to the political elite. As China seeks to reform its system, there are enormous possibilities and important risks for the United States. One risk is that America will be unable, or unwilling, to provide the resources to meet Chinese expectations. For their part, the Chinese must recognize, in the future as in the past, that foreign involvement cannot be the keystone of their development process. As a Chinese student in Zhejiang Province recently put it, "We must search for the 'middle way' between rejecting foreign experience and attaching too much importance to it."

NOTE

1. Foreign Broadcast Information Service, Nov. 30, 1984, p. K8, from *Xinhua*, Nov. 29, 1984.

2

The Context for Academic Exchange

Although this study focuses primarily on American academic exchanges with China in the late 1970s and early 1980s, it analyzes those exchanges in a comparative and historical context. Both China and the United States have scientific, technical, and educational relations that span the globe, and each country's present interaction with the other must be seen against the entire backdrop of those relations. For example, in academic year 1983–1984, 21,960 students from Taiwan were studying in the United States, more than from anywhere else. In that same year, the People's Republic of China was not among the top 10 in numbers of students studying in the United States, while strikingly smaller societies such as Malaysia, Korea, Japan, and Hong Kong were (this probably will change soon, as discussed in Chapter 3).[1] Placing America's academic relations with China in a comparative perspective helps distinguish the unique aspects of the relationship from the characteristics common to U.S. academic ties with Third World countries generally. Similarly, examining China's handling of its educational exchanges with Japan and the Soviet Union helps put the Sino-American relationship in perspective.

The Sino-American academic exchanges of the 1970s and 1980s were preceded by more than eight decades—from the 1870s to 1950—of educational and scientific interaction. The links between the two eras are strong. Personal connections, lessons learned, and patterns of interaction from the earlier period influenced the character of present activities; numerous characteristics of earlier exchanges endure today. In

15

many respects, the Sino-American educational relationship resumed in the 1970s and 1980s where it had left off in the early 1950s.

PRE-1950 SINO-AMERICAN ACADEMIC RELATIONS

Chinese academic relations with the United States have been closely linked to basic sociopolitical trends in China and the West since the mid-nineteenth century. For China, the question of how to relate to American and Western education and science has been tied to more fundamental questions: Can China change economically and still preserve valued elements of its culture? Which elites should dominate the Chinese polity? What values should its leaders embrace? How much economic growth should be sacrificed for equality? How dependent on the external world should China be? Will scientific and educational interaction with America and the West foster independence or dependence? As these questions suggest, Chinese political leaders and intellectuals have been, and will continue to be, ambivalent about ties to the West.

Americans, too, have viewed academic ties to China through the lenses of their own priorities and values. Educational relations with China have always served many purposes for many groups. For some, educational ties developed from missionary impulses, either secular or religious; for others, these links have served economic, political, or strategic interests; and for still others, China has represented a scientific and intellectual frontier important to the advancement of global knowledge.

Motivating all of these groups, however, has been the belief that China was malleable and that if they did not leave their imprint first, someone else would. The potential of educational ties with China has always sparked the imaginations of leaders and interest groups— American universities have been particularly responsive to Chinese students and scholars. At the same time, scientific, technological, and educational relationships have often served the aspirations of those who hope to impart their cultural and political values to the Chinese. Edmund J. James, president of the University of Illinois, summarized this notion early in this century:

China is upon the verge of a revolution. . . . Every great nation in the world will inevitably be drawn into more or less intimate relations with this gigantic development. . . . The United States ought not to hesitate. . . . The nation which succeeds in educating the young Chinese of the present generation will be the nation which for a given expenditure of effort will reap the largest possible returns in moral, intellectual, and commercial influence. . . . We may not admit the Chinese laborer, but we can treat the Chinese student decently, and extend to him the facilities of our institutions of learning.[2]

Americans were not the only ones to see educational and scientific links to China as avenues of influence; on occasion, our friends and competitors both have worried about the consequences of America's presumed influence. For example, in 1921, *The Daily Mail* of London carried an article that voiced concern about the long-term effect of Tsinghua (Qinghua) College's program to send students to the United States.

Educated under the American system, constantly reminded of the happy associations of their school days through the influential alumni organization, aware that they owe their scholarships to American justice, and saturated with American sentiment by five to eight years' residence in the country, they will look to the United States solely for cooperation in the troublous years to come."[3]

For *both* Chinese and Americans, such dynamics and expectations have made disillusionment an ever-present threat. That threat has materialized on many occasions. The Chinese government often expected more of returned scholars than they could deliver, and the returned scholars themselves did not always have the impact they anticipated or receive the treatment they felt was their due.[4] For Americans, China has been less malleable and results have been slower in coming than was hoped. If one lesson has emerged from the pre-1950 experience, it is that both sides must moderate their expectation that academic exchanges will produce immediate change. Both sides can anticipate ups and downs in their relationship.

Many of the patterns, trends, and issues that characterized Sino-American educational ties persisted throughout the pre-1950 era despite the almost continual political and social turbulence that China experienced since the 1870s. A number of these patterns are equally apparent today. (See Tables A-1 and A-2.)

Perhaps the most fundamental trend was China's continual interest in sending its students to study in the West. This was an enduring feature of Chinese educational policy throughout the late Qing Dynasty, the early Republic, the warlord era of 1915 to 1927, and the Guomindang years. In each period, the Chinese state had slightly different objectives in sending students abroad, but the practice was always motivated by a belief that China needed Western science, technology, and learning in its national effort to remain independent, improve its economic welfare, and enhance its power in the world.

Training in the West, particularly in the United States and Great Britain, conferred high status on the returned student. This bred resentment among graduates of less prestigious institutions in China, inflated the expectations of the select few who studied abroad, and produced in them what many Chinese considered arrogant behavior.[5]

In contrast to their government-sponsored counterparts, Chinese students able to pay their own expenses were variously encouraged and discouraged from going abroad by their political leaders; they frequently felt that their own government discriminated against them, both while they were abroad and after they returned, *if* they returned. This discrimination is an equally relevant issue in the 1980s, as evidenced in the open discussion of the problem of reabsorbing returned students and scholars in the official Chinese press today.

Most of the Chinese students who pursued long-term study leading to the completion of advanced degrees did so in the United States. In the pre-1950 era, approximately 30,000 Chinese students came to America, and at least 10 times as many studied in Japan, for reasons of proximity, cost, and cultural affinity. But during that time, Chinese students earned 20 times as many Ph.D.s in the United States as in Japan.[6] Although this reflects the different degree-granting structures in Japan and the United States, its practical effects were to concentrate academic status among graduates of American institutions. These American-trained Chinese have played a crucial role in promoting Western science in China and in reestablishing scholarly ties with the West in the 1970s and 1980s.

Chinese reformers, like Zhang Zhidong (Chang Chih-tung), long ago realized that simply sending younger students abroad to study was not enough to institutionalize change. It also was important to send more senior persons abroad. In Chang's words, "Much more benefit can be derived from study abroad by older and experienced men than by the young, by high mandarins rather than by petty officials."[7] Today's "visiting scholars," then, had their antecedents.[8]

Throughout the first half of the twentieth century, women constituted a fluctuating fraction of the Chinese students coming to the United States. In 1914, 11 percent of Chinese students in America were women, and by 1925, this percentage had risen to 39, a rather high level considering the era and China's prevailing traditions with respect to the education of women.[9] In 1983, 23 percent of PRC Chinese students and scholars in the United States were women. There are several possible reasons for the comparatively high proportion of women sent abroad in the pre-1949 era, including the greater percentage of undergraduates sent abroad by China at that time, the greater emphasis on social sciences and humanities, and the impact of missionary education in pre-Communist China.

Despite continual debate over the fields that Chinese students should pursue abroad, engineering remained the centerpiece of each pre-1950 regime's program in the United States. Almost without exception, Chinese regimes placed agricultural science at the bottom of the priority list. Natural sciences received continual heavy emphasis, and the humanities and social sciences were subject to fluctuating attention. Within the social sciences, economics generally held the most attraction.[10] (See Table A-2.)

In the past, as now, field "selection" reflected American funding priorities as well as the conscious choices of the Chinese state or of individual students. Because American funding was relatively plentiful for the natural sciences, Chinese students abroad were more frequently able to complete degree programs in these fields. In all fields, financial considerations continually intruded into the educational relationship. The Chinese often expressed astonishment at the cost of a foreign education, while Americans sometimes felt that China sent students abroad without adequate financial support,[11] as is the case today (see Chapter 5).

When central power was relatively weak, China's provinces took the lead in supporting students abroad. In such periods, each province tried to increase its own competitive position, which included building foreign ties and intellectual resources. In the early part of this century, provincial authorities aggressively promoted foreign study. More than half the Chinese students in Japan in 1906 held Chinese government scholarships, most from provincial governments.[12] A similar dynamic emerged with the renewal of Sino-American educational ties in the late 1970s and mid-1980s, when Chinese provinces were being given more responsibilities and power.

Despite the keen interest of many provinces in foreign study, approximately three-quarters of the Chinese students who went abroad between 1909 and 1945 came from five eastern provinces: Guangdong (Kwangtung), Jiangsu (Kiangsu), Zhejiang (Chekiang), Fujian (Fukien), and Hebei (Hopeh)[13] (see Table A-1). The actual geographic range was likely to be even narrower; the students were probably from the major metropolitan areas within these five provinces. This imbalance existed both because intellectual and economic resources were concentrated in the lower Yangzi Delta area and because many Chinese immigrated to the United States from southeastern China. Hence, this trend was further reinforced by the earlier groups of Chinese whose immigration to the United States from China's coastal areas gave subsequent travelers relatives in the United States from whom to draw support. As a result of these trends, China's heartland was effectively left out of this aspect of the educational interaction. The question remains: Did the United States build a relationship with China or only with the relatively cosmopolitan and urbanized coastal elite?

Although the Chinese expected students and scholars to return with Western knowledge, they did not want the travelers westernized in other ways. In the pre-1950 era, the Chinese authorities felt responsible for supervising the moral and political development of their students abroad and for assuring that students remained rooted in Chinese culture.[14] This provoked some problems. In 1944, for example, a major controversy erupted among American academics, the U.S. government, and the Chinese government over the Chinese Ministry of Education's assertion that "all the thoughts and deeds of self-supporting students residing abroad must absolutely be subject to the direction and control of the Superintendent of Students of the Embassy."[15]

In 1948 and 1949, the United States' new Fulbright Agreement with China provided access to China for U.S. scholars in all fields, albeit under the conditions of hyperinflation and civil war. The program was designed to include American graduate students in Chinese area studies, and grants were available to American researchers in all disciplines to do field projects.[16] During this two-year period, a few Americans taught in China, concentrating on language, American literature, and history. Alumni of the Fulbright Program (e.g., Derk Bodde, Arthur Steiner, W. Theodore de Bary, Harriet Mills, and Frederick Mote) contributed substantially to Chinese studies in the United States subsequently.

The global context, the economic and political circumstances in each society, and the leaders on both sides have changed, but many of the problems and objectives outlined above persist today. The Sino-American educational exchange programs of the 1970s and 1980s are more a renewal than a beginning.

SINO-SOVIET EXCHANGES, 1950–1960

Although the founding of the People's Republic of China in 1949 did not alter the fundamental goals and priorities of China's educational exchange policies, the decisive political realignment did produce significant changes in the destination of Chinese students going abroad and in the origin of foreign students entering China. The new Communist leadership swiftly centralized control over all levels of education throughout the country and moved to eliminate the "bourgeois" orientation of urban intellectuals. These developments, along with the Korean War and the Cold War, eliminated the United States as a potential destination for students and scholars. At the same time, China established exchange programs with the Soviet Union, which grew throughout the 1950s.

Estimates of the total number of Chinese trained in the USSR from 1950 to 1960 vary substantially. One source places the number of students at about 13,500 for the entire decade. Another source asserts that approximately 38,000 Chinese received training in the USSR between 1950 and 1967: 1,300 scientists, 1,200 instructors, 8,000 technicians, 20,000 workers, and 7,500 students.[17] By 1958, UNESCO statistics indicate that the Chinese comprised by far the largest concentration (nearly 5,000) of foreign students in the Soviet Union,[18] although during China's First Five-Year Plan (1953–1957), perhaps half the number planned actually went to the Soviet Union.[19] More than 3,200 students were still in the Soviet Union in 1960.[20]

Although China's strategic and political alignment changed greatly in 1950, many aspects of its foreign-study efforts showed considerable continuity with earlier programs. The Communists had the same objectives in sending students abroad, targeted many of the same fields for emphasis, and maintained the same role for the state in managing students abroad. Foreign students in China, too, showed the same dissatisfactions under the new regime. Like their earlier counterparts, Chinese students in the Soviet Union were supervised by the PRC embassy in Moscow and were assigned to educational institutions and academic disciplines according to Beijing's priorities. During China's First Five-Year Plan, about 70 percent of the Chinese students in the Soviet Union devoted themselves to scientific and engineering fields, while the small minority studying in other nations (principally in Eastern Europe) concentrated more on languages, history, literature, and the arts.[21] In this respect, the Communist regime significantly narrowed China's educational objectives during the 1950s. Although China consistently emphasized engineering and science in its academic exchanges from the 1870s to the 1950s, business, social sciences, and humanities received much greater emphasis during those years than they did in the 1950s.

Once in the Soviet Union, most Chinese students stayed from three to six years. As in the pre-Communist period, students returned from studying abroad with advantages that made them arrogant in the eyes of their peers and bred resentment among those who had been educated solely in China. In 1957, for example, the deputy director of the Institute of Mechanical Sciences said, "The stock of the student who has been to Russia rises sky high on his return. He gets a cushy job and a princely salary and enjoys all sorts of privileges, including meals, special messes, without having to prove his worthiness."[22] Upon returning, many of these foreign-trained Chinese worked in the many enterprises constructed with Russian assistance during the First Five-Year Plan.

As with Chinese study in the USSR, considerable uncertainty surrounds the number of Soviet students and scholars who went to China during the 1950s. One estimate puts the number of economic, cultural, educational, and technical experts who went to China during this period at more than 10,000.[23] Evidence points to relatively modest numbers of students. A first-hand report by Rene Goldman, a Polish student who studied in Beijing from 1953 to 1958, indicates that although his university traditionally had hosted many foreign students, he encountered no Soviet students until 1957, when two groups totaling more than 100 arrived.[24] Further evidence that the flow of Soviets to China was modest appeared in a 1957 Chinese news article that stated that an arriving group of 50 Russian students represented the largest group in the history of the exchange relationship up to that time.[25] Almost all the Soviet and Eastern European students were confined to Beijing,[26] while Korean and Vietnamese scholars apparently were spread more evenly across China.[27]

The presence of Soviet and Eastern European students in China did cause some friction. Some of the problems arose in the late 1950s as China tried to carve out an independent domestic development and foreign policy line during the Great Leap Forward. Other frictions reflected China's longstanding system for dealing with foreigners, which isolated them from the Chinese. All foreign students, including those from the Communist Bloc, lived in separate dormitories, ate different food, felt closely supervised and constrained in their choice of friends, and had generally rocky relations with the foreign affairs offices (*wai ban*) responsible for looking after them.[28] Indeed, with the modest resumption of educational exchange between China and the USSR in the 1980s, these frictions quickly reemerged.[29]

In 1958, Beijing's leaders issued revised guidelines for foreign students who wished to enter the People's Republic of China. Thereafter, according to Rene Goldman, China would admit only one or two students from any one nation who would "come for one or two years of study of the Chinese language."[30] By the early 1960s, following China's split with the USSR, virtually all of the Soviet and European students had been replaced by students of Asian, African, or Latin American origin,[31] a change that reflected a fundamental shift in Chinese foreign policy in the wake of the rift with Moscow.

As the United States expands ties with China, the earlier Sino-Soviet collaboration provides perspective on today's relations in two ways. First, the PRC's current interest in American and Western educational and scientific institutions stems, in part, from the rigidities of the Soviet-style educational institutions created in the 1950s. Thus, China is reacting against the separation of teaching from research, the noncompetitive allocation of research resources, the separation of technical training from broader social science and humanistic concerns, the deemphasis of management, and the overcentralization of university and research institute administration. Second, the Soviet experience suggests that a Western country enthusiastically exporting its experience to a China looking for a model can produce disillusionment in the Chinese. It is important that Americans be forthright with the Chinese and with themselves about the limitations on the applicability of our experience to their situation.

GLOBAL SETTING OF CURRENT SINO-AMERICAN EXCHANGES

The flow of students and scholars between China and the United States must be viewed in the context of each country's global scholarly connections. America and Asia are becoming increasingly interdependent, both in economic and academic terms. In 1982, America's trans-Pacific trade exceeded the flow across the Atlantic for the first time.[32] In academic year 1983–1984, Asia (including India) had 132,270 students in the United States, more than twice the number from the Middle East, which ranked second. Even more important, the rate of growth in the number of foreign students from Asia in America between academic years 1982–1983 and 1983–1984 (10.5 percent) was higher than for any world region.[33]

Taiwan (with 21,960 students), Malaysia (18,150), Korea (13,860), India (13,730), Japan (13,010), and Hong Kong (9,420) all had more students in the United States than did China (8,140) in academic year 1983–1984.[34] Note, however, that about one-third of the PRC Chinese who have come to the United States thus far have been nonmatriculated "visiting scholars" who are *not* counted in the figure just cited.

Although PRC students and scholars currently comprise a modest percentage of foreign students in the United States, China has made sending students here a major priority in its total exchange effort. According to imprecise Chinese statistics, since 1978 (presumably through 1983), 26,000 officially sponsored "students" (almost certainly including "visiting scholars") and an additional 7,000 self-paying students have studied in other countries. Already, this is probably double the number of Chinese sent abroad for study during the entire 1950–1977 period.[35] Of the total number of PRC students and scholars who have studied abroad since 1978, between 50 and 60 percent have come to the United States. Other partial data from the Chinese Ministry of Education confirm that the United States is a major target of the PRC's academic exchange plan. For example, between September 1982 and April 1984, 60 percent of the Chinese faculty from 28 key universities who were selected by the Chinese Ministry of Education to study abroad under the World Bank's University Development Project (see Chapter 4) have gone or will go to the United States (see Table A-3).

Statistics from the United States reflect the same trend. Between 1979 and 1983, 19,872 American student/scholar visas were issued to citizens of the PRC (see Table 3-1 in the next chapter). Although this figure probably includes slight double-counting (because the same individual could have received more than one visa in the period), it is 60 percent of the total Chinese students and scholars reported to have gone abroad.

Japan, in contrast, received less than 10 percent of the students and scholars that China sent abroad from 1979 to mid-1983. During that period, 1,439 PRC "government-sponsored" students and scholars went to Japan, as did an additional 805 privately sponsored (or "self-paying") students, for a total of 2,244 (see Table A-4).[36] A similar pattern emerges from the World Bank data cited above. Of the Chinese faculty selected to study abroad under the University Development Project, only 6 percent have gone or will go to Japan. In mid-1984, Chinese State Councillor Fang Yi was paraphrased by *China Daily* as having said, "Though some progress has been made in recent years, Sino-Japanese scientific cooperation and exchange remains a 'weak link' compared with the close ties between the two nations in finance, trade, and culture."[37]

Comparisons of the general foreign student population in the United States to the PRC Chinese who have come here reveal several differences that are examined in greater detail in Chapter 3. Among all foreign students here in academic year 1983–1984, 30 percent were women,[38] though in calendar year 1983, 23 percent of the Chinese students and scholars issued visas to travel to the United States were women (see Table A-5).

In other respects as well—field of study, visa status, and rate of growth—China displays patterns that are distinct from those of other countries. Although 8 percent of all foreign students in the United States studied physical and life sciences in academic year 1983–1984, 34 percent of Chinese officially sponsored students and scholars did so in calendar year 1983. Four percent of all foreign students in the United States studied in the health sciences during academic year 1983–1984, while 10 percent of officially sponsored Chinese students and scholars were in the health sciences in the United States during 1983.[39]

A dramatic difference exists between the visa status of Chinese students and scholars in the United States and that of all foreign students. In academic year 1982–1983, 84 percent of all foreign students here had F visas and thus were neither sponsored by their home government nor subject to America's requirement that they leave the United States for two years prior to any possible application for a change of residency status (see "two-year rule" in the Glossary).[40] In 1982, only 26 percent of Chinese students and scholars entering the United States had F-visa status. A full 74 percent of Chinese students *and* scholars issued visas in 1982 held J visas and more than 80 percent of them were subject to the two-year rule. Similar percentages held for Chinese students and scholars in 1983 (see Table 3-1). Thus, Chinese students and scholars probably are more likely to return to their homeland than are foreign students in general. Furthermore, the Chinese government assumes a potentially larger financial liability per given number of students and scholars in the United States and therefore has more incentive to push its "officially sponsored" students to find financial support abroad. As discussed later, this pressure has been considerable.

Finally, while the overall number of foreign students in the United States grew by less than 1 percent in academic year 1983–1984 and the number of South and East Asian students grew by 10.5 percent, the number of students from China increased by 30.7 percent between the academic years 1982–1983 and 1983–1984—from 6,230 PRC students in 1982–1983 to 8,140 PRC students in 1983–1984.[41] Such a high growth rate is not unusual for a new program starting with few students. The question is how rapidly that number will continue to expand.

Some evidence suggests that the swift growth will continue. In late 1984, Chinese State Councillor Zhang Jingfu announced that in 1985 China intended to boost by one-third the number of officially sponsored students *and* scholars sent abroad.[42] Finally, in January 1985, China's State Council issued "Draft Regulations on Self-Supported Study Abroad," which encourage any interested Chinese citizen to apply for permission to study abroad at his or her own expense, regardless of that person's academic qualifications, age, or employment status in China.[43] Although the impact of these regulations remains to be seen, it appears likely that many more students holding F visas will come to the United States from China.

In sum, China currently has identified the United States as the principal site abroad for educating its students and scholars. The rate of increase in the number of PRC students in America has been comparatively high and is likely to remain so in the near future, although the number of PRC students here is still small relative both to other foreign student populations in the United States and to China's size.

POLICIES, PERCEPTIONS, AND THE DYNAMICS OF ACADEMIC EXCHANGE
IN THE 1970s AND 1980s

The nature of the Sino-American academic exchange relationship since the 1970s has been decisively influenced by changing policies and perceptions in both China and America. Beijing's domestic and foreign policies have increasingly emphasized applied science, the role of universities as both teaching *and* research institutions, the training of younger persons, the utility of peer review, the competitive allocation of resources, and the importance of the management sciences. In some cases, these policy alterations in Beijing have been followed by changes in the kind and number of persons coming to the United States and in their fields of study. As mentioned above, in late 1984 and early 1985, Beijing decided to permit more persons to study abroad. Finally, in the spring of 1985, the government announced far-reaching reforms of the science, technology, and education systems, which were aimed at decentralizing the management and financing of these sectors and forging closer links between the economy and research activities.

The education reforms adopted in May and June 1985, which brought multiple changes for higher education, are already affecting Sino-American academic exchange and increasingly will influence it in the future. The reforms are designed to give Beijing enhanced control over general education policy by folding the former Ministry of Education into a new, higher-level State Education Commission with representation from other commissions and ministries.[44] At the same time, Beijing has given individual institutions of higher education more decision-making power over finance, personnel, curricula, teaching materials, and use of locally raised funds. Individual schools were authorized to admit students at the request of employers (who would pay tuition and costs) and admit "a small number" of self-paying students. These two new categories of student are in addition to those admitted under the central enrollment plan. In effect, schools are being given incentives to increase facility utilization and revenues by admitting paying students. Finally, institutions of higher education are being encouraged to establish economic relationships with business enterprises to link research more closely to production and to raise revenue for the institutions.[45]

These changes are likely to produce several effects on academic exchanges; indeed, some already are apparent. First, American universities and exchange organizations will be dealing more with leaders of individual institutions of higher education in China who are empowered to make decisions. Second, these leaders now have greater incentive to assess exchange arrangements from an economic perspective. If receiving a foreign scholar or sponsoring a relationship with a foreign entity does not appear economically beneficial to that institution, the institution will be less receptive than in the past when Beijing in effect covered local financial losses. Conversely, individual academic and research institutions in China may be more receptive to foreign research and cooperation (including field research) if they can see an economic advantage. Already foreign researchers are facing new (and frequently high) fees on a broad range of items and services. Third, because effectively implemented reforms will give individual Chinese institutions more autonomy, it may become harder for national exchange organizations in America to gain access to a broad range of individual institutions in China simply by dealing with central authorities in Beijing, unless Beijing underwrites the costs for individual institutions. All that can be said with certainty in early 1986 is that these reforms will affect academic exchanges in many ways.

No less important, American perceptions of and policies toward the People's Republic of China have changed since the 1970s. These shifts also have affected Sino-American academic exchanges. In the 1970s, U.S. policymakers viewed China primarily in strategic terms and saw it as a Marxist–Leninist state with no real inclination to reform and a fundamental ideological conflict with the West. But by the mid-1980s, Americans were impressed with China's apparent commitment to system reform and began to view China's problems and behavior as very substantially the products of its status as a Third World developing country. As perceptions have changed in the United States, policy concerning technology transfer has been liberalized and there has been increased involvement in economic development projects. This study now turns to the quantitative and qualitative manifestations of these changes in the realm of academic exchange.

NOTES

1. "IIE Survey Reports 338,894 Foreign Students in 1984 Academic Year," Institute of International Education (IIE) News Release, Sept. 5, 1984.
2. Edmund J. James, "Memorandum Concerning the Sending of an Educational Commission to China," quoted in full in Arthur N. Smith, *China and America Today* (New York: Fleming H. Revell, 1907), pp. 213–218, and cited in Mary Brown Bullock, "Scientific and Educational Relations Between the United States and the People's Republic of China: An Historical Perspective" (Colloquium Paper, Woodrow Wilson International Center for Scholars, Washington, D.C., March 20, 1984), p. 7.
3. Barry Keenan, *The Dewey Experiment in China: Educational Reform and Political Power in the Early Republic* (Cambridge, Mass.: Council on East Asian Studies, Harvard University, 1977), p. 18.

4. Y. C. Wang, *Chinese Intellectuals and the West, 1872–1949* (Chapel Hill: University of North Carolina Press, 1966), pp. 50 and 90–93.
5. Ibid., pp. 88–91.
6. Bullock, "An Historical Perspective," pp. 20–21.
7. Wang, *Chinese Intellectuals*, pp. 52–53.
8. Wilma Fairbank, *America's Cultural Experiment in China, 1942–1949*, Cultural Relations Programs of the U.S. Department of State, *Historical Studies: Number 1* (Washington, D.C.: U.S. Department of State, Bureau of Educational and Cultural Affairs, June 1976), pp. 100 and 119.
9. Wang, *Chinese Intellectuals*, p. 73.
10. Ibid., App. B, pp. 510–511.
11. Fairbank, *America's Cultural Experiment*, pp. 131–133.
12. Wang, *Chinese Intellectuals*, p. 55.
13. Ibid., p. 158.
14. Ibid., pp. 44–45.
15. Fairbank, *America's Cultural Experiment*, p. 125.
16. Ibid., p. 167.
17. A total of 40,000 Chinese went abroad for study in that same period. Stewart E. Fraser, "China's International, Cultural, and Educational Relations: With Selected Bibliography," in Hu Ch'ang-tu, ed., *Aspects of Chinese Education*, a joint publication of the Center for Education in Asia, the Institute of International Studies, Teachers College, Columbia University, and the East Asian Institute, Columbia University (New York: Teachers College Press, 1969), p. 66.
18. Josef Mestenhauser, "Foreign Students in the Soviet Union and East European Countries," in Stewart E. Fraser, ed., *Governmental Policy and International Education* (New York: John Wiley & Sons, 1965), p. 149.
19. Stewart Fraser, "Sino-Soviet Educational Cooperation: 1950–1960," in Fraser, *Governmental Policy and International Education*, pp. 199–200.
20. Ibid., p. 201.
21. Theodore H. E. Chen, "Governmental Encouragement and Control of International Education in Communist China," in Fraser, *Governmental Policy and International Education*, pp. 112–113; and Fraser, "Sino-Soviet Educational Cooperation," p. 200.
22. Fraser, "Sino-Soviet Educational Cooperation," p. 200.
23. Ibid., p. 201.
24. Rene Goldman, "The Experience of Foreign Students in China," in Fraser, *Governmental Policy and International Education*, p. 135.
25. Chen, "Governmental Control of International Education," pp. 115–116.
26. Ibid.
27. Goldman, "Foreign Students in China," p. 136.
28. Ibid., pp. 138–139; and Chen, "Governmental Control of International Education," pp. 117–118.
29. Daniel Southerland, "Exchange Program Ends: First Soviet Students in Peking Since '60s Trash Dorms, Abandon Studies," *The Washington Post*, Aug. 20, 1985, p. A-8: "The first Soviet students to study in Peking in more than two decades left here in an angry mood this summer after a frenzy of smashing beer bottles and dormitory windows, according to other foreign students. . . . Trained as China specialists and fluent in Chinese, the Soviets told others that their access to information here was limited and that their Chinese academic advisors at Peking University were useless."
30. Quoted in Chen, "Governmental Control of International Education," p. 119.
31. Goldman, "Foreign Students in China," pp. 135–140.

32. Jay Mathews, "Gateway to America Now Faces the Orient," *The Washington Post*, July 1, 1984, p. A-1.

33. IIE News Release, Sept. 5, 1984.

34. Mary Ellen Adams, Alfred C. Julian, and Krista Van Laan, eds., *Open Doors: 1983/ 84, Report on International Educational Exchange* (New York: Institute of International Education, 1984), p. 18.

35. "Renmin Ribao Reports on Chinese Studying Abroad," in *Daily Report: China*, Nov. 28, 1984, Foreign Broadcast Information Service (hereafter referred to as *FBIS*) (Springfield, Va.: National Technical Information Service, U.S. Department of Commerce), p. K23, from *Xinhua*.

36. Hiroshi Abe, "Chinese Students and Scholars in Japan " (Tokyo: National Institute for Educational Research, July 15, 1984), pp. 3–4.

37. "Fang Yi Views Technology Ties with Japan, U.S.," *FBIS*, May 4, 1984, p. A1, from *China Daily*.

38. IIE News Release, Sept. 5, 1984.

39. Ibid.

40. Douglas R. Boyan, Alfred C. Julian, and Krista Van Laan, eds., *Open Doors: 1982/ 83, Report on International Educational Exchange* (New York: Institute of International Education, 1983), p. 43.

41. *Open Doors, 1983/84* (New York: Institute of International Education, 1984), pp. 14 and 19.

42. "China Will Send More Students Overseas," *China Daily*, Nov. 30, 1984.

43. "State Council Rules on Self-Supported Study Abroad," *FBIS*, Jan. 15, 1985, pp. K12–K14, from *Xinhua*.

44. *FBIS*, June 14, 1985, pp. K6–K7, from *Zhongguo Xinwen She; FBIS*, June 18, 1985, pp. K1–K2, from *Xinhua*.

45. *FBIS*, May 30, 1985, pp. K1–K11, from *Xinhua; FBIS*, May 20, 1985, pp. K1–K7, from *Xinhua; JPRS* (Joint Publications Research Service), CPS-85-035 (April 15, 1985), pp. 75–80, from *Liaowang [Outlook]*.

3

Characteristics of Exchange Participants

There were 50 Chinese students and scholars in the first group to come to the United States after Sino-American educational exchanges resumed. They arrived in Washington, D.C., in late 1978, with only the slightest preparation for their experience in America. They had a difficult time. By the 1984–1985 academic year, the number of Chinese students and scholars in the United States had grown to about 14,000,[1] and, for the most part, they were doing very well. This rapid growth in the number of Chinese students and scholars in the United States is likely to continue in the immediate future; if it does, China may have more students and scholars in America by the early 1990s than any other country has.

An analysis of the personal profiles and academic characteristics of the PRC Chinese exchange participants reveals patterns with significance which transcends academic exchange. One of the major themes of this chapter—and indeed of the entire study—is that the character of the Sino-American academic relationship from 1979 through 1984 has been shaped very considerably by China's status as a developing country with academic ties to an economically and technologically advanced nation. The scientific and technological emphasis of the fields of study of the PRC Chinese in America, the unbalanced flow of students and scholars between China and the United States, the low priority accorded the study of agriculture by the Chinese, and American interest in pursuing work in the humanities and social sciences in the PRC all are characteristic of the academic relations between Third World countries and the United States. Although the Sino-American academic relationship has its own distinctive character, the broader similarities should not be overlooked or incorrectly ascribed to the PRC's political and social system.

The following analysis also reveals a number of exceedingly important attributes of the PRC Chinese students and scholars in America. First, Chinese students and scholars in America have adapted with remarkable speed to the competitive funding system in the United States. American universities (drawing funds from many sources) have become the largest single source of financial support for PRC students and scholars in the United States, with expenditures exceeding those made by the Chinese government itself. This development reflects funding patterns in American schools and the generally high quality of academic performance of PRC students and scholars on American campuses.

Second, of the PRC students and scholars who came to the United States during the 1979–1984 period, about two-thirds were in the physical and life sciences, engineering, and health sciences. This percentage is very high compared to other developing countries; it reflects China's concentration on science and technology as keys to modernization.

Third, although PRC students and scholars are scattered widely throughout the United States and attend institutions of higher education of every description, more than half come from three urban coastal areas in China (Beijing, Shanghai, and Guangdong Province). Finally, the PRC students and scholars who are coming to the United States are younger and younger. With long careers ahead of them, the impacts of their experiences in America, whatever they may be, will endure.

In contrast to the detailed information available on PRC students and scholars in the United States, comparatively little is available on American students and scholars in China. Nonetheless, even this limited information underscores the different purposes that the exchanges serve for the two nations. Of the American students and scholars who have gone to China for research and study, about two-thirds have been in the social sciences and humanities; their principal interest has been in Chinese culture, history, and society.

PRC STUDENTS AND SCHOLARS IN AMERICA

Numbers of PRC Students and Visiting Scholars, 1979–1984

Both American and Chinese records show that the number of Chinese exchange visitors coming to the United States grew dramatically

TABLE 3-1   J-1 and F-1 Visas Issued in the PRC, 1979 Through 1983

Year	J-1 Visas	F-1 Visas	Total
1979	807	523	1,330
1980	1,986	2,338	4,324
1981	3,066	2,341	5,407
1982	3,327	1,153	4,480
1983	3,328	1,003	4,331
Total	12,514	7,358	19,872

SOURCE: Consular reports, U.S. Department of State.

between 1979 and 1984. From 1979 through 1983, 19,872 scholarly exchange visas were issued to PRC Chinese. Of these, 63 percent were J-1 visas and 37 percent were F-1 visas. (See Tables 3-1 and 3-2 and visa definitions in the Glossary.) Actually, the number of Chinese who have come to the United States is smaller, since some scholars return to China during their course of study, are issued new visas before returning, and therefore are counted twice. Also, presumably, a few of these persons issued visas do not, in fact, come to the United States. It can be stated with certainty, then, that no more than 19,872 PRC students and scholars came to the United States during this period. One can safely infer that the number of such persons who have come to the United States during the 1979–1983 period is close to the 19,000 mark.[2]

In April 1984 the Chinese released fragmentary and imprecise data that set a lower figure for the total number of PRC exchange visitors who came to the United States from 1979 through 1983 (see note 2 in this chapter).[3] Slight double-counting in compiling statistics for this report may account for some of the discrepancy, but the main reason is thought to lie with the Chinese systems for collecting data and issuing exit permits. In May 1984, CSCPRC staff interviewed officials of the Chinese Ministry of Education (MOE), who spoke candidly of two problems. First, their information system is not automated; their statis-

TABLE 3-2   New and Continuing PRC Students and Scholars with J-1 Visas, 1979 Through 1983

Year	New	Continuing	Total
1979	891	134	1,025
1980	1,854	866	2,720
1981	3,210	2,358	5,568
1982	3,077	3,894	6,971
1983	3,190	4,550	7,740
Total	12,222		

SOURCE: USIA data tape.

tics are "not good." Second, the MOE is not in full control of the process by which exit permits are issued, since other ministries can also issue them—namely, the Ministry of Foreign Affairs, the Public Security Bureau, and the provincial and municipal bureaus of foreign affairs.[4] China's leaders clearly knew of the coordination problem, and in mid-1985 they took one step to ease it when a State Education Commission was established and the Ministry of Education abolished. This move obviously was directed at other problems as well, not merely at sending students abroad.

The annual total of scholarly exchange visas (both J-1 and F-1) issued from 1979 to 1983 peaked at 5,407 in 1981. This overall pattern, however, obscures differences between the two visa types. The number of J-1 visas increased rapidly through 1982 and then leveled off in 1983, presumably reflecting the start-up time needed to select and prepare students and scholars to go abroad under PRC government auspices. For students with F-1 visas, an immediate postnormalization surge was followed by a decline in 1982 and 1983. While a number of reasons may explain the drop, two factors appear to have been official Chinese government discouragement of privately sponsored arrangements at that time and tighter U.S. immigration restrictions.

Academic enrollments of Chinese students show the same kind of growth as visa statistics. According to estimates by the Institute of International Education (IIE) in its annual census of foreign students in America, 1,000 Chinese students were enrolled at American institutions of higher education in academic year 1979–1980. By academic year 1983–1984, this number had risen to 8,140.[5] These numbers include both J-1 *and* F-1 students; they do not include nonmatriculated "visiting scholars" who are not degree candidates. The latter group comprises a significant percentage of the PRC students and scholars coming to the United States on J-1 visas (Table 3-3).

More information is available on the J-1 visa holders than on F-1 visa holders. Most of it is drawn from the IAP-66 form required for all J-1s, which authorizes the student or scholar to enter a program for one year; the form is reissued annually, although it is unnecessary to obtain a new visa each year. With data collected from this form, it is possible to distinguish among students entering a U.S. program for the first time, continuing in the same program, and transferring to a different program. By 1983 the number of J-1s in the United States had reached 7,740 (Table 3-2). Each year the number of continuing J-1 students and scholars increased as more and more stayed to continue their studies. By 1982, continuing J-1s outnumbered the new ones.

From 1979 through 1983, the percentage of students among J-1s

TABLE 3-3   Percentage Distribution of PRC J-1 Students and Scholars by Category, 1979 Through 1983

Occupation	1979	1980	1981	1982	1983
Student	18	18	21	29	41
Trainee	2	4	3	2	2
Teacher	0	1	1	1	1
Professor	3	5	5	4	3
Research scholar	69	68	67	61	52
International visitor	3	3	2	3	2
Professional trainee	5	2	1	1	1
Total	100	100	100	100	100
N =	(1,025)	(2,720)	(5,568)	(6,971)	(7,740)

SOURCE: USIA data tape.

increased while the percentage of "research scholars" declined.[6] The increase occurred because many students remain for several years to complete their degrees and because the percentage of students among *new* visa holders has been growing since 1979 (see Table 3-4). Percentages in other categories ("trainees," generally sponsored by an American business or foundation; "teachers," who teach at levels other than college; "professors"; "international visitors," who usually are sponsored by an agency of the United Nations; and "professional trainees," generally in the health sciences) have remained approximately the same.

At present, there is no way to determine precisely and directly the number of PRC F-1 students in the United States each year. However, using the average length-of-stay information for F-1s (Table 3-5) and the

TABLE 3-4   Percentage Distribution of PRC J-1 Students and Scholars Entering New Programs, by Category, 1979 Through 1983

Occupation	1979	1980	1981	1982	1983
Student	16	20	21	31	43
Trainee	2	2	4	3	3
Teacher	0	1	2	1	1
Professor	3	5	5	5	4
Research scholar	71	66	63	55	45
International visitor	3	4	3	4	3
Professional trainee	4	1	1	1	1
Total	100	100	100	100	100
N =	(890)	(1,854)	(3,210)	(3,077)	(3,190)

NOTE: "Entering new programs" is a USIA appellation, which indicates persons who are entering the United States. If J-1 visa holders switch fields of study once they are already in the United States, they are *not* counted as entering new programs.
SOURCE: USIA data tape.

TABLE 3-5 Planned Length of Stay in United States of PRC F-1 and J-1 Visa Holders

Planned Length of Stay in United States (months)	Visa Type (percent)	
	J-1	F-1
3 or less	4	0
4–6	5	1
7–12	30	3
13–24	36	22
25–36	6	21
37–48	12	32
49–60	6	20
More than 60	1	1
Total	100	100
N =	(3,141)[a]	(927)[b]

[a]Percentage of missing data excluded from total is 2 percent.
[b]Percentage of missing data excluded from total is 3 percent.
SOURCE: Records of visas issued in 1983.

number of F-1 visas issued (Table 3-1), it is estimated that slightly more than 5,000 F-1 students from the PRC were in the United States at the end of 1983. Unfortunately, the relevant immigration document, the "I-20" (see Glossary), was not available for this study. It would be helpful to policymakers and analysts if the U.S. Immigration and Naturalization Service (INS) would computerize these data (as is understood to be the intention of the INS). It is too early to know what percentage of PRC F-1 students will return home, but it is known that a substantial number of all foreign students on F-1 visas either remain in the United States after obtaining their degrees or stay on in America without finishing their studies.

Projections of future trends in Sino-American exchange must be based on assumptions about the number of individuals the Chinese will send, the number the United States will admit, and the average period that different categories of PRC students and scholars will stay. Using the information on the *intended* lengths of stay for both visa categories (Table 3-5), the number of "new" and "continuing" students and scholars from 1984 through 1990 can be estimated.

One probable scenario assumes that the number of J-1 visas issued annually reaches 5,000 by 1986 and that the number of F-1s increases by 500 each year from 1984 to 1987. Under these circumstances (Table 3-6), slightly more than 19,000 PRC students and scholars would be in the United States at any one time by 1990, still fewer than the 21,960

TABLE 3-6 PRC Students and Scholars in the United States, Projected from Possible Increase, 1979 Through 1992

Year	J-1			F-1			Total in United States by Year
	New	Continuing	Total	New	Continuing	Total	
1979	891	134	1,025	523	0	523	1,548
1980	1,854	866	2,720	2,338	502[a]	2,840[a]	5,560[a]
1981	3,210	2,358	5,568	2,341	2,631[a]	4,972[a]	10,540[a]
1982	3,077	3,894	6,971	1,153	4,254[a]	5,407[a]	12,378[a]
1983	3,190	4,550	7,740	1,003	4,188[a]	5,191[a]	12,931[a]
1984	3,159	3,084[a]	6,243[a]	1,000[a]	3,553[a]	4,553[a]	10,796[a]
1985	4,000[a]	3,590[a]	7,590[a]	1,500[a]	2,828[a]	4,328[a]	11,918[a]
1986	5,000[a]	4,155[a]	9,155[a]	2,000[a]	2,977[a]	4,977[a]	14,132[a]
1987	5,000[a]	4,919[a]	9,919[a]	2,500[a]	3,783[a]	6,283[a]	16,202[a]
1988	5,000[a]	5,313[a]	10,313[a]	2,500[a]	4,895[a]	7,395[a]	17,708[a]
1989	5,000[a]	5,562[a]	10,562[a]	2,500[a]	5,635[a]	8,135[a]	18,697[a]
1990	5,000[a]	5,640[a]	10,640[a]	2,500[a]	6,010[a]	8,510[a]	19,150[a]
1991	5,000[a]	5,650[a]	10,650[a]	2,500[a]	6,120[a]	8,620[a]	19,270[a]
1992	5,000[a]	5,650[a]	10,650[a]	2,500[a]	6,125[a]	8,625[a]	19,275[a]

[a]Estimated.

SOURCES: Tables 3-1, 3-2, and 3-5 in this report.

students from Taiwan who were in the United States during academic year 1983–1984.[7] From the vantage point of mid-1985, however, this scenario appears conservative. During the first eight months of 1985, in Beijing alone J-1 and F-1 visas issued to PRC Chinese by the American Embassy doubled as compared with those issued during the same months in 1984.

Whether these projections prove accurate depends to a large extent on the policy decisions made by both the Chinese and American governments and on how they are implemented. In late 1984 and early 1985, the PRC government made two changes that should result in an increase in the number of PRC students and scholars coming to the United States: (1) In late 1984 China's State Council announced its intention to send one-third more "people abroad to study at State expense."[8] (2) In January 1985 the State Council issued "Draft Regulations on Self-Supported Study Abroad." These latter regulations signal Beijing's encouragement to Chinese students and scholars to make privately sponsored arrangements to study abroad.[9] The crucial questions in terms of the effect on the number of PRC students and scholars in the United States are how liberally these regulations will be implemented by Chinese officials at various levels and how American immigration authorities will respond.

Fields of Study

In general, PRC students and scholars come to the United States seeking training in scientific and technical fields. Over two-thirds of them have been in such fields as computer science, engineering, health sciences, life sciences, mathematics, and physical sciences (Tables 3-7 and 3-8).

This pattern represents a continuation of the pre-1950 era in some ways and a departure in others (see Table A-2). Then, as now, few Chinese studied agriculture and many studied engineering. In other areas the pattern was not repeated. Before 1950 a greater percentage of students and scholars came to America to study the humanities, social sciences, and business than was the case between 1979 and 1984. During the latter period, the percentage of students and scholars in the physical and life sciences became *much* greater than before 1950.

Parenthetically, many other countries also give limited attention to agriculture in programs that send students to America. As Sirowy and Inkeles document, agriculture consistently has been a low-priority field of study among all foreign students in the United States.[10] This pattern presumably reflects the usual bureaucratic weakness of agricultural

TABLE 3-7   Percentage Distribution of PRC F-1 Visa Holders by Intended Field of Study in United States, 1983

Intended Field of Study in U.S.	F-1 Visa Holders
Agriculture	1
American studies	—
Architecture	1
Business management	9
Computer science	13
Education	3
Engineering	23
English as a second language (ESL)	1
Health sciences	4
Humanities	15
Law	—
Library and archival science	—
Life sciences	5
Mathematics	5
Physical sciences	14
Social sciences	4
Other	2
Total	100
N =	(911)[a]

NOTE: The symbol "—" indicates a value less than 0.5 percent.
[a]Percentage of missing data excluded from total is 4 percent.
SOURCE: Records of visas issued in 1983.

ministries in the Third World, the low status of agriculture among urban intellectuals, and the fact that foreigners generally come to the United States looking for advanced knowledge not normally associated with agriculture. The seemingly lower priority for agriculture may also reflect the fact that American agriculture is energy- and capital-intensive and that much American agricultural training goes on in the Third World itself.

Considerable overlap exists in the fields studied by F-1 and J-1 visa holders, but there are important differences as well (Tables 3-7 and 3-8). The holders of F-1 visas (generally privately sponsored students) were more likely to study business management, computer science, and the humanities than were J-1 visa holders.[11] J-1s, in contrast, have more often studied the physical and health sciences. These patterns remained constant for J-1s from 1979 through 1984 (Table 3-8). Despite shifts in Chinese policy pronouncements promoting the importance of applied science, agriculture, management, and law, there was only a slight

TABLE 3-8 Percentage Distribution of PRC J-1 Students and Scholars by Field of Study, 1979 Through 1984

Field of Study	1979	1980	1981	1982	1983	1984
Agriculture	3	4	2	3	4	5
American studies	—	—	—	—	—	—
Architecture	—	—	—	—	—	—
Business management	1	1	1	1	2	2
Computer science	5	4	4	4	4	4
Education	1	2	2	2	2	2
Engineering	30	31	31	29	27	29
English as a second language (ESL)	—	1	1	1	1	1
Health sciences	9	10	11	11	10	11
Humanities	1	2	2	3	3	3
Law	—	1	1	1	1	1
Library and archival science	—	—	—	—	—	—
Life sciences	9	8	9	10	9	9
Mathematics	6	5	4	4	5	4
Physical sciences	29	25	24	24	25	22
Social sciences	4	3	4	4	5	6
Other	—	2	3	3	2	2
Total	100	100	100	100	100	100
N =	(1,000)	(2,714)	(5,565)	(6,971)	(7,740)	(2,277)

NOTES: The symbol "—" indicates a value less than 0.5 percent. Percentage of missing data is less than 1 percent for all years.
SOURCE: USIA data tape.

increase in the number of students and scholars in those fields who came to the United States from 1979 to 1984. This stability may signal, in part, the difficulty of implementing personnel policies that shift priorities.

Different categories of J-1 visa holders (e.g., student, trainee, teacher, research scholar) tended to be concentrated in particular fields and programs (see Table A-6). Although the two largest categories—students and research scholars—had similar distributions, more research scholars than students studied engineering and health sciences, while the opposite was true in the physical sciences. Each of the other categories of J-1s had a distinctive profile. Trainees tended to be sponsored by an American business or foundation for a specific training program, most commonly in agriculture and engineering. Teachers taught at a level other than college; many studied education and the humanities (including English), as well as engineering. Professors were concentrated in engineering, health sciences, and physical sciences. International visitors usually were sponsored by an agency of the United

Nations. The largest percentage of international visitors were in health sciences, as were professional trainees.

In recent years, Chinese women from the PRC who have come to the United States have been concentrated in American studies, library and archival science, health sciences, education, English as a second language (ESL), and the humanities (see Table A-7). Conversely, relatively few female PRC students and scholars were studying engineering, mathematics, and computer and information science. Virtually the same pattern of field distribution was evident among all women receiving graduate degrees in the United States during academic year 1981–1982.[12]

Personal Attributes: Geographic Variation

The majority of the PRC students and scholars who have come to the United States since 1978 are from a few areas of China, principally the cosmopolitan areas along the coast (Table 3-9). This pattern of concentration is similar to that of the pre-1950 era (see Table A-1). Of those who applied for F-1 visas in 1983, 75 percent listed Shanghai, Beijing, and Guangdong Province as their current address. Seventy-one percent of these students were *born* in those three localities.

This concentration may reflect several factors. Each of these places is the site of centrally run "key" educational institutions and government bureaucracies, and the populations tend to have higher incomes, higher average education levels, and longer histories of interaction with the West. In 1983, Beijing, Guangdong (in which the city of Guangzhou is located), and Shanghai were the only places in China with American consular officials in residence. Proximity to the embassy or consulates may also have been a factor: persons making private arrangements would be more likely to be able to file a visa application the closer their residence was to the American Embassy or consulate.

The geographic concentration of J-1s is only slightly less pronounced. Fifty-one percent listed Shanghai or Beijing as their current address in 1983. Trailing far behind in percentages of J-1s were provinces with cities (shown in parentheses) that traditionally have been very important economic and administrative centers: Guangdong (Guangzhou), Hubei (Wuhan), Jiangsu (Nanjing), and Sichuan (Chongqing and Chengdu). Each of these provinces contributed 5 percent of the J-1s in 1983. This pattern reflects the concentration of state educational, scientific, bureaucratic, and economic entities in these localities and the officially sponsored character of most J-1s.

TABLE 3-9 Percentage Distribution of PRC F-1 and J-1 Visa Holders by Birthplace and Residence, Compared to 1982 PRC Population Distribution, 1983

Province or Municipality in China	% of PRC's 1982 Population	Birthplace		Current Home	
		F-1	J-1	F-1	J-1
Anhui	5	—	2	2	3
Beijing	1	19	10	25	37
Fujian	3	3	3	2	1
Gansu	2	—	—	—	1
Guangdong	6	15	5	17	5
Guangxi	4	1	1	1	1
Guizhou	3	1	—	—	—
Hebei	5	1	3	—	1
Heilongjiang	3	1	2	1	1
Henan	7	—	2	—	1
Hubei	5	2	4	2	5
Hunan	5	1	3	1	2
Jiangsu	6	5	11	4	5
Jiangxi	3	—	2	—	—
Jilin	2	1	1	1	2
Liaoning	4	2	4	2	3
Nei Monggol	2	—	1	0	1
Ningxia	—	0	—	—	—
Qinghai	—	—	—	0	—
Shaanxi	3	1	2	1	3
Shandong	7	1	3	1	2
Shanghai	1	37	19	33	14
Shanxi	3	—	2	0	1
Sichuan	10	3	7	1	5
Tianjin	1	1	2	2	3
Xinjiang	1	0	—	—	—
Xizang	—	0	0	0	0
Yunnan	3	1	1	1	—
Zhejiang	4	2	7	2	2
Outside China	0	1	1	0	0
Total	100	100	100	100	100
N =		(947)	(3,180)	(944)	(3,150)

NOTES: Percentage of missing data excluded from F-1 and J-1 figures is less than 2 percent. The symbol "—" indicates a value less than 0.5 percent.

SOURCE: Population figures calculated from John S. Aird, "The Preliminary Results of China's 1982 Census," *The China Quarterly*, No. 96 (December 1983), pp. 616–617; records of visas issued in 1983.

The overrepresentation of Beijing and Shanghai is matched by disproportionately low numbers of students and scholars from other areas. Anhui, Henan, Shandong, and Sichuan are all significantly underrepresented (Table 3-9), as are China's five autonomous regions (Guangxi, Nei Monggol, Ningxia, Xinjiang, and Xizang), where ethnic minorities dominate the population. (It should be noted, however, that the combined population of the autonomous regions is less than 10 percent of China's total population.[13])

This pattern of geographic distribution raises several questions about China's development strategy and America's response. China, clearly, is concentrating its "human investment" in a few metropolitan and coastal centers. This has been true throughout most of modern Chinese history, although Mao Zedong sought to diminish this bias during most of his long rule. It seems likely that persons trained abroad will return to the same area of China from which they came, since Chinese organizations retain their personnel. Therefore, not only does the present Chinese development strategy concentrate economic resources and foreign investment incentives along the coast, it also concentrates intellectual talent there. This, in turn, raises the specter of the "two Chinas" so feared by Mao—a dynamic eastern seaboard and an inland left behind and, perhaps, resentful.

The implications of this Chinese strategy for the U.S. government and private institutions are unclear. On the one hand, concentrating American linkages in the most dynamic areas may maximize U.S. impact. On the other hand, building ties to inland institutions may help reduce the likelihood of becoming the target of a backlash from a lagging heartland. America's pluralism guarantees that no single approach will be adopted, but two major questions arise: How much will the inland benefit from the "open" policy? Will America's role become a contentious issue in Chinese domestic politics?

Personal Attributes: Socioeconomic Status

The first Chinese students and scholars began arriving in the United States in the "normalization" period only a few years after the official close of the decade of the Cultural Revolution. The opening to the West was part of the ever-expanding and continuing repudiation of the Cultural Revolution and the excesses of the entire period (from 1957 to 1966) that preceded it. In China, issues surrounding the role of universities, their staffing, curricula, and admissions all were under debate. Universities and research institutes were trying to retool and rebuild their faculties and research staffs after a long period of stagnation. In this setting, then, an examination of the socioeconomic characteristics of persons sent abroad in the 1979–1983 period assumes particular importance.[14]

In 1983 a large percentage of PRC students and scholars coming to the United States were from academe (Table 3-10). Among J-1s almost four-fifths were students, teachers, professors, or researchers, with college teachers or professors making up the largest percentage. A few doctors, journalists, and engineers also participated in exchanges. Over time, the percentage of J-1 visa holders who were students in China has increased, while the percentage who were university professors, researchers, and government officials in China has declined steadily (Tables 3-10 and 3-11).

The F-1 visa holders are a more diverse group. Although more than one-half are classified as academics, there are more "engineers," who usually work as technicians in China. Also, more F-1s are in the "other" category, which includes clerical, agricultural, and factory workers (Table 3-10).

In both visa groups the affiliations of students and scholars fall into clear patterns. In 1983, 71 percent of the J-1 visas were issued to applicants from a college or university (Table 3-12). That same year, 47 percent of this group came from "key schools" in China; that is, institu-

TABLE 3-10   Percentage Distribution of PRC J-1 and F-1 Visa Holders by Occupation in China, 1983

Occupation in China	Type of Visa	
	J-1	F-1
Student	21	26
Teacher—high school or below	1	8
College teacher or professor	42	16
Researcher	15	5
Administrator	1	—
Party/government cadre	1	1
Journalist	1	1
Engineer	9	15
Doctor	6	4
Musician, artist, etc.	—	5
Other	3	18
Total	100	100
N =	(3,113)[a]	(923)[a]

NOTE: None of the visa applications coded listed the applicant's occupation as "military."
[a]Percentage of missing data excluded from total is 3 percent.
SOURCE: Records of visas issued in 1983.

TABLE 3-11   Percentage Distribution of PRC J-1 Students and Scholars Beginning New Programs in the United States by Occupation in China, 1979 Through 1983

Occupation in China	1979	1980	1981	1982	1983
Undergraduate student	3	1	3	6	7
Graduate student	8	9	11	14	22
Teacher—secondary or below	1	1	1	1	1
University professor or researcher	57	63	59	55	48
Government official	15	10	10	10	8
Media	—	1	1	—	1
Musician, artist, or other performer	0	1	—	—	1
Other	16	14	16	14	12
Total	100	100	100	100	100
N =	(891)	(1,853)	(3,210)	(3,077)	(3,190)

NOTES: "Entering new programs" is a USIA appellation, which indicates the persons who are entering the United States. If J-1 visa holders switch fields of study once they are already in the United States, they are *not* counted as entering new programs.

The symbol "—" indicates a value less than 0.5 percent.

SOURCE: USIA data tape.

TABLE 3-12   Percentage Distribution of PRC J-1 and F-1 Visa Holders by Employer in China, 1983

	Type of Visa	
Employer in China	J-1	F-1
High school or lower school	—	1
College or university	71	56
National key institution	(47)	(21)
Other	(24)	(35)
Chinese Academy of Sciences	14	4
Chinese Academy of Social Sciences	1	1
Scientific organization	2	1
Hospitals	3	3
Media	1	1
Government	4	5
Finance or trade corporation	1	4
Performing arts troupe	—	4
Factory	1	19
Commune	1	—
Other	1	1
Total	100	100
N =	(3,101)[a]	(882)[b]

NOTE: The symbol "—" indicates a value less than 0.5 percent.

[a]Percentage of missing data excluded from total is 3 percent.

[b]Percentage of missing data excluded from total is 7 percent.

SOURCE: Records of visas issued in 1983.

tions that receive more money and better personnel from Chinese educational authorities and have high priority in China's development scheme (see Appendix D). Another 15 percent of J-1s worked for the Chinese Academy of Sciences (CAS) or the Chinese Academy of Social Sciences (CASS).[15] Only about 15 percent come from other institutions.

In contrast, more F-1s came from nonacademic organizations and fewer from key schools. Fifteen percent had a middle-school education or less, and another 14 percent came from technical schools (Table A-8). Of particular note, 19 percent were "factory workers" (see Table 3-12), although not necessarily low-level workers. One-half of this latter group list their field in China as business management, computer science, and engineering, and 43 percent have college degrees. Many in this group apparently are educated factory employees who want to study further in the United States so they can secure more responsible positions when they return to China. The fields they plan to study in the United States are engineering (44 percent), computer science (21 percent), business management (10 percent), and physical sciences (7 percent).

Personal Attributes: Age, Sex, and Marital Status

The age of Chinese exchange visitors varies considerably with the type of visa issued. Ninety-six percent of F-1s are under 40 years of age (see Table 3-13), whereas only 53 percent of J-1s are under 40. Over the years, China has increased the percentage of younger J-1 students and scholars it sends to the United States (Table A-9); the percentage of those below 30 years of age rose from 5 percent in 1979 to 34 percent in 1983. The dramatic increase in 1982 of the percentage of J-1s under age 30

TABLE 3-13 Percentage Distribution of PRC J-1 and F-1 Visa Holders by Age, 1983

Age	J-1 Visa	F-1 Visa
Under 20	—	5
20–29	31	58
30–39	22	33
40–49	32	3
50–59	12	—
60 and over	2	—
Total	100	100
N =	(3,192)	(949)

NOTES: The symbol "—" indicates a value less than 0.5 percent. Percentage of missing data excluded from totals is less than 1 percent.
SOURCE: Records of visas issued in 1983.

reflects the time necessary to select and train qualified students in the wake of the Cultural Revolution and the higher quality of the first graduating class selected through competitive college entrance exams in the late 1970s. As more younger persons have come to the United States, there has been a corresponding decline in the percentage of J-1s in the 40- to 49-year-old age cohort.

Many more men than women come from China as students and scholars. This also is true for all foreign students in America. In 1983, women received 23 percent of the American visas granted to PRC students and scholars (Table A-5). However, among F-1s the percentage of women was almost twice what it was among J-1s. Although the percentage of Chinese females among J-1s is lower than the percentage of women among all foreign students coming to the United States, the rate for F-1s is considerably higher.[16] There has been little change in the percentage of women among J-1s throughout the 1979–1984 period, in part because of the Chinese government's steadfast emphasis on science and technology, fields in which men tend to predominate, globally as well as in China.

In 1983, 63 percent of the PRC students and scholars were married— 73 percent of J-1s and 30 percent of F-1s (see Table A-5). Seventy-five percent of J-1s intended to stay in the United States 24 months or less, while 74 percent of F-1s intended to stay more than 24 months (Table 3-5).

These socioeconomic data raise two key issues. First, the F-1 visa holders' lack of official sponsorship and permanent employment in China, relative youth, and general lack of ties to China have led many observers in the PRC and elsewhere to expect fewer of them to return to China. China's intention to liberalize its policies on "self-supporting" students and scholars, then, has potentially important implications for U.S. immigration authorities. Second, if young people during the Cultural Revolution had not taken advantage of opportunities to study abroad in the late 1970s through 1981, by 1982 their prospects under the officially sponsored program had declined markedly. Whether they can go abroad under private sponsorship is unknown. A question for the future, then, is whether the members of this generation will be less supportive of the "open" policy and whether their attitudes will have a political impact.

Financing of PRC Students and Scholars in the United States

In August 1978, representatives from 25 American colleges and universities and five national education associations met in Washington,

D.C., to discuss arrangements for the exchange of American and PRC students and scholars. The meeting addressed the financial implications of such an exchange. The universities and the U.S. government expressed the view that the Chinese would have to pay the full cost of educating their students and scholars in the United States and that the Chinese authorities should be made fully aware of the considerable expense of such an undertaking before they embarked on the new course. Since then, the situation has evolved quite differently. PRC students, like foreign students in general, have been quite successful in gaining financial support at American institutions of higher education.

The authors of this report estimate total expenditure for all PRC students and scholars in the United States from 1979 through 1983 at about $337 million, with the annual outlay in 1983 exceeding $111 million (in U.S. dollars).[17] The patterns of financial support for PRC J-1 and F-1 visa holders reflect the nature of the two categories (Table 3-14). Of the J-1s applying for visas in 1983, 77 percent stated that their support came from either the Chinese government or an American university. Among applicants for F-1s, only 1 percent received any assistance from the Chinese government or a Chinese work unit, and only 12 percent received aid from an American university; 76 percent of the

TABLE 3-14 Percentage Distribution of J-1 and F-1 Visa Holders by Stated Source of Financial Support, 1983

Stated Source of Financial Support	All Students and Scholars	Type of Visa	
		J-1	F-1
Self, savings, or family in China	—	—	—
Chinese government or work unit	32	41	1
U.S. relatives or private individual	21	4	76
U.S. government	2	2	0
U.S. university	30	36	12
U.S. foundation/philanthropy	4	5	0
International organization	4	5	0
Other or combination of sources	8	6	11
Total	100	100	100
N =	(4,010)[a]	(3,068)[a]	(942)[b]

NOTE: The symbol "—" indicates a value less than 0.5 percent.
[a]Percentage of missing data excluded from total is 4 percent.
[b]Percentage of missing data excluded from total is 1 percent.
SOURCE: Records of visas issued in 1983.

F-1s said they would receive support from relatives in the United States or other individuals.

Considerably more detailed financial information is available on J-1s (see Table 3-15).[18] The total amount needed to finance Chinese J-1s from 1979 through 1983 was estimated at more than $189 million (in U.S. dollars). By 1983, the annual amount spent—about $67 million—was nine times the amount spent in 1979. This large increase was due principally to the rising number of students and scholars studying in the United States and to the escalating cost of education in America. Seventy-six percent of the total amount spent from 1979 through 1983 came from U.S. universities (42 percent) and the Chinese government (34 percent). In 1981, American universities for the first time provided more support for Chinese students and scholars than did the Chinese government (Table 3-16). Note, however, that two caveats apply to these figures. First, they probably understate the costs for American universities, because many J-1s are research scholars who may use university facilities but generally pay no fees for their use.[19] Second, the figures in Tables 3-15 and 3-16 undoubtedly understate the actual level of support by the U.S. government, foundations, corporations, and international organizations, because funds that these agencies channel

TABLE 3-15   Financial Support for PRC J-1 Students and Scholars by Source, 1979 Through 1983 (in thousands of dollars)

Source of Funds	1979	1980	1981	1982	1983	Total
PRC government	$3,968	$7,729	$15,011	$16,980	$21,211	$64,899
Personal funds	187	789	1,982	2,521	4,039	9,518
U.S. government	550	1,490	2,586	3,297	3,375	11,298
U.S. university	1,354	6,487	17,117	24,944	30,052	79,954
U.S. foundation	263	814	1,003	1,113	1,509	4,702
U.S. corporation	17	32	557	602	481	1,689
International organization	70	203	606	636	941	2,456
Other	983	1,725	2,951	4,565	4,930	15,154
Total	7,392	19,269	41,813	54,658	66,538	189,670
Total number of students and scholars	1,025	2,720	5,568	6,971	7,740	
Number of students and scholars for whom data on finances were available	808	2,235	4,520	5,791	6,523	

NOTE: Estimates were included for students and scholars for whom financial data were not available.
SOURCE: USIA data tape.

TABLE 3-16 Percentage Distribution of Sources of Financial Support for PRC J-1 Students and Scholars, 1979 Through 1983

Source of Funds	1979	1980	1981	1982	1983
Chinese government	54	40	36	31	32
Personal funds	3	4	5	5	6
U.S. government	7	8	6	6	5
U.S. university	18	34	41	46	45
U.S. foundation	4	4	2	2	2
U.S. corporation	—	—	1	1	1
International organization	1	1	1	1	1
Other	13	9	7	8	7
Total	100	100	100	100	100

NOTE: The symbol "—" indicates a value less than 0.5 percent. Figures have been rounded to the nearest percent.
SOURCE: USIA data tape.

to American universities through contract and grant mechanisms appear in these statistics as U.S. university funds.

Three factors have helped shrink the Chinese government's share of support for new and, particularly, for continuing J-1s (Table 3-17). First, the proportion of continuing students and scholars among J-1s has been growing each year as more and more students remain in the United States to complete long-term courses of study. Continuing students are more likely to win financial support. Second, the Chinese are presumably becoming more familiar with the American system and thus more adept at gaining support. Third, the Chinese government is

TABLE 3-17 Percentage Distribution of Sources of Funding for New and Continuing PRC J-1 Students and Scholars, 1979 Through 1983

Source of Funds	1979	1980	1981	1982	1983
New students and scholars:					
Chinese government	55	37	33	30	37
U.S. university	19	36	40	41	36
Other	26	27	27	29	27
Total	100	100	100	100	100
Continuing students and scholars:					
Chinese government	49	46	40	32	28
U.S. university	12	29	42	50	53
Other	39	25	18	18	19
Total	100	100	100	100	100

NOTE: Figures were rounded to the nearest percent.
SOURCE: USIA data tape.

TABLE 3-18   Percentage Distribution of Funds Spent on J-1 Students and Scholars, Excluding Those from the PRC, by Source of Funds, 1979 Through 1983

Source of Funds	1979	1980	1981	1982	1983
Foreign government	17	13	12	9	13
U.S. university	48	52	52	35	49
U.S. government	4	4	4	3	2
International organization	—	—	—	—	—
Personal funds	10	11	13	10	13
Other	21	20	19	44	21
Total	100	100	100	100	100

NOTE: The symbol "—" indicates a value less than 0.5 percent. Figures have been rounded to the nearest percent.
SOURCE: USIA data tape.

putting more pressure on its students and scholars to secure non-Chinese-government funding. The balance between Chinese government and American university funding for "new" J-1s is worth watching in the future. However, U.S. universities generally pick up about one-half of the total costs of all foreign J-1 visa holders in the United States, and foreign governments usually pay less than 15 percent of the total costs (see Table 3-18).

Although J-1s have been discussed as a group thus far, in fact there are important differences between the various categories within the J-1 group, the most salient of which is the distinction between students and research scholars. The Chinese government and American universities together provided about 80 percent of the support for J-1 *students* from 1979 through 1983 (Table 3-19). During this time, the Chinese government's percentage of support declined while the percentage of support from U.S. universities increased. A similar pattern of support was found for J-1 research scholars (Table 3-20). The PRC's percentage declined steadily from 1979 to 1983, though every year the PRC's support for J-1 scholars exceeded their support for J-1 students.

Conversely, a greater percentage of American university support went to students than to research scholars. Nonetheless, U.S. university allocations to Chinese research scholars rose from 1979 through 1983, in both absolute and percentage terms. In this same period, the percentage of U.S. university support for J-1 students multiplied by 2.5—for research scholars it doubled. By 1983, U.S. universities and the PRC government provided *equal* percentages of support for research scholars.

It is not possible to make very reliable estimates of how F-1 outlays

TABLE 3-19   Percentage Distribution of Funds Spent on PRC J-1 Students, by Source of Funds, 1979 Through 1983

Source of Funds	1979	1980	1981	1982	1983
Chinese government	57	30	20	20	30
Personal funds	5	5	6	6	7
U.S. government	2	5	5	3	2
U.S. university	21	48	62	62	53
U.S. foundation	—	—	—	1	1
U.S. corporation	—	—	0	—	—
International organization	0	0	1	1	1
Other	14	10	6	7	6
Total	100	100	100	100	100

NOTE: The symbol "—" indicates a value less than 0.5 percent. Figures have been rounded to the nearest percent.
SOURCE: USIA data tape.

would affect the totals contributed by the eight financial sources listed in Table 3-15. But it can be said that including such outlays would not materially increase the figures for the Chinese government's expenditures; the personal funds category would jump dramatically; and the U.S. university total would rise moderately.

The Chinese government has provided no official estimates of how much it believes it has spent to support officially sponsored students and scholars in the United States. Chinese estimates do exist for the cost of foreign study in general, although they are not detailed enough to per-

TABLE 3-20   Percentage Distribution of Funds Spent on PRC J-1 Research Scholars, by Source of Funds, 1979 Through 1983

Source of Funds	1979	1980	1981	1982	1983
Chinese government	64	51	44	41	38
Personal funds	2	4	4	4	5
U.S. government	1	6	5	7	6
U.S. university	19	30	36	37	38
U.S. foundation	3	3	2	2	3
U.S. corporation	0	—	—	—	0
International organization	2	1	1	1	2
Other	9	6	7	8	8
Total	100	100	100	100	100

NOTE: The symbol "—" indicates a value less than 0.5 percent. Figures have been rounded to the nearest percent.
SOURCE: USIA data tape.

mit in-depth analysis. In November 1984 Beijing announced that, "in the past six years, China has spent 290 million *yuan* ($116 million) to send 26,000 students to study in more than 60 countries. In addition, 7,000 have gone abroad at their own expense."[20]

Multivariate analysis (see Appendix E) can be used to determine the characteristics of J-1 visa holders who receive more or less money from the Chinese government and American universities.[21] The dependent variable is the amount of money received, and the independent variables are the characteristics of the J-1 visa holder. This analysis shows that, all other factors being equal, American universities have preferred to fund *continuing* students or scholars from China (Appendix E, Table E-1), and had an apparent preference for funding females. J-1 trainees and international visitors are least likely to receive funding at American universities, and J-1 students are the most likely.

Field of study also influenced funding. Students and scholars in the life and physical sciences tended to receive more money from American universities; lesser amounts, in descending order, went to health sciences, mathematics, law, and social sciences. Fields that appear to have had a negative impact on the amount received from American universities were architecture, agriculture, computer science, and engineering.

In contrast, the Chinese government basically supports those persons not as likely to be supported by American universities—more teachers and research scholars (Appendix E, Table E-2). Finally, the Chinese government funded more students and scholars in engineering, architecture, computer science, agriculture, library science, and humanities, in descending order, and was less likely to fund those in law and American studies.

In what context should American support for PRC Chinese students and scholars be viewed? First, U.S. universities generally pick up about half of the total cost of foreign J-1 visa holders, whereas foreign governments usually pay less than 15 percent of these costs. As shown in Tables 3-19 and 3-20, the Chinese government pays more than 15 percent for their J-1 visa holders. Second, the academic performance of Chinese students and scholars compares favorably to both foreign *and* domestic students (see Chapter 5). Their ability to compete successfully for financial assistance not only speaks well for them, but their efforts also enrich the intellectual climate in American academe. Third, many of the problems under investigation by students and scholars from China are important to American research objectives. In one sense, Chinese support for their students and scholars are subsidies to U.S. programs. Finally, the U.S. government has defined it to be in the national interest that China's modernization effort succeed. Since direct federal development assistance to China is not yet available, this educational relationship is the most direct contribution, aside from commercial transactions, that the United States can make to China's modernization.

The American educational community has been particularly concerned about four financial issues: (1) the adequacy of stipends provided by the Chinese government to its officially sponsored students and scholars; (2) the fact that many PRC officially sponsored students and scholars have had to remit a portion of their U.S. stipends and/or pay back their salary and travel advances to their home "unit" (the kickback issue); (3) the pressure applied by the Chinese government on its students and scholars to secure American support for their research and study in the United States; and (4) the frequency with which PRC students and scholars fail to purchase health insurance. Each of these areas is discussed in detail in Chapter 5, which deals with the role of American universities in the academic exchanges.

OVERVIEW OF AMERICAN STUDENTS AND SCHOLARS IN CHINA, 1979–1984

Numbers of American Students and Scholars

There is considerably less information about Americans who went to China from 1979 through 1984 than there is for PRC Chinese who came to the United States. The Chinese are in the best position to count Americans traveling to China, because visitors must first obtain visas from the Chinese. In practice, however, these Chinese statistics pose several problems, one of which is that an unknown number of American scholars travel to China on tourist visas and then undertake academic work while they are in China.

According to general information provided by the Chinese Ministry of Education (MOE), the number of Americans going to China for academic purposes grew rapidly from 1979 through 1983, although the total is much smaller than the number of Chinese coming to the United States for academic purposes. These figures do not indicate how many different individuals have traveled to China, since some stay for more than one year or across calendar years, and many have made multiple visits. If the repeat visitors constitute 10 to 20 percent of the total provided by the Chinese (Table 3-21), approximately 2,900 to 3,300 American students and scholars would have traveled to China for what the Chinese government considers academic purposes.

U.S. citizens actually taking courses at Chinese institutions of higher learning constitute only a modest percentage of total foreign enrollment

TABLE 3-21　American Students and Scholars Traveling to the PRC, by Category, 1979 Through 1983

Category of Scholar	1979	1980	1981	1982	1983
Scholars sent by CSCPRC	33	44	24	25	27
Fulbright scholars	0	0	0	10	0
Students sent by CSCPRC	29	10	21	14	10
Intercollegiate	36	179	183	200	about 200
Short-term	0	0	400	800	1,200
English teachers	0	0	0	0	200
Total	98	233	628	1,049	about 1,600

NOTE: This table, provided by the Embassy of the PRC, obviously is missing data—for correct figures on Fulbright scholars and CSCPRC students and scholars, see Tables 4-1 and A-11 and Chapter 4 in this report. For more recent aggregate figures, see *Beijing Review*, No. 31 (Aug. 5, 1985), pp. 13–14, which reports, "Some 3,500 American students [and scholars?] have come to China since 1979."
SOURCE: Embassy of the People's Republic of China.

in China. In late 1984, the MOE announced that there were 2,500 "foreign students for regular courses."[22] The number of such American students implied in Table 3-21 (for 1983) is only about 12 percent of this number (if one counts the categories of "Intercollegiate" and "Students sent by CSCPRC"). In "short-term" classes, which the Chinese say "are mainly in the Chinese language,"[23] the percentage of Americans is larger. In the MOE report of late 1984 cited above, then-Minister of Education He Dongchang said that there were 4,000 "foreign students for short-term studies. . . ."[24] According to the Chinese figures in Table 3-21, therefore, Americans appear to constitute a significant percentage of the foreigners in China for short-term study.

From 1981 through 1983 (see Table 3-21), between two-thirds and three-quarters of the American students and scholars who went to China were categorized as "short-term." This figure includes many American academics who have gone to China to lecture and teach (e.g., English teachers). In 1984 Li Tao, then director of the Foreign Affairs Bureau of China's MOE, underscored this point when he reportedly said, "Since 1979 China has invited hundreds of U.S. experts, most of them teachers of English, to lecture for one or two years in colleges."[25] In that same report, Li Tao also emphasized a critical dimension of the exchanges from the Chinese perspective—the role of the many American scientists who have gone to the PRC to lecture for short periods and contribute to the development of the natural sciences in China.

The disparity between the number of Americans going to China and that of Chinese coming to the United States is characteristic of America's exchange relationships with developing societies. It also reflects global patterns. For example, in academic year 1981–1982, a total of 30,552 American students were studying abroad. In the same academic year, there were 326,299 foreign students in the United States.[26] Sirowy and Inkeles make an important point concerning this global imbalance in exchanges, noting that in 1973, Asian nations sent 40.9 percent of all students who went abroad and received only 13.4 percent of the global total of foreign students. Conversely, North American nations sent 12.1 percent of all students going abroad and received 33.2 percent of the world total.[27]

Fields of Study

The patterns of study in Sino-American exchange are like those Sirowy and Inkeles observed worldwide: students from the Third World tend to focus on pure and applied science, while those from economically advanced nations are more often concentrated in the liberal arts disciplines.[28]

The field distribution displayed in Table 3-22 is based on reports from 30 American universities with Asian studies programs. The numbers should *not* be viewed in absolute terms, as they are only a small sample of American scholars. Nonetheless, they provide a rough approximation of the distribution of areas of interest among Americans who go to China for research. Predictably, the social sciences and humanities dominate, with approximately two-thirds of the researchers. Agriculture and engineering were the next most popular fields, with only a few scholars in each of the other categories. Of the American graduate students and faculty in Chinese studies who conducted or planned to conduct a month or more of research in the PRC from 1978–1979 through 1984–1985 (see Table 3-23), more than 50 percent were in history and literature, with an additional 17 percent in political science/ international relations.

PRINCIPAL FINDINGS AND CONCLUSIONS

Six broad conclusions emerge from this statistical characterization of Sino-American exchange. First, the academic relationship between the two countries from 1979 through 1984 has been shaped very considerably by a developing country establishing academic ties with an economically and technologically advanced country. The fields of study of

TABLE 3-22   Percentage Distribution of American Graduate Students and Faculty in All Fields Who Conducted or Planned to Conduct One Month or More of Research in the PRC, by Field, 1978–1979 Through 1983–1984

Field of Study	Percent
Agriculture	6
American studies	2
Architecture	3
Business management	2
Computer and information sciences	2
Education	1
Engineering	7
Health sciences	3
Humanities	26
Law	1
Library and archival sciences	—
Life sciences	3
Mathematics	3
Physical sciences	4
Social sciences	38
Total	100
N =	(392)

NOTE: The symbol "—" indicates a value less than 0.5 percent.
SOURCE: Questionnaire responses from Asian studies departments at 30 universities. Respondents were asked to estimate, "How many graduate students and scholars at your university *outside* of China studies have conducted research for one month or more in the PRC from academic year 1978–1979 through academic year 1983–1984?" Added to these data were figures, estimated by the same respondents, for students and scholars in China studies fields.

TABLE 3-23   Percentage Distribution of American Chinese Studies Graduate Students and Faculty Conducting or Planning One Month or More of Research in the PRC, by Field, 1978–1979 Through 1984–1985

Field of Study	Percent
Anthropology	7
Art history	5
Economics	6
History	28
Linguistics	5
Literature	25
Political science/international relations	17
Sociology	6
Total	100
N =	(199)

NOTE: Figures for 1984–1985 are those who planned to conduct research at time of survey.
SOURCE: Questionnaire responses from Asian studies departments at 30 universities.

the PRC Chinese in America, the uneven flow of students and scholars between China and the United States, the low priority accorded the study of agriculture for the Chinese, and Americans' interest in pursuing work in the humanities and social sciences in China are all characteristic of the academic relations between Third World countries and the United States. Although the Sino-American academic relationship has its own distinctive character, the broader similarities should not be overlooked or incorrectly ascribed to the PRC's political and social system.

Second, the clear imbalance in the flow of students and scholars moving between China and the United States *is likely to grow in the years ahead*. Growth processes already under way, and decisions made by the PRC government in late 1984 and early 1985 to send more students and scholars abroad will both contribute to this trend. Americans should not permit this imbalance to distract them from the more important issue of quality. Rather, they should concentrate on improving the quality of the experience that U.S. students and scholars have in China, and on making it possible for a broader range of Americans to go to China for long-term study and research. Access for both Americans in China and Chinese in the United States are discussed later, but it should be emphasized here that, over time, there will be an erosion of goodwill if Americans come to perceive a lack of *responsiveness* on the part of the Chinese.

Third, although it is not known how many PRC students and scholars return to China, the personal characteristics of the F-1 students suggest that many will seek to remain in the United States. The Chinese government's recent decision to permit more "self-supported" students to go abroad signals, in the authors' view, its willingness to accept this.

Fourth, American universities (themselves drawing funds from many sources) have been the single largest category of financial supporters of PRC students and scholars in the United States, contributing more than the Chinese government itself. American universities have funded the Chinese for several reasons, among them: the quality and competitive performance of PRC students (see Chapter 5), the comparative ease with which the Chinese have been absorbed into American university communities, and the important teaching and research roles played by PRC Chinese students in many graduate science programs.

Fifth, the geographic and institutional origin in China of PRC students and scholars coming to the United States raises questions about China's development strategy and U.S. involvement with it. Most Chinese who study in the United States are from three coastal areas and a small number of "key" schools. Although the implications of this are by no means self-evident, China's unity has long been dependent on the prevention of gross disparities between different regions of the country. Should such an imbalance develop and assume politically significant forms, the United States could become associated with the contested development strategy. This suggests that American institutions, in establishing ties with their Chinese counterparts, might profitably consider geographic and institutional diversification in the PRC. Indeed, the eagerness with which inland provinces now are seeking external ties may represent new opportunities for some American scholars and institutions.

Sixth, if American policy is aimed at training a Chinese generation that would be in place for a long time to come, the declining average age of PRC J-1s coming to the United States is significant. Because more and younger Chinese are coming to the United States, the effects of the present program—whatever they may be—will endure.

NOTES

1. The figure 14,000 comes from Guo-cang Huan, "Taiwan: A View from Beijing," *Foreign Affairs* (Summer 1985), p. 1074.

   The findings in this report are based upon both quantitative and qualitative information from program files, specific data sets described below, questionnaires, telephone and personal interviews, commissioned papers, and published sources. Each source has strengths and weaknesses, but together they provide a comprehensive view of Sino-American scholarly exchange. The details of the principal sources are described below. (Before proceeding further, the reader is advised to review the terms in the Glossary.)

   Records of Visas Issued to PRC Students and Scholars in 1983. The PRC persons of interest in this study fall into a number of categories. The largest proportion of them are students; next are research scholars, and the remainder are professors, trainees, teachers, or international visitors. Because all such persons must be issued visas from the American Embassy or consulates in China before they may travel to the United States, a survey of the application forms for Chinese citizens issued visas yields a complete count of all categories of persons traveling for scholarly reasons. The records of all visas issued during 1983 are stored at the American Embassy in Beijing and at the consulates in Shanghai and Guangzhou. Of the 4,391 F and J visas issued in 1983, 96 percent were located and hand-coded for this study. The names of individual subjects were not included in the coding process.

   An important strength of this information is that it covers both J-1 and F-1 visas. J-1 visas are issued to students, research scholars, teachers, trainees, and international visitors. Persons issued J-1 visas are considered to possess a higher level of scholarship and generally are subject to the "two-year rule" (see Glossary). In the PRC, these individuals generally are considered to be "officially sponsored." F-1 visas are issued *only* to students, and, for the most part, these individuals are supported by funds from relatives or personal sources. The Chinese generally refer to these persons as "self-paying" or "privately sponsored" (see Glossary), though the overlap between American visa categories and Chinese designations is imperfect. Therefore, it is possible to compare the attributes and activities of the Chinese in the two visa categories of interest in this study. A weakness of the visa data is that they are available only for 1983, since some earlier data were destroyed according to regulation, making it impossible to analyze trends over time. Because this type of information is so valuable, the Committee on Scholarly Communication with the People's Republic of China (CSCPRC) will continue to compile these data for subsequent years. Some time lag is inevitable since records for one year cannot be examined until the following calendar year.

IAP-66 Data Concerning J-1 Students and Scholars. The United States Information Agency (USIA) routinely collects information on the students and scholars who receive J-1 visas. This information is recorded on a form called the IAP-66, which is filled out annually by sponsors of these visa holders. For this study, 26,301 records from 1979 into 1984 were analyzed.

The principal strength of the USIA data is their existence over a period of several years, which permits analysis of trends. Also, they provide valuable information about the financial support provided by different types of sponsors. Unfortunately, fewer items of information are available for this data set than for the 1983 visa data. Moreover, F visa holders (all of whom are students and the great majority of whom are in the United States under private arrangements) are *not* included.

Questionnaires. In 1984, a questionnaire was sent to 391 American universities and colleges that were identified as having five or more Chinese students and scholars. Of these questionnaires, about 60 percent were returned; 55 percent of the total sent out were usable. The questionnaire provided information about how universities handle students from the PRC, including admissions policies, student adjustment, problems in health and housing, and financing. (See Appendix B for a complete list of responding institutions.)

To obtain information about American students and scholars traveling to China, another survey was sent in mid-1984 to 64 universities with Asian studies programs; 50 percent of these questionnaires were returned, a marginal response rate that limits the ability to generalize. However, this is one of the few sources available on Americans visiting China for scholarly purposes. These questionnaires were analyzed by hand, and many interesting qualitative comments were obtained. (See Appendix C for a complete list of responding programs.)

Other Sources of Information. To compare various programs that send students and scholars to China for study and research, telephone interviews were conducted with 11 individuals known to have received grants to study or to undertake research in China from the CSCPRC and from other programs. Additionally, onsite interviews were conducted with administrators and faculty at seven American universities and colleges (Appalachian State University, University of California at Berkeley, Hofstra University, University of Minnesota, Oberlin College, University of Pittsburgh, and Stanford University) to compile case studies on institutional experiences with U.S.–China exchanges. These schools were selected by the study steering committee, which sought to include a variety of types of institutions. Also, limited formal and informal discussions were held with representatives of the Chinese Embassy in Washington, representatives of China's Ministry of Education (MOE), and officials of the Chinese Academy of Sciences.

2. Table 3-2 shows that 12,222 "new" arrivals in the J-1 category came to the United States in the 1979–1983 period. This indicates that the double-counting problem is not great, because the total of 12,514 J-1 visas issued (in Table 3-1) is only slightly higher

than the figure of 12,222 for "new arrivals" in Table 3-2. If it is assumed that a person who interrupts his or her stay in the United States with a trip back to China is counted as a "continuing" student or scholar upon return to the United States, then most Chinese students and scholars appear to have stayed in the United States for the full duration of their studies, during the period under study. Furthermore, if it is assumed that the double-counting problem is no more severe among privately sponsored students (the 7,358 F-1s in Table 3-1) than for J-1s, this would mean that a total of about 19,000 Chinese students and scholars have come to study in the United States during the 1979–1983 period. Note, however, as time progresses, the double-counting problem is expected to become more severe, since more Chinese may have the opportunity to come to the United States for a second time.

3. Foreign Broadcast Information Service (*FBIS*), Apr. 24, 1984, p. B12, from *Xinhua*: "The ministry [of Education] sent the first group of 52 visiting scholars to the United States on December 26, 1978. . . . China has since sent 8,900 government-financed students to the United States, 3,600 of whom have graduated and returned. Most of the remaining 5,300 are visiting scholars and post-graduates. Another 4,000 Chinese students are studying in the United States at their own expense." This report, however, cannot be usefully assessed because the period covered by the figures is not precisely specified. As discussed later in this chapter, there appear to be serious gaps in China's statistical collection system.

4. Interview, May 23, 1984, Washington, D.C.

5. Mary Ellen Adams, Alfred C. Julian, and Krista Van Laan, eds., *Open Doors: 1983/84, Report on International Educational Exchange* (New York: Institute of International Education, 1984), p. 18; and *Open Doors: 1979/80* (New York: IIE, 1980).

6. This is consistent with the earlier 1981 findings of Thomas Fingar and Linda A. Reed, *Survey Summary: Students and Scholars from the People's Republic of China in the United States, August 1981* (Washington, D.C.: U.S.-China Education Clearing House, 1981), pp. 5 and 8 (hereafter referred to as *Survey Summary, 1981*).

7. IIE News Release, Sept. 5, 1984.

8. "China Will Send More Students Overseas," *China Daily*, Nov. 30, 1984.

9. *FBIS*, Jan. 15, 1985, pp. K12–K14, from *Xinhua*.

10. Larry Sirowy and Alex Inkeles, "University-Level Student Exchanges: The U.S. Role in Global Perspective," in Elinor G. Barber, ed., *Foreign Student Flows: Their Significance for American Higher Education*, Report on conference held at Spring Hill Center, Wayzata, Minnesota, April 13–15, 1984 (New York: Institute of International Education, 1985), pp. 60–61.

11. The seemingly low numbers of J-1 visa holders who intend to study computer science in the United States can be explained by the fact that the general category of "engineering" includes several computer-related subfields.

12. According to National Center for Education Statistics material, supplied by Tom Snyder.

13. John S. Aird, "The Preliminary Results of China's 1982 Census," *The China Quarterly*, No. 96 (December 1983), pp. 616–617.

14. When applying for an F-1 visa, a document called the "Student Data Form" is required to be completed. This document, which requests information on educational background, was not available for J-1s, and the educational background information frequently was missing for F-1s.

15. CAS released two (somewhat contradictory) figures which indicate that the Academy had sent well in excess of 3,000 persons abroad throughout the world by mid-1984 (see *Joint Publications Research Service* [hereafter referred to as *JPRS*], CPS-84–090, Dec.

20, 1984, P, S & M [Political, Sociological, and Military Affairs], pp. 51–52, from *Guangming Ribao*; also *JPRS*, CPS-84-090, Dec. 20, 1984, P, S & M, pp. 69–70, from *Xinhua*); CAS has provided CSCPRC staff with moderately detailed figures on scholars sent to the United States.

16. Twenty-nine percent of all foreign students in the United States in academic year 1983–1984 were female. IIE News Release, Sept. 5, 1984.

17. These estimates were computed based on a projected total number of F-1s and multiplied by the average annual amount spent per year per J-1. However, this calculus assumes that J-1s and F-1s cost the same on average (see Table A-10 for methods of calculation).

18. It was possible to determine the amount of money that a student or scholar received from different sources to cover tuition and room and board (but *not* air tickets). This information was available for about 80 percent of the J-1s from 1979 through 1983. It was assumed that this group is representative of all J-1 visa holders.

19. Fingar and Reed, *Survey Summary, 1981*, p. 23.

20. *China Daily*, Nov. 30, 1984.

21. Ordinary least-squares regression analysis was used, and variables that were significant to at least the .05 level of probability were included in the results.

22. *FBIS*, Dec. 13, 1984, p. K17, from *Xinhua*.

23. *FBIS*, Apr. 24, 1984, p. B12, from *Xinhua*.

24. *FBIS*, Dec. 13, 1984, p. K17, from *Xinhua*.

25. *FBIS*, Apr. 24, 1984, p. B12, from *Xinhua*.

26. *Open Doors, 1982/83*, pp. 1 and 86.

27. Sirowy and Inkeles, in *Foreign Student Flows*, pp. 36–37.

28. Ibid., p. 41.

4

Exchange Programs and Sponsors

On January 31, 1979, immediately after the establishment of diplomatic relations, President Jimmy Carter and Vice-Premier Deng Xiaoping signed a landmark "Agreement on Cooperation in Science and Technology" in Washington, D.C. This accord provided the umbrella under which subsequent federal scientific, technological, and educational exchanges have occurred. Subsumed under this agreement was an earlier "Understanding on Educational Exchanges," signed in October 1978 to provide for the exchange of undergraduate students, graduate students, and visiting scholars to undertake research and study in each country. Since the late 1970s, the Sino-American educational relationship has achieved high-level attention from many quarters in both societies, most recently during Premier Zhao Ziyang's January 1984 visit to America, President Ronald Reagan's spring 1984 journey to China, and Chinese President Li Xiannian's summer 1985 trip to the United States.

These agreements and the protocols that grew out of them prompted rapid increases in the number of individuals involved in academic exchanges.[1] But this growth also reflects the initiatives of an expanding range of governmental agencies and of private organizations on a national scale. This chapter describes the roles and activities of these diverse government and private organizations.[2]

The many national-level organizations engaged in academic exchange with China are motivated by a variety of considerations, and in many cases, by more than one objective. Initially, an important motivation of the U.S. government was strategic: to assure that China and the Soviet Union did not again cooperate in ways inimical to U.S. interests. Over time, the range of motivations has broadened. Some organizations value cultural and educational exchange as a means to promote mutual understanding. For others, access to China provides opportunities to contribute to change in the PRC,[3] which reflects, in some instances, secular missionary impulses. In many cases, the principal motivation of organizations has been to reinforce China's "open" policy and to familiarize the Chinese with Western technology and products. For still others, China is a place to be studied, yielding information that will contribute to global scholarship.

Chinese national organizations also have diverse, often multiple motivations for participating in exchange with the United States. Many Chinese view academic relationships with the United States in practical terms—such ties provide a quick way to augment China's skilled manpower pool and to overcome, to some extent, the damage done by the Cultural Revolution. For others, Western science and technology have an almost magical quality, offering a possible "solution" to China's heretofore intractable modernization problems. Finally, some Chinese see ties to prestigious American institutions as a way to enhance the visibility of their own institutions domestically and to win additional resources in the ongoing scramble for funding. The resumption of academic ties also has had a very personal meaning for many Chinese and Americans who share a desire to renew ties with institutions and colleagues that had been established in the pre-1950 era.

This chapter focuses on the national exchange programs of the U.S. federal government and of private agencies. As will be seen, public- and private-sector programs have complemented one another well. Initially, programs such as the National Program of the Committee on Scholarly Communication with the People's Republic of China (CSCPRC)[4] focused principally on providing single-year grants for individual research in China, with emphasis on Chinese studies and the natural sciences. Over time, new exchange programs of both the CSCPRC and other public and private agencies have diversified exchange opportunities by broadening the fields of exchange, providing multiyear grants, promoting collaborative research, assisting China in disciplinary and institutional development, and offering opportunities to teach in China. By the mid-1980s, all of these initiatives, taken as a whole, constituted a rather comprehensive framework for academic exchange.

Bilateral Agreements

Between 1978 and mid-1985, the number of bilateral accords in science, technology, or education between Chinese and American government agencies grew from 2 to 24 (see Appendix G). Following the normalization of U.S.–China relations, the U.S. executive branch promoted these bilateral agreements in the belief that it was important to institutionalize the Sino-American relationship rapidly. One way to do this was to give the major government agencies in each country a tangible stake in the relationship.

The resulting bilateral agreements cover a broad range of scientific areas: space technology, high-energy physics, environmental protection, earthquake studies, nuclear safety, transportation, statistics, and biomedical sciences. These agreements sparked varying degrees of activity. Because most are funded under existing agency budgets rather than through special federal appropriations, the degree of interchange that has occurred reflects the importance that agency heads placed on Sino-American technological and scientific cooperation and the visibility their agencies gain by promoting such ties.

Since the large number of agreements and diversity of activities precludes a thorough description of each, this section instead presents an overview of the most active bilateral programs and looks in greater detail at one innovative program, the Dalian National Center for Industrial Science and Technology Management Development.

As of 1985, some of the most vigorous bilateral agreements included the Protocol on Cooperation in the Field of Atmospheric Science and Technology (signed by National Oceanographic and Atmospheric Administration [NOAA] in 1979); the Protocol on the Field of Marine and Fishery Science and Technology (NOAA, 1979); the Protocol for Scientific and Technical Cooperation in the Earth Sciences (U.S. Geological Survey [USGS], 1980); the Protocol for Scientific and Technical Cooperation in Earthquake Studies (USGS and National Science Foundation [NSF], 1980); and the Agreement on Cooperation in the Field of Management of Industrial Science and Technology (U.S. Department of Commerce, 1979). Interactions between the U.S. Department of Agriculture and the PRC were extensive until November 1983, when activities under the 1979 Understanding on Agricultural Exchange were suspended after China failed to import the quantity of American grain called for in a long-term agreement.

One of the most innovative bilateral programs grew out of a 1979 protocol, signed by the U.S. Department of Commerce, China's State Economic Commission, State Science and Technology Commission, and Ministry of Education (MOE). Entitled "Cooperation in the Field of Management of Science and Technology," the protocol was designed to give China a mechanism for upgrading its management techniques. For the United States, the agreement satisfied a desire to respond to China's needs and to improve relations between the two countries. Some American observers, looking at the long range, saw the agreement as a way to "train a group of managers who would be familiar with American techniques and equipment, would be favorably disposed to deal with American companies, and who would continue to exercise both mental attitudes as they rose through the Chinese bureaucracy to more important positions."[5] The initial agreement expired in 1984 and was renewed for five years in April of that year.

As a result of this agreement, the National Center for Industrial Science and Technology Management Development was established at Dalian City, China, in 1979. The center now employs a staff of both Americans and Chinese and provides a 6- to 8-month curriculum similar to that in American business schools for about 200 Chinese mid-level managers annually. By the end of 1985, 87 Americans will have taught at the center. In the first four classes (through 1983), 750 individuals were trained. By the end of 1984, there were more than 1,000 graduates of the center throughout China. Of the 750 trainees in the first four classes, about two-thirds were factory managers or were otherwise involved in management. Of the remaining one-third, about half were science managers and half were college teachers. The largest single group of Dalian graduates is employed in the Beijing area.[6] The most notable graduate of the center to date is Wang Zhaoguo, the former director of an auto plant who became head of China's Communist Youth League and now (late 1985) is director of the General Office of the Central Committee of the Chinese Communist Party. Another graduate is Ye Qing, vice-minister of China's Coal Ministry. Hong Yuandong, deputy mayor of Dalian City and also a graduate, acknowledges the role of the center in alumni's success, noting: "It's not true that the training was the sole reason for our promotions, but I cannot deny the basic fact that it helped."[7]

The Dalian Center now also offers an 8- to 10-week course for senior Chinese executives. In May 1985 the State University of New York at Buffalo began operating a master's of business administration program at the Dalian Center, with the two governments agreeing to provide a total of $2 million for this new program during its first five years. "The Chinese students will spend their last semester at the Buffalo campus and will take internships in American companies as part of their academic requirement."[8]

The center has been highly successful from a number of perspectives. Although both Chinese and foreign observers believe that China's modernization effort requires persons trained in business and management sciences, China sends only a small number of officially sponsored PRC students and scholars to study these fields in the United States. The Dalian program provides another way to meet that need. The success of the center is also reflected in the value the Chinese place on admission, the increasing authority exercised by graduates in their work units, and the high-quality American academics who wish to participate in the program. Finally, alumni of the Dalian Center sometimes work together on common problems. Some of the center's alumni, in Shanghai for instance, get together to address difficult business investment decision problems. Graduates also seem to be establishing "horizontal" ties that may facilitate cooperation among bureaucratically separate Chinese organizations with related functions.[9]

Overall, the bilateral agreements display various degrees of activity and quality. From the perspective of building a network of agency ties between China and the United States, the agreements have achieved their principal aim. The bilateral agreements are important in two respects. First, inevitably, there will be ups and downs in the U.S. relationship with China over time; the web of interagency ties provides added stability to the relationship. For instance, in mid-1983, when bilateral political relations were at a low ebb, healthy educational ties continued unabated. Second, the bilaterals, based as they are on *mutual* benefits, are one way in which America can play a positive role in China's economic and scientific advance, at least until such time as development assistance may become available.

The U.S. government also is integrally involved, to varying degrees, with other national-level exchange activities with China.

The Fulbright Program

Following the 1947 launching of the Fulbright Program, China became the first country with a Fulbright Agreement.[10] The current National Fulbright Program is authorized by Public Law 87-256 of 1961. Grants are awarded to citizens of the United States and other countries for educational activities that include university lectureships, advanced research, graduate study, and teaching in elementary and secondary schools. The CSCPRC-administered National Program for Advanced Study and Research in China (see below) is part of the graduate study and advanced research component of the Fulbright Program with respect to China. Worldwide, the Board of Foreign Scholarships is responsible for setting program policy, supervising Fulbright exchanges, and approving Fulbright participants. The board is composed of educational and public leaders appointed by the President of the United States. The U.S. Information Agency (USIA) administers the Fulbright Program, with the U.S. Embassy in Beijing supervising the program locally.

In addition to the CSCPRC-administered National Program described below, there are other important facets of the Fulbright Program in China. The Council for International Exchange of Scholars (CIES) in Washington, D.C., is under contract with the USIA to organize publicity, to receive and process applications, and to make recommendations to the Board of Foreign Scholarships for sending Americans to Chinese universities as Fulbright lecturers in fields that include the following: American literature, American history, business management, economics, law, political science, and sociology.[11] CIES also brings some Chinese researchers and teachers to American universities.

From 1980 through 1984, CIES sent 73 American lecturers (see Tables A-11 and A-12) to 12 Chinese universities, colleges, and institutes in eight cities (see Table A-13). Of the Chinese institutions, Beijing University and Shanghai Foreign Languages Institute received the most lecturers. The program's early focus on American studies and English language in 1980 and 1981 has expanded to include law, economics, political science, business, library sciences, and several other fields in 1984 (see Table A-12).

From 1980 through 1984, CIES brought 22 Chinese lecturers (see Table A-14) and 45 Chinese researchers (see Tables A-15 and A-16) to the United States. The Chinese lecturers have lectured on topics pertaining to the study of China, while the researchers generally have undertaken research on the United States.

While also administered through the Board of Foreign Scholarships, some Fulbright funds are also appropriated for the U.S. Department of Education (USED), where the Office of Postsecondary Education (Center for International Education) administers the Foreign Language and Area Studies Training Program. This program is designed to promote and improve modern foreign language training and area studies in American education. Grants are available in these areas: Doctoral Dissertation Research Abroad, Faculty Research Abroad, Group Projects Abroad, and Seminars Abroad, as well as Foreign Curriculum Consultants.[12] With the exception of Foreign Curriculum Consultant grants (which bring educators from other countries to the United States to help develop language and area studies curricula for American schools), all other grants under the program are to send Americans abroad.[13] The CSCPRC receives monies from USED for the National Program to fund Doctoral Dissertation Research Abroad and Faculty Research Abroad in the area of modern foreign languages and area studies. The competitions administered by USED are conducted separately from those of the CSCPRC. Interested applicants may apply to either or both of these organizations. From Fiscal Year (FY) 1980–1981 through 1983–1984, USED selected 17 people in its Doctoral Dissertation Research Abroad Program to conduct research in China. Eight of those students also were selected by the CSCPRC and are included in the total number of CSCPRC graduate program grantees.

From FY 1980–1981 through FY 1983–1984, 13 individuals were selected by the USED Faculty Research Abroad Program to conduct research in China. Three individuals listed in the department's records also were selected by the CSCPRC and have been included in statistics for the National Program (discussed below).

The Fulbright Program in China, as is the case with the Fulbright Program worldwide, has difficulty in attracting enough high-quality American applicants, especially younger persons.[14] Several factors cause this problem, including the low stipends that deter Americans with young families from participating in the exchange. Young faculty also find that in their attempt to gain tenure at U.S. universities and colleges, a year abroad as a Fulbright lecturer does not necessarily enhance their prospects at many institutions.

The Fulbright Lecturer Program is particularly important because it emphasizes the fields of American studies, American literature, American history, and economics. More recently, limited attention has been given to sending Americans to lecture on business management, library science, law, and political science. Few students in these fields are sent abroad by the PRC, though the fields are critical to China's capacity to understand the United States and to the success of Beijing's educational and economic goals.

National Science Foundation

The NSF inaugurated its program of Sino-American scientific cooperation in December 1980 by signing the U.S.–China Protocol on Cooperation in the Basic Sciences with the Chinese Academy of Sciences (CAS) and the Chinese Academy of Social Sciences (CASS).[15] Activities under the protocol are coordinated by the U.S.–China Joint Working Group on Cooperation in Basic Sciences, staffed by Americans from NSF and Chinese from CAS, CASS, and MOE.

Currently, emphasis in this program is on cooperative research in a wide range of disciplines.[16] The NSF program provides support for scientific cooperation between the United States and China through joint seminars and joint research projects. Since the inception of the program, joint research projects have been undertaken in fields that include the following: archaeology, applied mathematics, astronomy, engineering sciences, linguistics, international studies, materials science, natural-products chemistry, systems analysis, plant studies, earth sciences, and information sciences. Between December 1980 and November 1984, the program supported a total of 43 cooperative research projects and 12 joint seminars and workshops.

The NSF cooperative program has several notable strengths. Because many projects are conducted over two-year periods and involve researchers from both nations, access problems are less likely to arise. One scientist who received grants (at separate times) from the CSCPRC and the NSF indicated that the multiyear character of research projects under the NSF program permits scientists to tackle more complex projects in a sustained and comprehensive manner than is possible under the single-year grants from the CSCPRC. Another notable feature of the NSF-funded joint research projects is that between December 1980 and November 1984, 16 of the projects directly involved Chinese university researchers.[17] This is consistent with Beijing's desire to improve the research capabilities of Chinese universities.

On November 13, 1984, the fourth meeting of the U.S.–China Joint Working Group on Cooperation in Basic Sciences was held in Washington, D.C. That meeting expanded the scope of cooperation under the Basic Sciences Protocol to encompass *all* fields of basic science, engineering, and social sciences eligible for joint support by the two sides. Previous cooperation had been limited to certain fields by mutual agreement. Extension of the protocol for a second five-year period will occur in April 1986.[18]

CSCPRC PROGRAMS

The CSCPRC was founded in 1966 under the joint sponsorship of the American Council of Learned Societies (ACLS), the National Academy of Sciences (NAS), and the Social Science Research Council (SSRC). With the outbreak of China's Great Proletarian Cultural Revolution late that year, 1966 was not an auspicious time for Americans to try to develop scholarly dialogue with academics in China. Nonetheless, the CSCPRC's founders hoped that monitoring intellectual developments in China and fostering interpersonal ties where possible would pay off when political circumstances changed. Such a change occurred in February 1972 when President Richard M. Nixon and Premier Zhou Enlai signed the Shanghai Communique. In the wake of that communique, both governments recognized the CSCPRC as an agency to facilitate scholarly exchange programs. In 1972 the CSCPRC began a multidisciplinary exchange program. By the spring of 1985, 40 American delegations had visited China and 50 Chinese delegations had traveled to the United States (see Appendix H).

In September 1978, USICA (U.S. International Communication Agency, which was called U.S. Information Agency before April 1978 and after August 1982) designated the CSCPRC to administer the National Program for Advanced Research and Study in China in anticipation of the October signing of the "Understanding on Educational Exchanges." In this Understanding, the United States expressed the wish to send 10 "students" to China in January 1979 under the new National Program and 50 additional "students" under the same program by September 1979, "as well as such other numbers as the Chinese side is able to receive."

At about the same time, the U.S. government decided to grant an unlimited number of academic visas to Chinese students and scholars who were accepted into bona fide academic programs in American institutions of higher education. As a result of this decision, there has been no direct relationship between the number of Americans going to China and the number of Chinese coming to the United States. American academic ties with China, therefore, are fundamentally different from those with the Soviet Union, which maintain a strict numerical equality of "person-months." The American decision not to require such numerical correspondence in its educational exchange relationship with China was wise. However, that decision does diminish CSCPRC capacity to negotiate access for National Program students and scholars.

Since its inception, the National Program has received funding from the NSF, USIA, the National Endowment for the Humanities (NEH), and USED. Total budget allocations during program years 1978–1979 through 1984–1985 have exceeded $7.4 million, of which 17 percent has come from NSF, 48 percent from USIA, 18 percent from NEH, and 18 percent from USED.

The National Program consists of two components: a graduate program and a research program, both of which support long-term research and study in China. From January 1, 1979, to July 1, 1985, about one-third of the total number of National Program grantees were in the graduate program, and approximately two-thirds in the research program (see Table 4–1).

More than one-half of all grantees have been in the social sciences

TABLE 4-1   CSCPRC National Program Grantees, by Program
Category and Program Year, 1978–1979 Through 1984–1985

Program Year	Graduate Program	Research Program	Total for National Program
1978–1979[a]	6	7	13
1979–1980	22	30	52
1980–1981	10	30	40
1981–1982	16	22	38
1982–1983	18	21	39
1983–1984	8	30	38
1984–1985	11	27	38
Total	91	167	258

NOTES: Program year 1978–1979 began January 1, 1979; all other program years begin on July 1 of each year.
   Extendees are *not* included in this table.
SOURCE: CSCPRC National Program files.

(including history) and the humanities (Table 4-2). In the social sciences (see Table A-17), there has been little change in the yearly number of grantees in anthropology, economics, political science, and sociology, despite the 1981 controversy over field work in China.

National Program grants have been awarded to individuals from 85 U.S. institutions of higher education and 16 other institutions. Fifty-two percent of total grants awarded went to individuals from 12 U.S. universities (see Table A-18), reflecting the large percentage of graduate students selected from the major East Asian Studies centers. About one-half of National Program grantees have been from publicly supported schools.

Like the Americans who went to China under the pre-1950 Fulbright Program, scholars under the National Program have been concentrated in China's capital. The principal host units for more than one-half of National Program grantees were located in Beijing, and about 10 percent were in Shanghai. The remaining one-third were widely distributed among China's provincial-level units (see Table A-19). Of the 29 provincial-level units, only 8 have not served as principal host for a National Program grantee from January 1, 1979, to April 1, 1985. Some of these 8 units—Guangxi, Heilongjiang, Henan, Jiangxi, Ningxia,[19] Shanxi, Xinjiang, and Tibet—have had grantees working in them.

Former participants point to both strengths and weaknesses in the National Program; what some view as strengths are problematic to others. In the view of participants, the main strengths were the capacity of the program to make initial contacts with a broad range of Chinese

TABLE 4-2   Percentage Distribution of CSCPRC National Program Grantees by Field Designation, for Program Years 1978–1979 Through 1984–1985

Field of Study	Graduate Program	Research Program	Total for National Program
Agriculture	3	2	3
Business management	0	1	—
Computer science	0	1	—
Education	1	0	—
Engineering	0	2	1
Health sciences	2	4	3
Humanities	30	12	18
Law	7	1	3
Library/archival sciences	0	0	0
Life sciences	0	13	8
Mathematics	0	2	1
Physical sciences	1	13	8
Social sciences[a]	37	39	38
Other	19	13	15
Total	100	100	100
N =	(121)	(198)	(319)

NOTES: Figures were determined by counting fields of study indicated by National Program grantees on their applications. Since many grantees indicated two fields, the "N" of 319 is higher than the total number of grantees (258). Percentages were rounded to the nearest 1 percent.

Program year 1978–1979 began on January 1, 1979; all other program years begin on July 1.

The symbol "—" indicates a value less than 0.5 percent.

[a]Includes history.

SOURCE: CSCPRC National Program files.

host units, CSCPRC's "connections" in China, and the prestige presumably conferred on winners of a national, peer-reviewed, high-quality grant competition. Some participants were critical of the National Program's requirements for minimum and maximum grant periods, its nonreciprocal nature, the long lead times required for participants in the program, and self-censorship of difficult research projects by faculty and scholar applicants. Some respondents also criticized the close ties to officialdom in both countries that were praised by others, illustrating the double-edged quality of such links. Close ties to officialdom may be essential to solve one scholar's problem while they may subject other scholars to unwelcomed attention.

The CSCPRC also has run the reciprocal "Distinguished Scholar Exchange Program" (DSEP) since 1979.[20] Like the National Program,

DSEP is a national-level, peer-reviewed competition. Under DSEP, equal numbers (in terms of person-months) of Chinese and American scholars travel in each direction annually. DSEP has a distinctive nomination procedure; half of the Americans who go to China are nominated by the Chinese and half of the Chinese who come to the United States are nominated by the Americans. Under the DSEP program, 129 Chinese came to the United States (see Table A-20) and 164 Americans traveled to China (see Tables A-21 and A-22) from 1979 through 1985.

Among both Chinese and Americans, the distribution of fields of study offsets the "natural" proclivities of each side (Table 4–3). Among Americans going to China under DSEP, there is a higher proportion of natural scientists than is the case in either the National Program or the university-to-university programs (see Chapter 5). There is a higher proportion in the social sciences and humanities among Chinese coming to the United States under DSEP than there is among the total number of students and scholars the Chinese government chooses to send abroad.

TABLE 4-3   Percentage Distribution of American and Chinese DSEP Grantees by Field Designation, 1979–1980 Through 1984–1985

Specific Field Designation	Chinese Grantees[a]	American Grantees[a]
Agriculture	1	2
Business management	1	—
Computer science	2	1
Education	1	0
Engineering	12	11
Health sciences	4	1
Humanities	11	10
Law	0	1
Library/archival sciences	0	—
Life sciences	8	9
Mathematics	3	4
Physical sciences	20	17
Social sciences	27	26
Other	10	14
Total	100	100

NOTES: Program years begin on July 1.

Figures were determined by counting fields of study indicated by grantees on their applications. Since many grantees indicated two fields, the total "N" is higher than the total of grantees (129 Chinese and 164 Americans).

The symbol "—" indicates a value less than 0.5 percent.

[a]Figures have been rounded to the nearest percentage point.

SOURCE: CSCPRC Distinguished Scholar Exchange Program (DSEP) files.

In recent years the CSCPRC began several initiatives that reflect new directions in academic exchanges with China. First, in early 1984, the CSCPRC began to administer the Science, Technology, and Economic Development Program for the National Academies of Sciences and Engineering, an initiative in applied science and technology with China's State Science and Technology Commission (SSTC). Under this program, American applied scientists from industry and academe in the United States are brought together with their Chinese counterparts from production ministries and other research institutes. Together, the two groups have held workshops on agricultural and energy technologies and on issues of science and technology management. This program responds to China's emphasis on applied science and attempts to involve American industry more extensively in academic exchange with the PRC.

As a second initiative, the CSCPRC and NAS opened a representative office in Beijing in July 1985. Functioning as a liaison body, the office will coordinate the academic, scientific, and technical exchange activities with CAS and other relevant Chinese organizations. The office is supported through specific grants to NAS from the Henry Luce Foundation, the Andrew W. Mellon Foundation, and the Ford Foundation. Additional support is provided through a general grant to NAS from the John D. and Catherine T. MacArthur Foundation to promote and maintain nongovernmental programs between the scientific communities of the United States and the PRC. This ongoing presence is one more indication that the Sino-American relationship is becoming institutionalized. Both sides are building the infrastructure necessary to support a larger and more interactive relationship.

Finally, the CSCPRC and the Chinese are now exploring the possibility of establishing a long-term research presence in several Chinese urban and rural localities. If such sites are established, they could involve multidisciplinary teams, conceivably composed of Chinese and American scholars. This plan would give American and Chinese scholars important opportunities to observe change at the local level, over time, both individually and in teams. This is a significant research need that should be addressed regardless of the fate of this particular plan.

These three new CSCPRC initiatives reflect some of the exciting changes occurring in Sino-American academic relations: greater emphasis on applied science, the creation of institutions in China that will facilitate academic interchange, and the opportunity for sustained multidisciplinary research in particular localities in China.

The national-level programs discussed above are fairly comprehensive, and overlap among them is not a serious problem. Nonetheless, they leave three areas of academic need unmet. First, a flexible travel grants program would be a valuable aid in facilitating the participation of American scholars in Chinese conferences, especially in the sciences. Second, American natural scientists lack adequate support to conduct their own individual research in China. The NSF and the CSCPRC, with their limited resources, have a fairly high rate of proposal rejection (about 4:1). Both organizations have indicated that, were additional monies available, significantly higher numbers of worthwhile proposals could be funded. Finally, there is very little federal support for programs in the applied sciences, technology, and agriculture.

CHINESE UNIVERSITY DEVELOPMENT PROJECT AND OTHER ACTIVITIES OF THE WORLD BANK

Because the World Bank is an international organization designed to promote worldwide economic and social development, its activities generally fall outside the scope of this study. However, the Bank is undertaking education projects in China in which many American scholars are participating. As of mid-1985, the World Bank was actively involved in projects on university development (particularly equipment and instrumentation), agricultural education and research, television education, and rural health and medical education. In addition, the Bank has plans for programs designed to upgrade provincial universities, technical education, instructional materials, and curriculum design (see Appendix I).

One World Bank program, the Chinese University Development Project, has extensive American professional and administrative participation. Under the program, Chinese faculty are sent to the West or to Japan for study or training. According to Chinese MOE figures covering the period from September 1982 to April 1984, 60 percent of the 1,182 Chinese faculty who received these awards had gone or planned to go to the United States (see Table A-3).*

The four-year project, administered by the Chinese MOE, is funded with a $200-million loan and credit agreement with the International Bank for Reconstruction and Development (World Bank) and the International Development Association. The project focuses on 28 major Chinese universities (see Table A-3), attempting to strengthen their

---

*As of March 31, 1985, the MOE reported that 1,532 students and visiting scholars had been sent abroad under this project. Of that total, 894 (or 58 percent) went to the United States (see Table A-23, Part II).

undergraduate and graduate teaching programs in physics, chemistry, computer science, engineering, and biology. The project also supports research development programs at these universities through the creation of 47 key laboratories and establishment of research and analytical centers on the university campuses.

Two panels advise the Chinese MOE on the overall implementation of the project. One is the Chinese Review Commission chaired by Zhang Guangdou, eminent hydraulic engineer, vice-president of Qinghua University, and member of the Chinese Academy of Sciences. Working with the Chinese Review Commission is the International Advisory Panel chaired by physicist Dale R. Corson, president emeritus of Cornell University and member of the National Academy of Engineering. The National Academy of Sciences in Washington, D.C., provides an administrative base for the International Advisory Panel. This panel is composed of specialists from the United States, the United Kingdom, France, Germany, Japan, and The Netherlands.

The International Advisory Panel works with the MOE, the Chinese Review Commission, and the administrations of the project universities in the following areas:

1. The selection of teaching and research equipment to be procured with project funds;
2. The updating of undergraduate curricula, the designing of graduate programs, and the development of research programs;
3. The further training of university faculty of the designated universities through the selection and placement of fellows for study outside of China;
4. The improvement of university management in five specific universities; and
5. The expansion of managerial capacity of the MOE in the areas of statistics, accounting, monitoring and evaluation, and the preparation of future sectoral investments.

One of the most important functions of the International Advisory Panel is to work with the MOE and the project universities in the selection and appointment of subject area foreign specialists for short-term technical assignments in China. The foreign experts consult on graduate and undergraduate curriculum development, advise on the development of research programs, conduct seminars, lecture, and help strengthen university management programs.

This program is important for a number of reasons, not the least of which is that it reflects China's desire to strengthen the research capabilities of its universities. Such capabilities had, to a considerable extent, deteriorated in the years after 1949 because of the strategy of concentrating research in the Chinese Academy of Sciences and ministerial research institutes. Moreover, the focus of the University Development Project on instrumentation in the basic sciences is filling a major gap that must be closed if effective research is to be conducted in China.

CHINA-RELATED ACTIVITIES OF AMERICAN PRIVATE PHILANTHROPIC ORGANIZATIONS: AN OVERVIEW

In his excellent overview entitled "American Philanthropy and Educational Exchange with the People's Republic of China,"[21] Francis Sutton notes that, overall, American foundations have devoted and continue to devote only modest resources to international activities.

Tradition and the tax laws have continued to make the total output of American philanthropy impressive. But it is notorious that most of it goes to local and national causes and purposes with perhaps not more than 2% going to foreign parts or to international matters in the U.S. . . . The interests of a few large foundations may give an impression of a special vocation for international matters among the endowed foundations, but in fact the number of foundations among the more than 22,000 in this country that have regular international programs is very small. . . . A reasonable guess at average recent levels of foundation international giving would be of the order of $100 million. . . . The rise of corporate philanthropy to totals comparable with foundation philanthropy seems not to have brought any major additions to international activities. . . . But, by and large, the maxim that charity begins at home has been at least as loyally maintained by corporate philanthropy as by the other forms of American philanthropy.[22]

Nonetheless, with the normalization of Sino-American relations, American philanthropic foundations are again viewing China as a particularly attractive site for their international activity.

This attraction is rooted in both past and present circumstances. First, some of the organizations most involved in China today (e.g., the Rockefeller Foundation[23] and the China Medical Board) were heavily involved in China prior to the Communist victory. Gratified by the impact of their previous philanthropic work in China, such organizations view renewed involvement as desirable. Second, foundations continually are in search of new and exciting activities and, as Sutton points out, respond to public enthusiasms. The new relationship with the PRC has captured the interest of large segments of the American populace, and foundations are responding accordingly.[24] The comparatively rapid "opening" of China in the 1970s and 1980s presented foundations with many important opportunities, particularly in China's education sector where the Cultural Revolution and the isolation of the previous 20 years had exacted a particularly heavy toll.

Beyond the charitable objective of relieving human distress, foundations generally pursue three other goals, singly or in combination, in their international activities: they seek (1) to strengthen American expertise in areas of strategic importance to the United States; (2) to enhance economic and social development in the belief that this will promote well-being, political stability, and international peace; and (3) to improve international understanding.[25] All three of these goals have helped draw foundations to China.

In supporting activities in China, American foundations historically have emphasized the liberal arts and natural, agricultural, and medical sciences. Today, foundations support programs to train Chinese students in the humanities and social sciences, particularly law, economics, international studies, and sociology. These fields fit comfortably with long-standing foundation proclivities; they are also areas on which the Chinese placed virtually no emphasis until very recently. Foundations, therefore, perceive an important gap to be filled and, as with agriculture and medical projects in China, these funding patterns also fit well with their traditional priorities and past work in China.

Because foundations are so numerous and their range of activities so broad, this report provides an overview of only some of the larger and more innovative philanthropic activities in the three broad fields that have received particular emphasis: education, health and medical sciences, and culture and the arts.

Education

The education-related activities of American philanthropic organizations in China have focused on the social sciences and humanities. Foundations currently are supporting the training of the Chinese personnel needed to build or to reconstitute fields that were neglected or undermined in the PRC and are helping to develop library resources. To improve understanding of China among Americans, U.S. philanthropic organizations have spent sizable resources on training American China specialists, on supporting academic research on China, and on underwriting conferences and seminars. The following discussion is *not* a comprehensive account of all American foundation educational activity in the PRC or of its total support for Chinese studies in the United States. It is an overview intended to convey the breadth and magnitude of foundation involvement with China.

The programs of the Asia Foundation are typical of foundation efforts to develop the social sciences in China and to strengthen Chinese libraries. From 1979 through 1983 the foundation sponsored 109 Chinese in the United States and 55 Americans in China at a cost of more than $600,000. It has focused its resources on law, international relations and strategic studies, international trade, international communication, and science and technology planning.

In cooperation with China's Ministry of Foreign Affairs, the foundation provided advanced training for young diplomats in American universities. In the field of international relations and strategic studies, it has sponsored senior research fellows (normally for a year) at major American universities. The foundation also has been helping China's College of Foreign Affairs develop its faculty by sending its lecturers to American universities and by inviting American professors to lecture in China. A similar project in international trade has helped train 13 younger lecturers for the Beijing Institute of Foreign Trade and has brought several American professors to lecture there under foundation auspices.

To encourage closer economic relations between the United States and China, the Asia Foundation has been cooperating with the Ministry of Foreign Economic Relations and Trade by offering advanced training in American business law to ministry staff members.

The foundation has also promoted journalism education. Three senior members of the New China News Agency each spent a year as visiting scholars, while two other veteran newspapermen participated in the Nieman Fellowship Program at Harvard. Young journalism lecturers received advanced training in an American university. Finally, one of the major undertakings of the foundation has been its Books for Asia Program, which distributes books and professional journals to libraries in China.[26]

The Ford Foundation not only has been a major force in the development of Chinese studies in the United States but also has consciously sought to contribute to the development of fields in China that are central to that country's economic success and "open" policy. Consistent with both Chinese and American priorities, activities funded by the foundation have centered on the fields of law, economics, and international relations. Total Ford Foundation commitments for China-related activities during the Fiscal Years 1979–1984 approximate $7 million, and in late 1984, commitments were running at the rate of more than $1.5 million per year.[27]

With respect to economics, the Ford Foundation has been working with the Chinese Academy of Social Sciences (CASS) in the area of economics management since 1979. In 1985 the foundation supported an expanded program on economics education and research in China involving seven Chinese university economics faculties and the institutes of economics in CASS. The program will offer young Chinese teachers and researchers year-long training in economics in the PRC and a doctoral fellowship program for selected Chinese in North American universities, and it will sponsor collaborative research projects. The foundation expects to commit approximately $800,000 for this program in 1985 and 1986; these funds may be augmented by monies from other sources. The program will be managed on the U.S. side by a committee cochaired by Professors Gregory Chow of Princeton University and Dwight Perkins of Harvard University, with administrative support from the CSCPRC. The foundation also has been working with the Chinese Academy of Agricultural Sciences and other Chinese institutions to strengthen research and training in agricultural economics. In 1983 it provided the Agricultural Development Council with $290,000 for this purpose.

In the field of law, the Ford Foundation has been active since 1981, when it provided funds for three American scholars to lecture in China and supported a conference in Beijing on the role of law in the United States and China, the first such conference since 1949. In 1983 the foundation provided a two-year grant of $575,000 to the U.S. Committee on Legal Education Exchanges with China (USCLEEC), chaired by Professor R. Randle Edwards of Columbia Law School. USCLEEC's programs include the exchange of legal scholars (including Chinese students doing advanced legal education degree work in the United States), U.S.–Chinese law conferences, and library development, as well as the acquisition of Chinese legal materials for American libraries.[28]

The Ford Foundation has also helped fund major conferences on international issues; supported visits to the United States, Asia, Africa, and Latin America by scholars from CASS and other Chinese institutions; and financed visits to China by American specialists on Latin America and Africa. It has contributed funds to a variety of CSCPRC programs, most notably DSEP, its Social Sciences and Humanities Panel, and the representative office in Beijing.

Finally, in international relations the Ford Foundation played a pivotal role in the 1984 establishment of the Committee on International Relations Studies with the People's Republic of China (CIRSPRC).

CIRSPRC was created at the initiative of several foundations concerned with international relations; it is administered by the Institute of International Education (IIE) in New York. Chaired by Robert Scalapino of the University of California at Berkeley, the committee sees its mission as helping to strengthen China's principal institutions of international relations research, training, and policy analysis while promoting collaboration between American and Chinese specialists. As of summer 1985, the committee had received funding from the Ford Foundation, the Rockefeller Foundation, and the Rockefeller Brothers Fund (RBF) totaling $1.1 million. The committee initially planned for a three-year program but anticipates that it could extend to five years.

CIRSPRC limits its activities to the following topics:

- contemporary international political, security, and strategic issues;
- contemporary international economic issues;
- comparative government in relation to linkages between domestic political and economic factors and international relations in various world regions;
- modern international relations history;
- international relations theory and research methodologies.

The committee is working initially only in Shanghai and Beijing with the following Chinese institutions: the Shanghai Institute of International Studies, the Shanghai Academy of Social Sciences, Fudan University, the Chinese Academy of Social Sciences, the Institute of International Relations (Ministry of Foreign Affairs), the Beijing Institute of International Strategic Studies (Ministry of National Defense), the Institute of Contemporary International Relations, the Center for International Studies (State Council), and Beijing University. CIRSPRC hopes eventually to establish relationships with institutions outside these two major cities.

Program activities include advanced training in the United States for PRC scholars, lecturing and collaborative research in China by Americans, study tours for staff members of Chinese or American institutions, research conferences and workshops, and library development and materials exchange. In February 1985, CIRSPRC agreed in principle to fund 11 Chinese candidates for graduate degree study and 7 visiting scholars (from eight different Chinese institutions) for academic year 1985–1986.[29]

Illustrating the wide range of American educational philanthropy in China is the work of the Trustees of Lingnan University, a New York-based organization that functions as a foundation. Trustees of Lingnan University was incorporated in New York State in 1893 to support the development of a college in Canton (Guangzhou) that later became Lingnan University. After 1949 the Arts and Sciences Schools of Lingnan were merged with Zhongshan University, which then moved to the former Lingnan campus. Subsequently, the American board of trustees functioned as a foundation, supporting the education of Chinese elsewhere in Asia, and worked chiefly with institutions of higher education in Hong Kong.[30] The Trustees resumed activity in the PRC in 1979 and have concentrated on projects at Zhongshan University, initially with emphasis on sociology and management.

In 1979 the Trustees made the first of several grants to assist CASS in reestablishing sociology as a discipline in China, and allocated funds for workshops and advanced study for Chinese scholars at the University of Pittsburgh and elsewhere. Grants also were made in 1979, 1980, and 1982 to support English as a Second Language (ESL) work in China and the United States.

After 1981 the Trustees gave particular attention to efforts by Zhongshan University to build a department of sociology. In 1981, two grants totaling $70,000 were made for a variety of initial needs: extended research stays and shorter study tours in the United States and Hong Kong for prospective sociology faculty members, lecturing at Zhongshan by American and Hong Kong scholars, and essential equipment purchases. In 1982 and 1983, renewal grants included support for field studies in China by Zhongshan students.[31] The Trustees began a series of annual grants to the university's new business management department in 1982, and in 1984 provided modest assistance to the chemistry department in order to strengthen general science education. In total, the Trustees of Lingnan University has provided more than $500,000 to Zhongshan University, most of which was designated for faculty advanced study and research in the United States, Hong Kong, or elsewhere in Asia. Finally, Trustees of Lingnan University has awarded grants to the Chinese University of Hong Kong (CUHK) to help pay for study there in sociology, business management, comparative literature and language, and related fields by persons from various PRC universities and colleges.

The activities of the Henry Luce Foundation show the degree to which Christian missionary impulses and the American belief in the transforming power of education have merged, particularly in the nineteenth and early twentieth centuries, to undergird philanthropic interest in education in China and the education of Americans about China. Born in Shandong Province in the late nineteenth century, Henry R. Luce was the son of a Presbyterian minister who was considered one of the founders of Yenching University, the buildings of which are now part of Beijing University. Luce became the cofounder of Time Incorporated and editor-in-chief of Time Magazine. He established the Henry Luce Foundation in 1936.

From 1978 to 1984 the Luce Foundation's work with respect to China fell into three categories: (1) grants under the Luce Fund for Asian Studies; (2) grants under the Luce Fund for Chinese scholars; and (3) general program grants to a variety of educational institutions, including exchange organizations. During this period, the foundation spent more than $4 million for these programs.

One primary exchange activity of the Luce Foundation—the Luce Fund for Chinese Scholars—was established in 1981 with $1 million, and an additional $1 million was allocated in late 1983 to assure the continuation of the fund through academic year 1986–1987. The purpose of this fund is to bring senior Chinese humanities scholars and social scientists (for periods of six months to one year) to one of 17 leading Chinese studies centers in the United States. Part of the philosophy in setting up the fund was to help counterbalance the heavy emphasis on science and technology in American exchanges with China.

The Luce Foundation also contributed to the USCLEEC's Law Library Development Program and has funded an Educational Testing Service project with China's Ministry of Education to improve selection and admission in China's higher-education system.

Although not a foundation, the United Board for Christian Higher Education in Asia has also contributed to educational development in China through its philanthropic activities. The board is an association of 10 Protestant denominations that, prior to 1949, had established 13 Christian universities in China. In 1979, when the U.S. government resolved American property claims with China, the board received monies from that settlement and decided to spend these and other revenues on educational projects in the PRC.[32] Board expenditures for its China program totaled $1,895,000 from 1981–1982 through 1984–1985.[33]

Following its 1980 agreement with China's MOE, the United Board has established major working relationships with Shaanxi Teachers University and Sichuan University to help establish two regional library centers by providing books and periodicals and by training librarians and other faculty. The board also has contributed to the development of humanities and social science faculty and other scholars from other Chinese institutions of higher education. At these other institutions the board occasionally also has provided aid for library development and the exchange of visiting professors.

Since the beginning of its agreement with the MOE, the board has sponsored (directly or indirectly) 141 scholars, 44 of whom were under 1984–1985 grants. Most United Board grants are made at the request of

PRC institutions of higher education on behalf of their social science and humanities faculty who are assured of jobs on their return.

Not only have long-established philanthropic organizations played an important role in recent educational work in China, new foundations are being established to promote such activities as well. One striking example is illustrated by the work of Santa Clara University Professor Shu-Park Chan (Chen Shubo). Chan has reached agreement with Chinese authorities to establish the China Experimental University in the Shenzhen Special Economic Zone near Hong Kong.[34] With Chan as the university's first president, a China Experimental University Foundation has been established (with plans to establish an office in Japan), and according to the foundation, "The Chinese Government has pledged 500 acres of land and U.S. $100 million for the construction. . . ."[35] However, the university will rely on non-PRC sources to cover operating costs, equipment, overseas staff salaries, travel, and so forth. There already are many indications that other Chinese institutions will seek similar kinds of American involvement in their development.

American foundations and philanthropic organizations have also worked to increase Americans' understanding of Chinese culture, history, and contemporary society. The Ford Foundation's involvement with China began in the early 1950s with efforts to develop Chinese studies in American universities. Since 1952 the foundation has invested some $40 million in support of major university centers of Chinese studies; the collection, storage, and distribution of Chinese language library materials; and the joint committees (now combined) of the SSRC and ACLS for the study of Chinese civilization and contemporary China.[36] Its contributions to the CSCPRC were mentioned earlier.

Along with Ford, the Andrew W. Mellon Foundation also has been a major contributor to Chinese and East Asian studies in the United States through its support of research and training projects conducted by the American Council of Learned Societies and through grants to organizations such as the Asia Foundation and the Association for Asian Studies. From 1978 through October 1984, the Mellon Foundation contributed $4.8 million toward these activities.[37]

The Luce Foundation has also supported studies on China through its Luce Fund for Asian Studies. The fund, established in 1975, was designed to stimulate new research on America's relations with East Asia and Southeast Asia. Ten major university centers of Asian studies participated in this program, receiving a total of $3 million over a six-year period. Several projects dealt with various aspects of U.S.–Chinese relations. Although the Luce Foundation discontinued this program, it still considers requests for support of specific projects on an ad hoc basis under its general program grants.[38]

The Wang Institute of Graduate Studies, although a relative newcomer to the philanthropic community, has begun programs of great importance to Chinese studies. In 1983 the Wang Institute initiated its Fellowship Program in Chinese Studies to support "full-time, postdoctoral research on any period or area of Chinese Studies in humanistic and social sciences." During the years 1984 and 1985, 13 fellows received grants totaling $250,000; the 1985–1986 academic year budget has been increased to $200,000. Fellows can use these grants as they see fit in conducting their research, and several have used part of their funds for work in the PRC. While American citizenship is not required of the applicant, he or she must hold a doctoral degree in a relevant discipline and have knowledge of China through academic accomplishment and proficiency in the Chinese language or in another relevant foreign language. The Wang Institute will sponsor two conferences in 1986, one concerning ancient China and the other focusing on linguistics.[39]

One of America's most pressing needs in Chinese studies and its relations with the PRC is the enhancement of the Chinese language capabilities in the United States. One U.S. organization, the Geraldine R. Dodge Foundation, has tackled this problem head-on in some of America's secondary schools. The Dodge Foundation's China Initiative has enabled 36 high schools (1983–1984) to offer Chinese language courses through grants totaling $1.4 million, plus an additional $200,000 for curriculum development and teacher workshops.[40]

Some of America's foundations have turned their attention to the more general need to educate the American public about China. One of the most notable organizations is the Johnson Foundation of Racine, Wisconsin. Since its establishment in 1959, the foundation has held, at its Wingspread Conference Center, approximately 40 China-related conferences involving both Chinese and Americans from many professions. Wingspread conferences have addressed such varied topics as teaching about China in the schools, U.S.–Chinese relations, and science, agriculture, education, urban planning, and the media in China.

Many of the foundation's programs were carried out in cooperation with the National Committee on United States–China Relations, Inc. (see below), the CSCPRC, and the China Council of the Asia Society. From 1979 to 1984, the foundation contributed about $177,000 to China programs through Wingspread conferences. The results of these conferences have reached large audiences through the foundation's radio programs and the publication of many conference reports.[41]

Health and Medical Sciences

During the nineteenth century and the first half of the twentieth, the medical projects of philanthropic organizations were among the most conspicuous activities of Americans in China. Although these activities were criticized by some Chinese both before and after Liberation as vehicles for "cultural imperialism," the medical legacy of this earlier era still influences today's China. In his Foreword to *China Medical Board and Peking Union Medical College* by Mary E. Ferguson, Raymond B. Fosdick, president of the Rockefeller Foundation from 1936 to 1948, articulated a rationale for philanthropic medical activities both in China and elsewhere.

In creating the Peking Union Medical College we were far wiser than we realized. The concept of modern medicine which was introduced there set in motion influences in China that cannot be stopped. The conflict of ideologies— what Gibbon called "the exquisite rancor of theological hatred"—does not relate to medicine, for health is something that all men desire, and there is no limited supply for which nations must compete. Modern medicine is one of the ties that bind the human race together regardless of ideologies and boundary lines. It is one of the rallying points of unity and is thus a foundation stone in the ultimate structure of a united society.[42]

Writing in 1951, Fosdick noted that China and the International Health Division had been the two most enduring interests of the Rockefeller Foundation.[43] Through its creation of the China Medical Board (discussed below) and the board's construction of Peking Union Medical College (PUMC), the Rockefeller Foundation's activities had considerable medical and scientific impact in the pre-1950 era. When China's post–Mao Zedong leaders became receptive to American philanthropy, the Rockefeller Foundation's renewed involvement was a natural continuation of its earlier interests.

From 1980 through May 1984 the Rockefeller Foundation allocated more than $1.3 million in grants to the PRC. Most of these funds were dedicated to projects on population and plant genetics.[44] The foundation's population-related assistance to China has given training opportunities to Chinese scientists, financial support for returning Chinese scientists to continue studies begun during training abroad, grants enabling selected Chinese institutions to do work in reproductive biology, and support and assistance for CAS and the Chinese Academy of Medical Sciences (CAMS). From 1979 to mid-1984 the foundation awarded fellowships to 22 Chinese scientists to spend 36 fellowship years studying in Western laboratories, primarily in the field of reproductive biology. To CAS's new Institute of Developmental Biology, the foundation contributed $350,000 toward the costs of designing and equipping a modern laboratory facility.[45]

The Rockefeller Foundation's involvement in medicine in China began in 1914, when the foundation established the China Medical Board "to take up medical work in China as recommended by the Commission [the 1914 Rockefeller Foundation Commission sent to China to 'Survey Current Medical Work and Education']. . . ."[46] The China Medical Board quickly reached an agreement with the London Missionary Society to purchase the Union Medical College in Peking in July 1915. During the next three decades and more, PUMC was built into one of Asia's premier medical and training centers. It was nationalized by the PRC in early 1951.

Following China's opening to the West in the late 1970s, the China Medical Board resumed its support of medical training and institutional development in the PRC. The board's first allocations went to the institution it supported prior to Liberation, now called Capital Medical College.[47] In 1980 the board allocated $250,000 for architectural advice on the design of a teaching hospital at Capital Medical College and $300,000 to replace pipes and boilers in the old PUMC Hospital.

In August 1984 the board reported that since 1979 it had allocated a total of approximately $9 million for the following purposes: a series of grants to Chinese medical schools to enable doctors to come to the United States for one year's study, for matching funds to eight Chinese medical schools for overseas fellowships, for matching and nonmatching funds to eight Chinese medical schools for research, for permanent matching endowment grants to seven Chinese schools for medical library support, and for a permanent matching endowment to Capital Medical College in Peking. In addition, various nonmatching funds have been allocated to the Chinese institutions involved, as well as funds for capital improvements.[48]

Other philanthropic organizations have also been significantly involved in cooperative medical training programs with the PRC. The Arthur M. Sackler Foundation and affiliated organizations have financed 16 grants that allow Chinese professionals to study in American universities for periods of 1 year to 18 months. Covering the academic years 1980–1981 through 1983–1984, the grants are part of a larger understanding with China's Ministry of Public Health. Nine grants were for students to enroll in programs of advanced English for technical interpreters and translators at Georgetown University. A second program provided grants to seven qualified doctors of medicine and other specialists in biomedical fields for postgraduate studies. Total expenditures by the Sackler Foundation and affiliates on Chinese academic-related programs and activities for the period 1980–1981 through 1983–1984 were $190,000.[49]

Project HOPE, an American private voluntary organization, is helping the Chinese improve their health care and medical education systems by creating or strengthening regional specialty care centers at leading medical universities. Since 1983, Project HOPE has helped the Chinese establish pediatric intensive-care units, learning resource centers, a new four-year nursing program, and a master's-degree program in health administration, and has trained Chinese health professionals in stomatology (oral and facial surgery), coronary surgery, intensive care, neonatal care, preventive dentistry, hospital administration, biomedical engineering, and adult heart surgery. During this time more than 75 medical educators from leading U.S. universities and hospitals have helped their Chinese colleagues incorporate the latest medical advances into the health care system. Project HOPE has also helped improve learning resources in China by donating more than 75,000 textbooks to health sciences libraries throughout the country.[50]

Culture and the Arts

A major portion of American philanthropic support for art and cultural education activities with China has gone to the Center for United States–China Arts Exchange. Established October 1, 1978, the center is a nonprofit national organization that promotes and facilitates exchanges of specialists and materials in the literary, performing, and visual arts between the United States and the PRC. The primary objective of the center is to stimulate public interest in the arts of both countries and to encourage collaboration among American and Chinese artists.

Initial funds for the center came from the Ford Foundation, the Rockefeller Brothers Fund (RBF), and the Henry Luce Foundation; Columbia University contributes office space and some direct costs. The center is not a funding organization; it relies on contributions of money, materials, and services from foundations, corporations, and individuals to carry out its programs. The anticipated expenses for FY 1984–1985 were approximately $530,000, $3\frac{1}{2}$ times the expenditure during the center's first year of operation.[51]

The center's programs have focused on bringing Chinese to the United States and sending Americans to China to lecture, teach master classes, and give and attend performances. The response to these performances in both countries suggests that the center has had an enduring impact directly on Chinese and American audiences. In May 1983 Arthur Miller's *Death of a Salesman*, directed by the playwright, opened in Beijing and drew full houses until the fall of that year. The production had the largest audience of any Western play in recent Chinese history. Isaac Stern's film *From Mao to Mozart*, a project facilitated by the center, brought the reality of the Cultural Revolution home to a broad American audience.[52]

The Atlantic Richfield Foundation not only has contributed to the Center for United States–China Arts Exchange, it also made a grant of $177,000 to the Museum of the American Indian for an exhibition of American Indian arts that was held in China in 1981.[53]

The Asian Cultural Council, the only foundation in the United States devoted exclusively to Asian-American cultural exchange in the arts, has contributed to the Center for United States–China Arts Exchange, but also has initiated numerous fellowship exchange programs of its own. The council has provided grants to both Chinese and American artists and specialists to support the teaching of the arts, attendance at workshops, travel, and observance of cultural activities. From 1978 to 1984 the council provided about $133,000 in grants to fund more than 40 musicians, dancers, visual artists, photographers, architects, theater specialists, and scholars and to support several performing arts troupes, artistic publications, and art exhibitions.[54] The council has provided grants to both Chinese and Americans to support teaching of the arts, workshop attendance, travel, observing of performances, and art exhibitions.

The Rockefeller Brothers Fund, in addition to its general support of the Center for United States–China Arts Exchange since 1978, has approved $475,000 to support the United States–China Arts Education Project, an innovative joint undertaking of the center and Harvard University's "Project Zero."[55] Over three years, the Arts Education Project will conduct a comparative study of arts education in the United States and the PRC. The study will include the exchange of arts educators. The Arts Education Project is the direct result of a project supported by the RBF in 1982 with a grant of $60,500 to the Center for United States–China Arts Exchange. Those funds were used to cover the costs of sending eight American specialists to Beijing and Shanghai in connection with a conference on arts education at the secondary-school-age level jointly sponsored by the center and the PRC Ministries of Culture and Education.

In summary, American foundations and philanthropic organizations have concentrated their activities in and about China on the social sciences, humanities, health sciences, culture and the arts, and, to a limited extent, agriculture. These initiatives are part of a larger purpose—to facilitate economic and social development and to enhance mutual understanding, thereby promoting world peace. This broad objective sets foundation programs apart from other American programs in China. First, the foundations seek to identify areas of need unmet by other national-level initiatives. Second, the foundations have emphasized directly strengthening and developing Chinese institutions to a much greater degree than have federal programs. Finally, they have sought to develop American competence on China through fellowships and institutional support.

The efforts of philanthropic organizations like the Ford, Mellon, and Luce foundations have greatly influenced the development of the entire Chinese studies field in the United States. In China, the past and present programs of the Rockefeller Foundation, the China Medical Board, and the Ford Foundation have had and will continue to have considerable impact.

One further effect of foundation activity is worthy of mention. Paradoxically, although there is great continuity between the pre-1950 project themes of some foundations and their present activities in China, the central imperative in foundation programs today is to identify and promote *new* initiatives. The tendency within other national-scale bureaucracies involved with exchanges is to preserve successful *old* programs. The dialectic between these two impulses serves the nation well.

PROFESSIONAL ASSOCIATIONS

In the course of this study, inquiries were sent to more than 50 professional associations identified in a directory* of the American Association for the Advancement of Science (AAAS) as having international academic or educational programs (see Appendix F). The plethora of professional associations in the United States makes it impossible to describe all their activities; those reported below simply illustrate the range of programs currently under way. These activities include delegation trips and study tours as well as joint conferences and symposia across a wide range of fields, including education, political science, library and information science, agriculture, cancer research, physics, psychology, engineering, computer graphics, metallurgy, and basic health sciences.

---

*1983/84 *Directory of the AAAS Consortium of Affiliates for International Programs.*

Four professional associations appear particularly active in academic exchanges with the PRC: the AAAS; the American Physical Society (APS) (discussed in detail in Chapter 7); the Computer Society of the Institute of Electrical and Electronics Engineers, Inc. (IEEE-CS); and the American Society for Metals (ASM). Other associations, such as the American Political Science Association (see Chapter 7) are just beginning cooperative activities with the PRC.

Since November 1978, when the Board of Directors of the AAAS traveled to China, the AAAS and the China Association for Science and Technology (CAST) have exchanged several delegations, with emphasis on joint symposia and study trips. Most recently, a joint symposium, "Science in China's Past: Recent Discoveries," was held at the 1984 AAAS annual meeting in New York. The papers presented at the meeting focused on the reconstitution of ancient metallurgical processes by studying artifacts (archaeological metallurgy), studies of traditional Chinese medicine, and new research issues in the history of Chinese science influenced by archaeological discoveries. During the summer of 1984, a delegation of American scientists visited China to participate in a joint symposium on arid lands issues at the Institute of Desert Research in Lanzhou. In the future China plans to send a CAST management techniques delegation to the United States and an arid lands delegation to the AAAS annual meeting.

Aided only by small grants from NSF in 1978 and the International Foundation in 1981, the AAAS has borne its portion of the costs of its exchange program with CAST. The association's arrangements with CAST are typical of such exchange agreements: the sending side pays international transportation and the receiving side the domestic costs.[56]

The American Coordinating Committee of the American Physical Society has participated since fall 1983 in a small but unique exchange program with the PRC. This undertaking places experienced Chinese Ph.D.-level scholars in American universities so that they can gain experience in modern research techniques. The uniqueness of the program lies principally in the fact that the scientists are carefully selected, mature physicists (ages 35 to 50) who are capable of assuming leadership roles in physics upon their return to China. The Chinese scholars are selected by CAS in cooperation with China's MOE. The American Coordinating Committee then matches them with prominent professors in American universities on the basis of their current research interests and abilities. After their arrival in the United States, the visitors participate as a group in regular "Chinese scholar meetings" to share experiences and plan for the future. The areas of research being emphasized in this particular program are condensed-matter physics and atomic, molecular, and optical physics. In 1984, 14 Chinese scholars were working at American universities under this program.

Under a financing arrangement stipulated in a Memorandum of Understanding signed by APS, MOE, and CAS, China would pay all travel expenses between China and the United States. During the first year of the program, the Chinese also would pay the stipends of the MOE scholars and the Americans would pay the stipends of the CAS scholars ($12,000 each, per year). Thereafter, the Americans would assume responsibility for all stipends. Another feature of the program is that the Chinese offered to pay all expenses for U.S. host professors to visit China for up to one month each, thus advancing the goals of the program by directly exposing American professors to Chinese research interests.

U.S. universities pay the American share of the stipends wherever possible, supplemented by funds from an Exxon Educational Research Grant ($20,000 per year). Other monies for running the program come from three separate sources: (1) The American program manager is a professor at the City College of New York, which donates a portion of annual administrative expenses. (2) APS contributes financially to various administrative expenses and travel in the United States. (3) The New York Academy of Sciences pays the costs of periodic meetings of the scholars in New York City.[57] This program shows how many academic activities with China represent the collective efforts of many groups.

Since 1979 the American Society for Metals has sent one delegation to China and received two delegations from the Chinese Society of Metals. The international airfares of the Americans traveling to China and domestic costs of the Chinese while in the United States generally were borne by the employers of the participating ASM members. This type of industrial support for exchange with China is widespread. Many companies have devoted considerable resources and employee time to hosting Chinese groups and permitting their employees to participate in a variety of educational endeavors related to China. ASM has also cosponsored three conferences that included Chinese scholars; one of these, the U.S.–China Bilateral Metallurgical Conference, was held in Beijing in November 1981.[58]

The Institute of Electrical and Electronics Engineers, Inc. (IEEE), a transnational organization with a quarter of a million members worldwide, started sending annual delegations to China in 1977 for the purpose of technical and cultural exchange. In addition, nine IEEE-society-based study groups have visited China since 1978, delivering lectures on a variety of topics in the fields of circuits and systems, communications, computer technology, control systems, magnetics, power engineering, quantum electronics, and radar/microwave theory. In 1978, IEEE began hosting Chinese delegations to the United States. The interests of these groups have encompassed many disciplines. During its centennial year, IEEE received a group composed of representatives from three of its sister societies in China. Over the past few years Chinese representatives have attended many IEEE conferences, and IEEE has sponsored or cosponsored three conferences in China: the First International Conference on Computers and Applications (June 1984), the International Conference on Properties and Applications of Dielectric Materials (June 1985), and the China 1985 International Conference on Circuits and Systems (June 1985). On July 17, 1985, IEEE celebrated the establishment of its first section in China, the IEEE Beijing Section, with a membership of 133.[59]

As the preceding examples illustrate, the principal exchange activities of professional associations have been delegations, conferences, and symposia. In the case of the American Physical Society, they have also included a program to bring Chinese scholars to the United States for long-term study. Much of the activity by professional associations actually involves interested members. Very often, the members themselves or their employers pay for these efforts, making it impossible to estimate either the magnitude of their financial commitment or the numbers of persons participating in such programs.

OTHER EDUCATIONAL EXCHANGE ORGANIZATIONS

Institute of International Education

Founded in 1919 with a staff of four, the Institute of International Education (IIE) now administers 163 programs for governments, foundations, corporations, universities, binational agencies, and international organizations. As of 1984, its budget was $92 million; it had a staff of 300 in its New York City headquarters, six regional U.S. offices, and six overseas offices. IIE recently has expanded its activities in the PRC, including the mid-1985 opening of a seventh overseas office in Guangzhou.

The China Guangdong Consultative Center of Talent Development, a provincial government agency, joined with IIE in 1984 to open the IIE/Guangdong American Study Information Center in Guangzhou, which provides counseling and advisory services to Chinese students considering study or training in the United States. The office, which formally opened in October 1985, offers the counseling and a reference library to Chinese students without charge. Both parties share administrative costs of the office, which is administered by a policy guidance committee composed of one representative of each party. Codirectors hired by IIE head the office, which will be staffed by Chinese personnel and American volunteers. The Luce Foundation has provided major support for this project; additional funds have been contributed by the United Board for Christian Higher Education in Asia and Trustees of Lingnan University.[60]

National Committee on United States–China Relations, Inc.

The National Committee on United States–China Relations, Inc., was founded in 1966 by interested American citizens. The National Committee was established in the twin beliefs that public education about China was essential if relations between the two countries were to improve and that a public body should be established to stimulate serious policy discussion of Sino-American relations. The National Committee's membership and leadership have always been drawn from a broad cross-section of America's business, academic, public service, and community leaderships. National Committee funders are USIA, USED, the Luce Foundation, RBF, the Ford Foundation, the Kettering Foundation, and NEH, as well as other foundations, corporate sponsors, and private contributors.[61]

With its 1972 hosting of China's Ping-Pong team in the United States, the National Committee, which had played a modest domestic role in public education about China, became an organization central to exchanges with the PRC. The initial exchanges were principally in athletics, the performing arts, and education. Over time, the National Committee sharpened the focus of its activities, with exchanges in the performing arts managed, for the most part, by the Center for United States–China Arts Exchange referred to above. Public education activities in the United States have been handled by the China Council of the Asia Society. By 1976 the National Committee was primarily concerned with exchanges in the areas of public policy, governance, and international affairs. More recently, economic management and development, communications, and education have also become high priorities.[62] From 1972 to 1985 the National Committee sent 63 delegations comprising 1,288 persons to China and has received 91 delegations with a total of 1,077 members from the PRC. Since 1972, when the National Committee's exchanges started, the organization has spent about $6.4 million. Not all of these funds have been devoted to exchanges of delegations—some have been allocated to other programs, such as those mentioned below.

Two National Committee programs deserve special mention: the Scholar Orientation Program and the Binational Dialogue. From its inception in the summer of 1980 through mid-1985, the Scholar Orientation Program involved more than 300 Chinese scholars. The program brings together Chinese scholars and professionals studying in American universities or research institutes for a 12- to 14-day series of lectures and seminars on American history and government and social and economic systems. Meetings with leaders in all branches of U.S. government, business, professional, and university affairs are an integral part of the program, as are visits to East Coast sites of historic and cultural interest. Chinese participants have been drawn from various professions, with the majority representing law, economics, management, journalism, foreign policy, American history, and English language and literature.[63]

The National Committee's Binational Dialogue, carried out in conjunction with the Chinese People's Institute of Foreign Affairs, is an annual series of gatherings that bring together a core group of distinguished citizens—decision makers and opinion leaders of both countries.[64] The first meeting was held in Tarrytown, New York, in September 1984. The second took place in Tianjin, China, in October 1985.

The principal rationale of the Binational Dialogue is a belief in the need for continuing, high-level, and unofficial discussion with PRC leaders on international questions. Moreover, it was hoped that this forum would acquaint leaders in both countries—particularly the potential leaders of the future—with one another's needs, problems, and aspirations. Finally, generational change in China made the latter consideration particularly important, as explained by a representative of the National Committee:

On the Chinese side, a historic transition is now under way. The generation conversant with the United States through pre-1949 education is passing from the scene. This generation was crucial in helping reestablish the links between the two societies and in interpreting America to China's political leaders. Few people familiar with the United States are today in sufficiently influential positions to take the places of the members of that generation.[65]

Yale-China Association

Founded in 1901, the Yale-China Association is a private, nonprofit organization that administers programs designed to enhance education and research in China and to improve American understanding of China and the Chinese people. The association is independently incorporated and is administered and funded separately from Yale University. The Yale-China Association is affiliated through cooperative agreements with Hunan Medical College and Huazhong Normal University in the PRC and with the Chinese University of Hong Kong.[66]

The association's principal activities are its English-language-teaching and medical exchange programs. Participants in the English-language-teaching programs, which began in 1980, spend two years in China. American participants in the medical exchange program, which started in 1979, spend from 1 month to 1 year in China; Chinese participants visit New Haven for 6- or 12-month stays. The Yale-China Association also has occasionally funded individual Chinese scholars to work at Yale. From 1979 through 1984, the Yale-China programs had 63 American and 26 Chinese participants. Total expenditures during that period were close to $500,000.[67]

During the 1980–1984 period, about 5,000 Chinese students and scholars have received English language instruction and exposure to American culture from the Yale-China teaching programs. Fourteen Chinese physicians have carried out research or clinical observation at Yale, and 14 Yale physicians have taught and conducted research in China under the association's Medical Exchange Program.[68]

The association is financed by private contributions, revenues from Claims Settlement with China, corporate and foundation grants, NEH Challenge Grant monies, and income from the association's endowed funds.[69]

In addition to the exchange organizations mentioned above, there are many other programs of importance, including Stanford University's U.S.–China Relations Program, Volunteers in Asia, the Oberlin–Shanxi Project, the United States–China People's Friendship Association, and the Council on International Educational Exchange.

Conclusions and Observations

1. The fundamental concept underlying the American government's promotion of bilateral agreements with Chinese governmental counterpart agencies has been the belief that it is essential to institutionalize the Sino-American relationship rapidly. One way to do this is to give the major bureaucratic entities in each country a tangible stake in the relationship. Bilateral agreements, and the linkages between American private-sector agencies and all levels of Chinese society, have provided added stability to the bilateral relationship. Nonetheless, because the relationship is still fragile, the maintenance and further strengthening of institutionalized ties is important.

2. On balance, the programs of the U.S. government, private Ameri-

can foundations, professional associations, and other organizations complement one another well. Nonetheless, three areas of academic need remain unmet: (1) There is no flexible travel grants program that would facilitate the participation of American scholars, especially in the sciences, in Chinese conferences. Foundation and federal funds for this purpose could be used effectively. (2) American natural scientists lack adequate support for engaging in their own individual research in China. (3) There is very little federal support for programs in the applied sciences, technology, and agriculture. More resources should be made available for these three purposes.

3. National-level exchange initiatives with China rapidly became involved in the development of institutions and programs after normalization. Because efforts to build institutions and to develop disciplines are designed to produce change, they inevitably create controversy in the society involved. Many of the programs discussed in this chapter focus on the social sciences and humanities, disciplines that embody values that were controversial in China before 1949 and are still so. The Chinese have historically wrestled with the problem of how to modernize without sacrificing the values central to their own national identity. It is essential, therefore, that American institutions facilitate change in a manner that is neither disruptive nor overbearing.

4. As American agencies become increasingly involved in institutional development in the PRC, they should remain mindful that American institutions require adequate support to help U.S. citizens better understand China and to promote American scholarship in and about China. Such investments paid off handsomely in the past. In the 1970s both the American public sector and the private sector were able to move rapidly to establish and consolidate extensive ties with China because both sectors had made major human and financial investments in Chinese studies during the 1960s and 1970s. Given today's rapidly expanding opportunities, there is an even greater need to maintain and enhance the American capacity to understand Chinese society, history, and culture. The United States needs to maintain, and indeed strengthen, the Chinese studies infrastructure of libraries, Title VI language and center grants, and opportunities for language study and research in Taiwan, Hong Kong, and the PRC (see Chapter 6).

5. Change in China is creating new possibilities for study, cooperative and multiyear research, applied-science cooperation, and American involvement in PRC education. Given the diversity of America's academic ties with the PRC, national leadership is needed in order to assess emerging exchange opportunities, to monitor trends in the relationship, to mobilize economic and intellectual resources, and to focus

attention on the issue of access. Therefore, there continues to be a need for an institution such as the Committee on Scholarly Communication with the People's Republic of China that has performed these functions in the past.

NOTES

1. Douglas R. Boyen, ed., *Open Doors: 1980/81, Report on International Educational Exchange; Open Doors: 1981/82; Open Doors: 1982/83;* and *Open Doors: 1983/84* (New York: Institute of International Education, 1981, 1982, 1983, 1984, respectively), Table 2.6.

2. This chapter is based on the authors' compilation and analysis of information from the following sources:

    The program files of the Committee on Scholarly Communication with the People's Republic of China—Records covering 1979 through 1984 for participants in the CSCPRC's National Program for Advanced Study and Research in China and Distinguished Scholar Exchange Program (now called the Visiting Scholar Exchange Program [VSEP], but referred to in this study as DSEP) have been computerized and analyzed in much the same manner as the United States Information Agency (USIA) and visa application data sets used in Chapter 3.

    Letters to foundations and professional associations—Requests for information on contributions to Sino-American educational exchanges were sent to 54 professional associations and 51 foundations. Responses were received from 25 professional associations and 32 foundations (see Appendix F).

    Additional Sources—Quantitative information about the participants in the Fulbright Program and other activities was provided by the USIA, the U.S. Department of Education (USED), the Institute of International Education (IIE), and the Council for International Exchange of Scholars (CIES). In addition, telephone interviews were conducted with all federal agencies having bilateral agreements with the PRC, and questionnaires were sent to 64 Asian studies programs at American universities.

3. For an excellent discussion of these impulses throughout history, see Jonathan Spence, *To Change China: Western Advisers in China, 1620–1960* (Boston: Little, Brown, 1969).

4. The CSCPRC's National Program for Advanced Study and Research in China offers support for visits to China by scholars and advanced graduate students in the sciences, engineering, social sciences, and humanities. The National Program has two components: (1) the graduate program, which offers support for individuals with an M.A. (or persons enrolled in a graduate or equivalent professional study program) to either enroll in courses or conduct dissertation research at Chinese universities; and (2) the research program, which supports individuals with a Ph.D. or the equivalent to conduct research in China.

5. U.S. Department of State cable, unclassified sections, No. 03901, March 1984.

6. Ibid.

7. Wendy Lin, "China Joins with U.S. Universities in Effort to Teach High-Level Managerial Skills," *Chronicle of Higher Education* (Jan. 23, 1985), p. 36.

8. Ibid.

9. U.S. Department of State cable, unclassified sections, No. 12806, June 1985, pp. 1–4. See also, Richard W. H. Lee, "Training Ground for a New Breed of Professionals," *China Business Review* (May–June 1985), p. 42.

10. Wilma Fairbank, *America's Cultural Experiment in China, 1942–1949*, Cultural

Relations Programs of the U.S. Department of State, *Historical Studies: Number 1* (Washington, D.C.: U.S. Department of State, Bureau of Educational and Cultural Affairs, June 1976), pp. 153–155.

11. CIES, *Annual Report, 1983*, p. 18.
12. *Fulbright Program Exchanges, 1983*, p. 25.
13. From FY 1980–1981 through FY 1983–1984, the Foreign Curriculum Consultant program has brought a total of three Chinese professors to the United States for 10 months each, one during FY 1980–1981 and two during FY 1981–1982.
14. Beverly T. Watkins, "'The Fulbrights,' Prestigious and Romantic, Are Having Trouble Luring Young Scholars," *Chronicle of Higher Education* (June 1985), pp. 23–25.
15. National Science Foundation, Division of International Programs, "U.S.–China Cooperative Science Program: Program Announcement and Guidelines for Preparation of Proposals," December 26, 1984, p. 1.
16. U.S. Department of State cable, No. 366456, December 1984, p. 2.
17. Ibid.
18. Rose Bader, program manager, National Science Foundation U.S.–China Cooperative Sciences Program, Apr. 10, 1986.
19. One National Program grantee received an extension that enabled him to spend considerable time in Ningxia, although his principal host for the initial grant was located in Beijing.
20. This program was known as the Senior Scholar Lecturer/Researcher Program during the 1979 program year. DSEP is a CSCPRC program that provides opportunities for American and Chinese scholars to lecture, conduct seminars, engage in collegial discussion, explore prospects for research in their discipline, or initiate actual research projects. The program is open to American scholars at the full or associate professor levels, or their equivalent, whose visits will make significant contributions to development of academic exchanges in a discipline, especially collaborative research projects.
21. Francis Sutton, "American Philanthropy and Educational Exchange with the People's Republic of China," prepared for the Conference on Sino-American Educational and Cultural Exchange, at the East-West Center, Honolulu, Hawaii, February 1985.
22. Ibid., pp. 1–3.
23. Mary Brown Bullock, *An American Transplant: The Rockefeller Foundation & Peking Union Medical College* (Berkeley: University of California Press, 1980).
24. Sutton, "American Philanthropy and Educational Exchange," p. 27.
25. Ibid., pp. 1–32.
26. The above information comes from a letter from Robert S. Schwantes, Executive Vice-President, The Asia Foundation, October 1, 1984; and the *Bay Area East Asia Newsletter*, Vol. 6, No. 3 (November 1984), p. 2. Updated in October 7, 1985, letter from Robert S. Schwantes.
27. "The Ford Foundation and China" (New York: The Ford Foundation, September 1984).
28. *Ford Foundation Letter*, Vol. 14, No. 5 (Oct. 1, 1983), pp. 4–5. Updated in telephone conversation with Peter Geithner's office, Oct. 16, 1985.
29. Douglas P. Murray, "CIRSPRC's First Year," *China Exchange News*, Vol. 13, No. 2 (June 1985), pp. 2–4. Updated in Oct. 1, 1985, letter from Douglas P. Murray.
30. Douglas P. Murray, "Foundation Support for Sociology in China: The Trustees of Lingnan University," in *China Exchange News*, Vol. 12, No. 4 (December 1984), p. 16. Updated in Oct. 1, 1985, letter from Douglas P. Murray.
31. Ibid.
32. Ibby Turnipseed, United Board for Christian Higher Education, phone conversation, Oct. 9, 1985.

33. Information from letter of C. T. Hu, China Program Director, United Board for Christian Higher Education in Asia, July 6, 1984.
34. *FBIS*, Aug. 8, 1984, p. R4, from *Tianjin Ribao*.
35. *China Experimental University Newsletter*, Vol. 1, No. 2 (1985), p. 3.
36. "The Ford Foundation and China" (New York: The Ford Foundation, September 1984).
37. Letter from James M. Morris, program director, Andrew W. Mellon Foundation, Oct. 16, 1984. Updated by James M. Morris's office in telephone conversation, Oct. 1, 1985.
38. Information from letter of Terrill E. Lautz, program officer, Henry Luce Foundation, Inc., Nov. 5, 1984. Updated in telephone conversation with Terrill E. Lautz, Oct. 22, 1985.
39. Information from letter of Margaret C. Fung, director, Wang Institute of Graduate Studies, Nov. 19, 1984, telephone conversation with Dr. Fung, July 1985, and letter received on Oct. 3, 1985.
40. Information from letter of Scott McVay, executive director, Geraldine R. Dodge Foundation, Oct. 31, 1984. Updated in telephone conversation with Scott McVay's office, Sept. 30, 1985.
41. Information from letter of Rita Goodman, vice-president, The Johnson Foundation, June 6, 1984.
42. Mary E. Ferguson, *China Medical Board and Peking Union Medical College: A Chronicle of Fruitful Collaboration, 1914–1951* (New York: China Medical Board of New York, 1970), p. 5.
43. Ibid., p. 13.
44. Letter from Jonathan Wiener, Information Service, The Rockefeller Foundation, May 29, 1984.
45. The Rockefeller Foundation, "Rockefeller Foundation Assistance to China in Population Matters." Mimeographed, June 1984.
46. Ferguson, *China Medical Board and Peking Union Medical College*, p. 21.
47. In 1985 the old name of Peking Union Medical College was restored.
48. Letter from Patrick A. Ongley, president, China Medical Board of New York, Inc., Aug. 27, 1984, and telephone conversation with Dr. Ongley, July 1985.
49. Information from letter of Curtis C. Cutter, executive director, Foundation for Nutritional Advancement, Aug. 31, 1984.
50. Information from letter of William B. Walsh, Jr., vice-president, operations, the Project HOPE Health Sciences Education Center, Sept. 25, 1984, telephone conversation, and letter from Kristen Foskett, director of public affairs, Project HOPE, Oct. 9, 1985.
51. Information from letter of Chou Wen-chung, director, the Center for United States–China Arts Exchange, Sept. 26, 1984, and *U.S.–China Arts Exchange Newsletter*, Vol. 5 (Summer 1984), p. 15. Updated in telephone conversation with Susan L. Rhodes, assistant director at the center, Oct. 18, 1985.
52. Ibid.
53. Letter from Eugene R. Wilson, executive director, Atlantic Richfield Foundation, Oct. 31, 1984.
54. Letters from Ralph Samuelson, associate director, Asian Cultural Council, Sept. 7, 1984, and Oct. 4, 1985.
55. Project Zero is a research unit at the Harvard Graduate School of Education that is devoted to the study of creativity and artistic thinking, and is named "Zero" because when philosopher Nelson Goodman founded the project in 1967, very little was

known about the cognitive and developmental processes involved in artistry. Information from Project Zero pamphlet and letters from William F. McCalpin, program associate, Rockefeller Brothers Fund, Oct. 1, 1984, and Sept. 30, 1985.

56. Information from letter of Lisbeth A. Levey, coordinator, AAAS China Exchange Program, American Association for the Advancement of Science, Dec. 22, 1984.

57. Information from letter of Mildred S. Dresselhaus, president, American Physical Society, Nov. 27, 1984, and letter from W. W. Havens, Jr., executive secretary, APS, Oct. 7, 1985.

58. Information from letter of Sarina Pastoric, manager, Society Activities, American Society for Metals, Nov. 27, 1984, and telephone conversation with same, July 1985.

59. Information from telephone interview with Barbara Ettinger, Institute of Electrical and Electronics Engineers, Inc., Aug. 12, 1985, and letter, Oct. 10, 1985.

60. Memo from Peggy Blumenthal, IIE, Apr. 26, 1985; telephone conversation with Peggy Blumenthal, Aug. 29, 1985; and letter from same, Oct. 1, 1985.

61. Information from telephone conversation with Jan Berris, vice-president, National Committee on United States–China Relations, Inc., July 17, 1985.

62. Jan Berris, "International Relations Programs of the National Committee on United States–China Relations," *China Exchange News*, Vol. 13, No. 2 (June 1985), pp. 6–8.

63. Information from letter of Janet A. Cady, program director, National Committee on United States–China Relations, Inc., Sept. 3, 1984. Also, information from Jan Berris, vice-president of the National Committee, July 17, 1985, and letter, Oct. 10, 1985.

64. Berris, "International Relations Programs of the National Committee on United States-China Relations," p. 7.

65. Ibid.

66. "Yale-China Association: Annual Report, 1983–1984," inside cover.

67. Information from letter of John Bryan Starr, executive director, Yale-China Association, Jan. 17, 1985, and telephone conversation, Oct. 23, 1985.

68. "Yale-China Association: Annual Report, 1983–1984," p. 4.

69. Ibid., p. 3.

5

Exchange on Campus

The speed with which Chinese students, scholars, and institutions have adapted to the American university scene since 1978 is one of the most notable features of Sino-American academic exchange. When the first PRC students and scholars applied to American schools, admissions officers and graduate departments had to make admissions decisions with virtually none of the standardized student information on which they normally rely. Transcripts from Chinese institutions frequently were unavailable; when available, they were not readily interpretable by admissions officers. The Chinese provided no standardized test scores to assess applicants' academic preparation, potential, and English language competence. Indeed, the very idea of rigorous grading and testing had been anathema to the Cultural Revolution radicals who had literally closed down China's institutions of higher education from late 1966 until the early 1970s. Even with Mao Zedong's death in late 1976, many Chinese were reluctant to embark on a path of strict academic evaluation that a few short years before had been denounced as "revisionist."

Equally problematic for universities was China's desire to send to America many nonmatriculated "visiting scholars," often scientists who sought knowledge at the scientific frontiers that had advanced dramatically during the isolation of the Cultural Revolution decade. Universities found this group difficult to deal with because of their age and comparatively senior status and because they were not enrolled in regular courses. Financial and social questions also were of concern. Would PRC students and scholars be able to adapt to the social milieu of the

American campus? Would they be able to compete for scarce financial resources?

By 1985 many of these problems had been substantially ameliorated and the questions answered affirmatively. All parts of the Graduate Record Examination (GRE) have been administered in China since October 1982, and the Test of English As a Foreign Language (TOEFL) is used routinely, though many persons still encounter difficulties in actually getting to the test sites and paying for the examinations. American university officials have a better understanding of Chinese grading systems, and today's graduates of Chinese institutions are selected much more methodically for study abroad under the officially sponsored program than were those sent in the late 1970s. Finally, although "visiting scholars" still comprise a significant percentage of the Chinese coming to the United States for study, the percentage of younger students is rising. In short, the Chinese have adapted rapidly to the American system, and PRC students and scholars generally are doing well.

Colleges and universities (drawing funds from a variety of sources) have become by far the biggest institutional financial supporters of PRC students and scholars in the United States, as seen in Chapter 3 (Table 3-16). In the wake of normalization, institutions of higher education signed many interinstitutional agreements with Chinese counterparts. Although these agreements are very important, the majority of exchange participants in both countries are not involved in them. Against the backdrop of these expenditures and the proliferation of interinstitutional ties, this chapter addresses the following questions: How are PRC students and scholars distributed in the United States and among different types of American educational institutions? What problems, financial and other, have arisen in the process of accommodating the needs of PRC students and scholars in the United States and those of Americans in China? How has the academic performance of PRC students and scholars been perceived on American campuses? What historical and other factors account for the proliferation of interinstitutional ties between American and Chinese educational institutions? Are these linkages generally working effectively and, if not, why? Can such relationships be modified to better serve American academic interests?

PRC Students and Scholars on the American Campus

Regional and Institutional Distribution

The great majority of PRC students and scholars come to the United States from comparatively few geographic areas in China and are drawn heavily from China's "key" educational institutions (Table 3-12 and Appendix D). But in the United States they are dispersed throughout almost all the states in the Union; indeed, one is struck by the very substantial geographic reach of China's academic presence in the United States (see Table A-24). The range of programs in which they are involved is equally broad; they attend all types of American schools of higher learning, from junior colleges to graduate institutions, with programs that range from vocational training to liberal arts and humanities studies.

Information on the intended destination in the United States of all PRC students and scholars is available only for 1983.[1] Overall, PRC students and scholars were somewhat more likely to be in the Middle Atlantic and Pacific regions than would be expected from either population size or the number of colleges and universities in those areas. Within these regions, New York and California had the highest percentages of PRC students and scholars, reflecting traditional settlement patterns of Americans of Chinese origin (see Table A-25). The American South receives relatively fewer students and scholars than would be expected based either on concentration of population or on institutions of higher education. Geographic patterns are different for the two visa categories. F-1 visa holders, who are generally in the United States under private and family arrangements, are more concentrated in California and New York than are the J-1 visa holders, most of whom are officially sponsored by the PRC government. J-1s tend to be distributed in a way that reflects American university fellowship support while distribution of F-1s tends to reflect the residential patterns of Americans of Chinese origin.

PRC students and scholars who received visas in 1983 *intended* to go to 440 different American schools (see Table A-26). Although there were three times as many J-1s as F-1s, F-1s mentioned more schools than did J-1s. F-1s attend a broader range of American institutions than J-1s do, because their academic level is more heterogeneous and there are many undergraduates in this group (see Tables A-26 and A-27). Also, because fewer F-1s study in fields targeted by the PRC government, more American schools are relevant to their needs.

J-1 visa holders, in contrast, were interested in a much narrower range of institutions. Seventy-six percent of this group intended to go to one of America's top 100 research universities,[2] whereas only 38 percent of the F-1s planned to do so (see Table A-28). This trend reflects the research focus and more selective character of the official Chinese program. Since officially sponsored PRC students and scholars are likely to play significant roles in development upon their return to China, it will be important to observe how their attendance at a comparatively small number of leading American institutions will affect their future career mobility, attitudes toward the United States, and future patterns of academic exchange. Equally important is the question of how this generation of American-trained Chinese will interact with their peers trained solely in the PRC and with the previous generation trained in the Soviet Union.

Funding PRC Students and Scholars on the American Campus

The Adequacy of Stipends American university officials estimate that PRC stipends for officially sponsored students and scholars are about $460 per month, with some variation for local cost of living.[3] There is ample evidence that many administrators and faculty at American universities and colleges believe that these stipends are inadequate, particularly in high-cost urban locales. In a questionnaire designed for this study, universities were asked about their perception of the adequacy or inadequacy of the PRC's stipend level for officially sponsored students and scholars. Two-thirds of the 112 respondents (usually the foreign student advisors at these universities) thought stipends were inadequate. This represents an increase compared with survey findings of Fingar and Reed which indicated that 42 percent of the respondents thought PRC stipends were not adequate.[4] The increase may reflect a number of factors: the rising costs of education in the United States, the reluctance of the PRC to raise stipend levels, and the increasing unwillingness of American institutions to waive stipend-level requirements for PRC students. The university respondents estimated that the average total stipend needed was about $680 per month—$220 per month more than the estimated amount of PRC stipends cited above.

From the perspective of American academics, low stipends cause several problems: they promote group living that hinders English language acquisition and encourages cultural isolation, they force PRC students and scholars to seek housing in unsafe buildings and neighborhoods, and they reduce the likelihood that they will purchase health insurance or participate in field trips and other educational activities. Finally, many universities have minimum financial support requirements for *all* foreign students, and administrators consider it inequitable to exempt PRC students from these requirements. Stanford University Vice-Provost Gerald Lieberman, for instance, recently described that university's response to this problem:

The stipend which the Chinese Government gives ranges between $420 and $450 a month. This is obviously substantially below our foreign student budget. . . . We have signed visa certificates for these students with increasing reluctance. Effective for 1985–86 we will no longer be able to do this. . . . It is inequitable for students from all the other countries and violates our own policy. We require all other foreign students to verify funds from Stanford or outside sources, up to the official budget in order to have a visa certificate issued.[5]

Health insurance is an equally critical financial issue. Many PRC visitors simply do not understand the potential cost of illness in American society, nor do Americans understand the responsibilities of the Chinese government in paying medical costs. Discussion with Chinese Embassy officials in Washington suggests that the PRC assumes no financial liability for privately sponsored (or self-paying) students and scholars in the United States. For officially sponsored students and scholars (see Glossary), the Chinese government may pay most medical costs if the person was officially selected by the PRC, but not all officially *sponsored* students and scholars are officially *selected*. The PRC government will insure these officially *selected* people for up to $10,000. If medical costs exceed that amount, the PRC's position is that the individual should return to China. Of course, it is in precisely such cases that individuals may be too ill to return.[6]

American universities may contribute to this problem by failing to require health insurance. More than 60 percent of the universities responding to the CSCPRC survey do require health insurance for exchange students and scholars, but that figure also indicates that many universities do not require it. Still other institutions require health insurance for students but not for visiting scholars and persons at the institution for short terms. The experience of one such uninsured scholar illustrates the problems this can cause. In early 1985 a PRC scholar hosted by a major American university was seriously injured and rapidly accumulated more than $6,000 in medical bills. The Chinese authorities reportedly assumed no liability and the scholar was not covered by the American host institution's health insurance plan, which did not insure visitors who stay for less than three months. With no other source of funds, individuals at the host institution were trying to raise money from private sources to pay these bills. The definitive way to prevent such situations is for all American colleges and universities to require all foreign students and scholars to show proof of adequate medical coverage.

Higher stipends and health insurance could improve the well-being of PRC students and scholars in many ways. But even if stipends are raised, there is no guarantee that the Chinese would use the added increment for better housing, educational materials, or health insurance. Many respondents mentioned that PRC students and scholars are frugal, and, indeed, many seek either to save American currency or to use it to purchase items not generally or easily obtainable in China. In 1984 such articles were referred to as the "eight great items" (color television, stereo, refrigerator, typewriter, washing machine and dryer, camera, and either a bicycle or a sewing machine).[7] That the Chinese might use stipends in these ways does not weaken the recommendation that stipend levels be raised. They should be.

The Issue of Financial Remissions to China

Some Americans have been concerned that many officially sponsored PRC students and scholars are remitting the portion of their fellowships in excess of the official Chinese government stipend level to their home work unit. Two separate interviews with officials of the Chinese Academy of Sciences (CAS) in 1984 helped clarify the situation. At that time, different Chinese organizations apparently had varying policies on the remissions of stipends, and some may have applied their guidelines unevenly within organizations. In 1984, for example, the CAS apparently offered a choice to students or scholars going abroad. Option "A" permitted the person who was awarded financial assistance in the United States to keep approximately $450 per month, which was roughly equal to the official Chinese stipend level. Above that level, the individual remitted 85 percent to his or her work unit and kept 15 percent for personal use—this amounted to an 85 percent income tax on amounts in excess of the official Chinese stipend level. The student or scholar who chose this option was then entitled to keep the "start-up allowances" provided to officially sponsored individuals and did not have to repay the subsidies and continuing wages provided by the work unit to family members who stayed at home (e.g., for housing and medical care). Under option "B", the officially sponsored PRC student or scholar could keep all of the American fellowship but had to repay the home unit for all subsidies and wages he or she directly received during the period abroad, as well as subsidies family members received during that time. Apparently it made financial sense to switch to option "B" when American aid reached about $600 per month. The Chinese officials said that this policy was in place to adjust for the financial benefits that PRC students and scholars abroad and their families in China continued to receive from the work units, and so to prevent "double dipping." Moreover, the officials also expressed some concern about students and scholars abroad having a standard of living too far above the level of colleagues in China.[8]

Since 1984, the Chinese may have modified these policies somewhat. A more recent study concluded:

The policies on kickbacks to the Chinese government of money received from American institutions has evolved over time as both Chinese and Americans have registered complaint. No longer are Chinese required to return to their government all, or even a percentage, of what they receive above $5,000. The current policy, reported to us informally by some who are subject to it, requires students and scholars to remit to their own work unit in American dollars the equivalent of their Chinese salaries for the period they were in the United States.[9]

Whether such arrangements are universal, applied consistently within organizations, or subject to change, they engender the perception among Americans that officially sponsored PRC students and scholars are not the only beneficiaries of American university fellowship support. Both the practice and perception are harmful to PRC exchange visitors. American universities and faculty are discouraged by such practices from providing partial grants to officially sponsored PRC students and scholars, believing that most of the increment over the official Chinese government stipend level goes to the home unit. Nonetheless, in the end, what PRC students and scholars do with their money is their own business, as is the case with all students. American institutions should require that China's official stipends be adequate and recognize that they cannot regulate how the money is spent.

PRC Students and Scholars: American Funding and Perceptions of Quality

The financial policy of the Chinese government in sending students and scholars abroad was stated clearly by Chinese Ministry of Education (MOE) officials in a 1984 interview: "Get more accomplished with less money" (*Shao hua qian, duo ban shi*). Officers of the MOE noted that when the exchange program began, the Chinese government paid about two-thirds of the cost. Now this contribution (in percentage terms) has been reduced because many PRC graduate students can obtain fellowships after their first year in graduate school. CSCPRC interviewers were told that there is "no need for more than one year."[10]

The basic premise underlying this position is that officially sponsored students and scholars should not need more than one year of PRC support if they are good. For "research scholars," the one-year limit to PRC support is rigid. One official of the Chinese Embassy has specified MOE policy on funding research scholars:

The Ministry [of Education] will provide one year [of] financial support to the scholars selected in 1984 and afterwards. In case a scholar finds it professionally necessary . . . to go on with his program in the United States for some more time, and he can manage to get [American] financial support for this extra period, then, with the approval of relevant authority, he is permitted to extend the duration of his stay for a limited period not more than one year. The Ministry of Education hopes that, with this change, the scholars will be encouraged to work still harder. . . .[11]

The MOE's policy toward officially sponsored students is slightly more flexible, depending on the student's field of study and the availability of American support. For instance, if a student in physics does not secure American funding after two years, MOE officials view that person as unlikely ever to do so and thus will not continue government support. But in some fields such as agriculture and law where American financial support is less readily available, the MOE appeared willing to make exceptions on a case-by-case basis.

Some Americans believe that these policies are undesirable because they encourage PRC students and scholars to become inordinately preoccupied with funding, discourage them from taking noncredit English language courses, and are insufficiently sensitive to the vagaries of funding in graduate departments. However, as long as American universities allocate financial support competitively on the basis of merit, it is difficult to object when the Chinese government employs the same criteria.

The academic performance of Chinese students and scholars suggests that they are indeed generally working hard enough to fulfill the PRC government requirements. In CSCPRC's questionnaire to American Universities and Colleges, respondents (usually foreign student advisors) were asked, "Generally speaking, how do the grades of students from the PRC compare to [other categories of students on campus]?" Forty-four percent of the college and university officials who responded to that questionnaire said that Chinese students' grades were "better than" those of "all graduate students." Ninety-seven percent said that Chinese students' grades were "better than" or "the same as" all graduate students.[12] These perceptions of quality are consistent with the success of PRC students in the competition for support. Maddox and Thurston report:

Repeatedly at the schools where we interviewed, we were told that the top physics students—despite often serious language difficulties—were Chinese. In fact, in some science departments, non-Chinese students have begun to complain that their Chinese colleagues are so good that they are throwing off the curve.[13]

Maddox and Thurston also quote one science faculty member who ranks PRC graduate students at the top of the class.

It is because the quality of students that come is so high that enthusiasm continues. If the quality were poor, it wouldn't last. Basically, it's because these kids come with the sole purpose of study. They aren't special agents of the government. They're here solely to study and learn. They do 100 percent—150 percent—of what they're asked to do.[14]

Visiting scholars have been a more heterogeneous and difficult group for American universities and colleges to deal with than students, and their performance is less easily measured. In the humanities and social sciences, there are no systematic data on how American scholars perceive their Chinese counterparts. Visiting scholars in the natural sciences received a generally favorable assessment in a survey conducted by University of Southern California chemist Otto Schnepp. The survey was addressed to faculty who have dealt with visiting scholars at seven American universities—Stanford University, University of California at Berkeley, University of California at Los Angeles, University of Chicago, University of Minnesota, University of Southern California, and University of Wisconsin. About 70 percent of the visiting PRC scholars in Schnepp's sample "would be welcomed back if they were to wish to return to the host research group" on the American campus where they previously had been.[15] A similar percentage of the visiting PRC scholars were reported to have "made significant contributions to the research they participated in."[16]

Although visiting scholars, particularly in the natural sciences, are perceived to have made contributions to some American research, some American faculty members also cite problems that arise because the visiting scholars tend to be older and less adaptable than the students, with academic needs that are less easily met by regular university programs. All of these factors combine to impose heavy demands on visiting scholars' American faculty hosts. Overall, however, the American academic community believes that the presence of PRC students and scholars in the natural sciences on campus has enriched academic life in the United States.

INTERINSTITUTIONAL ARRANGEMENTS

Formal exchange agreements between American and Chinese institutions have been one important vehicle for Sino-American exchange. From 1979 through 1984 there was a proliferation of agreements between American and Chinese universities and research and administrative entities. These offer American scholars and students potential avenues of access to a wide variety of institutions and localities in China. For some PRC institutions, these ties have become the principal vehicle by which they send their students and scholars to the United States. The majority of agreements, however, are substantially underutilized on both sides, symbolizing good intentions but little actual accomplishment. The task ahead is to identify the most vigorous interinstitutional arrangements and to strengthen them.

Of the 216 American universities and colleges that returned usable questionnaires (i.e., usable, as opposed to partially completed or blank questionnaires), 81 reported signing at least one interinstitutional agreement with a Chinese counterpart some time from 1979 to 1984.[17] This figure is fairly close to that given in a statement by the Chinese MOE in spring 1984: "About 100 U.S. universities have regular exchange programs with their Chinese counterparts to carry out joint research projects."[18]

The 81 American universities reported 214 agreements—an average of 2.6 agreements each (see Tables A-29 and A-30). CSCPRC's survey also showed that 123 Chinese institutions were reported to have at least one agreement with an American counterpart (see Table A-31). Since there were 211 agreements, each Chinese institution had an average of 1.7 agreements. Fifteen percent of the 125 Chinese institutions with at least one agreement were not colleges or universities, but organizations such as CAS, media institutions, some ministries, and administrative entities such as the Hubei Provincial Bureau of Education.

In the United States, impetus for these ties has come from several sources: historical and personal ties, a highly motivated Chinese studies community, and enthusiastic central university administrations. In China, university administrators initially saw such arrangements as a way to rapidly increase opportunities for their students and faculty to go abroad without securing vast quantities of scarce foreign exchange. Also, particularly during periods in which Beijing has emphasized the decentralization of educational administration, Chinese universities find such relationships useful means of avoiding the cumbersome central bureaucracy in the capital that controls the official student-abroad program. For some Chinese administrators, ties to American schools also are highly valued as a means of boosting the image of their institutions.[19]

For every American university that has set up an exchange with China, there are dozens that have not. In some instances, institutions (particularly smaller prestigious schools) have consciously decided not to establish such interinstitutional ties. These institutions have opted against doing so because they believe that top-notch scholars and students from China (particularly in the natural sciences) will apply anyway,[20] and that their faculty probably would have adequate opportunity to undertake research in the absence of such agreements. Moreover, individual departments fear that they might lose their traditional independence in the admission of students and be subject to pressure. Finally, in some cases, the institutions simply have no history of establishing such ties.[21]

Past relationships, both institutional and individual, are one factor shaping today's exchanges. For example, Oberlin College had a religious and educational presence in the Shanxi, Ming County Middle School, from the late 1800s until 1951. Ironically, Shanxi Province Vice-Governor Wang Zhongqing, the same official who dismantled Oberlin's program in the 1950s, personally arranged and paid for former Oberlin representative Ellsworth Carlson's 1979 return to the province in order to discuss the resumption of relations. Although Oberlin's ties in the 1980s are not religious in character, its exchanges are with two of Ming County Middle School's institutional descendants—Shanxi Agricultural University and Taiyuan Engineering Institute.

Americans of Chinese origin in U.S. universities have played, and are playing, a critical role in developing academic linkages and cooperative research projects with China. Although only one of the seven American universities visited in the course of this study cited faculty members of Chinese origin as *the* initial impetus for developing exchanges with China, four of the seven identified Chinese-American faculty as a very prominent factor in implementing the relationships, because they serve as bilingual, cross-cultural communicators, have extensive networks of personal ties in China, and retain a great sense of obligation to Chinese culture and society.

The personal and professional interests of Chinese studies faculty have been equally critical at these seven institutions. These faculty members have promoted interinstitutional ties because they seek to create research opportunities for themselves and their students as well as for the larger university community. Many also find appealing a sense of participating in China's experimental policies.

For university administrators, forming ties to China was motivated by a desire to internationalize the campus, to expand research opportunities, to create new programs that generate local interest and visibility, to satisfy their own personal intellectual interests, and, in a few cases, to raise university revenues. The central administration at Hofstra University, for example, believes that acting as a go-between for American firms that want to establish economic ties with Chinese enterprises will both enhance the university's access to China's intellectual circles and produce new university revenues.[22] According to the *New York Times*, "The university would receive a commission for each agreement it negotiated between China and a United States business."[23]

The flow of students under interinstitutional agreements suggests that the agreements are perhaps a comparatively more important vehicle for American students and scholars than for the Chinese. The 81 institutional respondents to the CSCPRC survey reported that, in academic years 1979–1980 through 1983–1984, a total of 838 PRC Chinese have come to American schools under these agreements. During the same period, 506 American students and faculty were reported to have gone to China under these arrangements. Although the PRC Chinese outnumber the Americans by a ratio of 1.6:1.0, this is much less of a disparity than exists in the overall Sino-American academic relationship. However, many of the Americans going to China under these arrangements go for short periods of time, and they frequently go to teach rather than to conduct their own research.

Of the 214 reported interinstitutional agreements, 49 percent appear to have no exchange participants moving in either direction. This inactivity can be traced to three circumstances. First, universities frequently have little funding with which to send either their students or faculty to China (see Table A-32). Indeed, in each of academic years 1983–1984 and 1984–1985, well over one-half of responding institutions had none of their own funds for sending undergraduates, graduate students, or faculty to China. Thus, students and faculty generally must find external support if they are to participate in their school's exchange program. Respondents also were asked how many students and faculty were supported by funds "administered by your university" (e.g., Fulbrights or Foreign Language and Area Studies fellowships). Eight of the 19 responding Asian studies centers had such funds, and each of the 8 supported from one to three persons in each of the two academic years 1983–1984 and 1984–1985.

Ironically, the responses to the questionnaires suggest that university support is much more available to bring Chinese students to the United States than to send American faculty and students to China. For American faculty and graduate students, most universities operate on the assumption that good projects can be funded externally.

A second impediment to the development of interinstitutional agreements has been the linking of generally comprehensive American universities with less comprehensive Chinese institutions. Almost all American universities have departments of political science, anthropology, and sociology, as well as numerous departments in the natural sciences—but this is not so in the PRC. Although changing slightly, most Chinese institutions are substantially less comprehensive. This means that only a few of the American institutions' faculty members see any natural "fit" between their interests and ongoing work at the particular Chinese institution with which their university happens to have a relationship. The location of the Chinese institution further shrinks the number of potentially interested faculty. Among those institutions whose fields are matched, only some American faculty will be interested because the location of the Chinese institution may be irrelevant to their research. Finally, the number of qualified faculty and graduate students in any given American school is reduced further because very few Americans speak Chinese (see Chapter 6).

The third problem affecting interinstitutional agreements involves the needs of American scholars who want to conduct research in China. A Chinese institution involved in such agreements generally finds that its American partner wants to send social scientists and humanists to do research, not to enroll in classes. These researchers (whether faculty or graduate students) want to conduct field research or, at a minimum, gain access to archives outside the individual Chinese institution's control that are not routinely open to foreigners. Because the Chinese unit has little leverage over external organizations, American schools wishing to send their students and faculty to China frequently fail to obtain the desired access. Even when access is eventually granted, the American institution becomes involved in protracted discussions encumbered by poor communication. Chinese institutions often feel overburdened by the need to negotiate with an endless number of external organizations to facilitate the research needs of the Americans. PRC administrators wonder why America cannot simply send people to study language, work quietly in the institution's library, undertake joint research in a laboratory, or teach classes in fields of interest to the Chinese. All of these factors adversely affect the likelihood of successfully undertaking social science research in China and decrease both the willingness of people to participate in these programs and the availability of funds to underwrite them.

The very character of the comprehensive American university makes it exceedingly difficult to establish linkages that promote mutual responsiveness. Maddox and Thurston summarize the problem well:

Often, the Chinese university is interested in sending scientists to the United States while the American university is interested in sending social scientists or humanists to China. Were the Chinese university to have difficulty accepting the social scientist or humanist, few of those with whom we spoke in American science divisions seem willing to refuse a Chinese scientist in order to force Chinese acceptance of the social scientist or humanist.[24]

This suggests that one way to establish highly responsive linkages is on a more specialized level, between departments or, for example, engineering schools. At this level, interests of the Chinese and Americans would presumably overlap enough to make both sides eager to meet one another's requirements.

The problems that affect interinstitutional programs are balanced by some equally important strengths.[25] First, these arrangements generally involve the American student or faculty member with a less cumbersome application and placement bureaucracy than when they must deal with national bureaucracies. They are more flexible in terms of the length and purposes of the stay in China. Because of this flexibility, these local programs permit a broader range of academics to undertake work in China. Second, if the agreement involves an explicitly reciprocal exchange of individuals, the Chinese tend to exert themselves more to meet the needs of the Americans, because they see a clear connection between accommodating the Americans and the continuation of the exchange. Third, some CSCPRC interviewees believed that research that would not have found favor among the national bureaucracies in Beijing was possible when local decision makers had control. Some field research (e.g., anthropology) is more effectively conducted when not subject to the scrutiny of either Chinese or American national bureaucracies. Finally, by raising money locally, these agreements can broaden the financial base of academic exchanges with China beyond resources provided by national-level organizations.

As shown in the discussion above, interinstitutional agreements are an important channel by which American students and faculty can go to China for a broad range of purposes and gain access to many geographic areas. Nonetheless, many of these linkages have difficulties, and it is essential to strengthen the most viable programs if this valuable pluralism is to be preserved. It would be undesirable (even if it were possible) to centralize, at the national level, the selection and funding of *all* American scholars and students going to China.

How can the most promising of these programs be strengthened? One potentially useful approach would be more specialized agreements, for instance, between departments, though this could weaken the university's leverage in bargaining for access in other fields. Another approach might be for several American institutions to pool their slots in China and devise a joint application and selection process. This would create more options for individual American faculty and students, permit more intensive use of available slots, enhance the competitiveness of the application process, and simultaneously maintain some of the flexibility that makes local arrangements attractive. Such a consortium would be a more potent bargaining entity with the Chinese. Once consortia are established, federal, state, and institutional funds should be focused on them. An organization such as the CSCPRC could play a useful role in catalyzing cooperation among American universities and promoting expanded access to Chinese materials and society.

For such cooperative interinstitutional arrangements to be effective, there must be a strong link between meeting Chinese requests and the accommodation of the American institutions' needs in China. There is no contradiction between developing and expanding ties with China while at the same time requiring that the Chinese satisfy legitimate American requests. Indeed, a pattern of unilateralism almost certainly would erode long-term American support for these relationships. The importance of Chinese responsiveness was clearly stated in the 1984 correspondence from a program director at a major American university to the vice-president of one Chinese institution of higher education:

We have done our best to be equitable and collaborative partners in our linkage and we are pleased to be able to offer full support to three of your students studying here. We would hope that in return your College could provide the support needed by one of our graduate students at [X University]. Our efforts in searching for new sources of financial support to continue the linkage are being negatively influenced by this difficulty in access to materials and facilities for thesis research.[26]

Principal Conclusions and Recommendations

1. The stipends provided officially sponsored students and scholars by the Chinese government are inadequate. Low stipend levels force many of these students and scholars to live in poor-quality, high-density housing with other Chinese. This, in turn, is inimical to English language acquisition, physical security, and overall educational opportunity. Finally, it is unfair to other foreign students who must comply with university rules regarding minimum stipend levels for foreign students. The Chinese official stipend level should conform to the current figures listed in the Institute of International Education's annually updated publication, *Costs at U.S. Educational Institutions*. Although there can be no assurance of how increased stipends will, in fact, be spent, adequate stipends make it possible for PRC students and scholars to improve their physical situation and educational experience. All American colleges and universities should require proof of adequate medical coverage for all foreign students and scholars.

2. Interinstitutional agreements (either at the university or department level) are excellent channels for some American universities and colleges to gain scholarly access to China. These linkages help mitigate the geographic bias in the recruitment of officially sponsored PRC Chinese who come to the United States, and afford opportunities for more

American scholars to undertake academic work in many areas of China. Nonetheless, these channels for Americans have been underutilized and many linkages are moribund. To more fully realize the potential of these relationships, increased financial support for Americans to go abroad is required, cooperation among American universities to utilize available "slots" is desirable, and more Chinese responsiveness and commitment are necessary to meet the research needs of American scholars. The pluralistic character of the Sino-American academic relationship is one of its greatest strengths.

NOTES

1. Where these individuals "intend" to go is generally where they in fact go. The I-20 and IAP-66 forms are specific for a given institution. To enroll in another school, the individual needs a new I-20 or IAP-66. These documents are valid for only a limited period of time.
2. A list of the top 100 research universities in the United States was obtained from *Federal Support to Universities, Colleges, and Selected Nonprofit Institutions, Fiscal Year 1982*, Surveys of Science Resources Series (Washington, D.C.: National Science Foundation, March 1984), Table B-4, pp. 47–48.
3. Patrick G. Maddox and Anne F. Thurston, "Academic Exchanges: The Goals and Roles of U.S. Universities," prepared for the Conference on Sino-American Educational and Cultural Exchange, East-West Center, Honolulu, Hawaii, Feb. 18–22, 1985, note 35 on p. 53.
4. Thomas Fingar and Linda A. Reed, *Survey Summary: Students and Scholars from the People's Republic of China in the United States, August 1981* (hereafter referred to as *Survey Summary, 1981*). A joint project of the Committee on Scholarly Communication with the People's Republic of China and the National Association for Foreign Student Affairs (Washington, D.C.: 1981), p. 24.
5. Memorandum from Gerald J. Lieberman, February 1985.
6. David M. Lampton, interview with Chinese Embassy official, July 2, 1985, Washington, D.C.
7. Maddox and Thurston, "Academic Exchanges," p. 43.
8. Otto Schnepp, Michel Oksenberg, and David M. Lampton, interviews in China.
9. Maddox and Thurston, "Academic Exchanges," p. 46; see also footnote 36, p. 53.
10. Interview with MOE officials, May 23, 1984.
11. Correspondence, Aug. 18, 1984.
12. See *Survey Summary, 1981*, pp. 13–14 and Table 8 for similar findings of the earlier survey.
13. Maddox and Thurston, "Academic Exchanges," p. 25.
14. Ibid., p. 26.
15. Otto Schnepp, University of Southern California, "The Chinese Visiting Scholar Program in Science and Engineering." Report prepared for the National Science Foundation (unpublished), p. 16.
16. Ibid., p. 15. "Significant contribution" was defined as "concrete contribution to at least one research paper published in a refereed journal."
17. For earlier information, see Fingar and Reed, *Survey Summary, 1981*, pp. 49–52.
18. *FBIS*, Apr. 24, 1984, p. B13, from *Xinhua*.

19. Factors that led to the establishment of these interinstitutional relationships were analyzed in intensive interviews at seven American universities and colleges— Appalachian State University, the University of California at Berkeley, Hofstra University, the University of Minnesota, Oberlin College, the University of Pittsburgh, and Stanford University—and also extracted from commissioned case studies analyzing the impact of exchanges on specific fields of study and research (see Chapter 7). The onsite interviews were conducted and analyzed by Kyna Rubin, Acting Director of the National Program, CSCPRC. These seven institutions were selected by the study's Steering Committee, which sought to include a variety of types of American colleges and universities in the cases.

20. Maddox and Thurston, "Academic Exchanges," pp. 25–26, report, "Interestingly enough, the quest for high quality students in the sciences is not a motivation for the establishment of formal exchange programs. American universities have been able to attract high quality students in the sciences without the institution of special programs. . . . This does not, in the main, hold true for the social sciences and humanities."

21. Correspondence from Professor Clarence Allen, Mar. 23, 1984.

22. David E. Sanger, "China Engages Hofstra U. To Arrange Deals with American Companies," *New York Times,* Dec. 3, 1984, pp. B1 and B6.

23. Ibid., p. B1.

24. Maddox and Thurston, "Academic Exchanges," p. 37.

25. CSCPRC staff conducted interviews with 11 persons who had undertaken research in China under the auspices of both the CSCPRC's National Program and other kinds of programs (including interinstitutional exchanges). These interviews and others conducted at seven American universities and colleges indicate that interinstitutional agreements have several strengths.

26. Correspondence, Sept. 12, 1984, p. 2.

6

Language Training
in Chinese and English

Throughout this study, the issues of language competency and language learning for both Americans and Chinese have come up repeatedly. The opportunity to live and work in China has made it possible for Americans to immerse themselves in the environment in which the living language of nearly one-quarter of the world's population is spoken. In the process of this immersion, Americans also learn a great deal about Chinese society, history, and culture. Similarly, for Chinese, the chance to live in the United States promotes greatly improved English language skills and a better understanding of American society and culture. These opportunities may be among the most important if least measurable benefits of Sino-American academic exchange. Because these opportunities are so important, this chapter addresses issues of language training in each society that influence the ability of both sides to derive maximum benefit from the academic exchange.

An assessment of the massive program to promote the study of English in the PRC is well beyond the scope of this study. The program under way in China almost certainly is the largest effort ever launched to teach the citizens of one country a foreign language. A recent Chinese publication estimated that approximately 50 million Chinese were learning English in mid-1985.[1] As part of this English language training

The authors of this report would like to thank William M. Speidel and Ronald Walton for their comments on an earlier draft of this chapter; though they are not, of course, responsible for any errors of fact or interpretation.

effort, uncounted numbers of Americans (and other English-speaking foreign nationals) have gone to the PRC to teach English (see Table 3-21). More research is needed concerning the scale and effects of this attempt to popularize English in China.

Assessment of Language Preparation of American Students and Scholars Who Go to China

Systematic and reliable information on the Chinese language skills of American students and scholars who go to China is scarce. The Center for Applied Linguistics has developed a "Chinese Proficiency Test" (CPT), which now is available for administration.[2] But neither this nor any other source could provide time-series data that would enable a reliable assessment of the Chinese language proficiency of American students and scholars going to China. Nor is there yet any rigorous way to compare the quality of various Chinese language training programs. Since there is no central source of time-series information, the authors of this report relied on data derived from examinations of applicants to the CSCPRC's National Program for Advanced Study and Research in China (hereafter referred to as the National Program) and the experiences of American teachers of Chinese language.

Taken together, these sources offer a clear, if dismaying, picture—the Chinese language proficiency of many Americans going to China is not high. Although this is only one of many deficiencies in America's foreign language programs, problems are particularly severe for Chinese and other less commonly taught languages. The study *Beyond Growth: The Next Stage in Language and Area Studies* summarized Americans' overall competence in foreign languages:

High-level competency in the less commonly taught languages is difficult to achieve and maintain, and the number of Americans who have done so is too small. The competency of many presumed language and area specialists is inadequate. Too many students are graduating with too low a level of language competency.[3]

One well-informed assessment of Americans' proficiency in Chinese comes from Professor Gregory Chiang of Middlebury College, who has been responsible for administering and assessing the Chinese language proficiency test for graduate student applicants to the National Program since its inception. This competitive, national-level program draws applicants from a broad array of America's leading universities and colleges. But the applicants' language skills generally do not match their other credentials. In a recent year's report on the Chinese language proficiency test results, Professor Chiang noted:

Although language ability should not be considered the sole criterion for selecting the applicants, one is not likely to be able to conduct meaningful research in China without some language competency. Generally speaking, the level of this year's [student] applicants' language training is disappointingly low. Therefore, one of the better among the group is not necessarily equipped to study at a Chinese institution of higher learning.[4]

Chiang went on to add that applicants who wish to undertake research on Confucius, Daoism (Taoism), metaphysics of the Song (Sung) Dynasty, and so on have no classical Chinese language training at all, or score very poorly on the test. Moreover, candidates with contemporary research topics cannot read simplified characters.

Why are so few Americans truly fluent in the Chinese language? Beyond the immediate explanation—the Chinese language is difficult and time-consuming to learn—the reasons are not complex, although the solutions may well be. First, not enough people study Chinese. Second, many begin to study Chinese too late in their careers. Third, of those who do undertake such study, most do not study long enough to become truly proficient. And fourth, most students are never—or only briefly—immersed in a Chinese-speaking environment, a critical part of attaining fluency.

The first, most basic problem is that comparatively few Americans are enrolled in Chinese language classes, although the number has grown recently. According to the American Council on the Teaching of Foreign Languages, Inc. (ACTFL), in the fall of 1976 a total of 1,629 students in American *public secondary schools* were enrolled in Chinese language courses; in the fall of 1978 that figure fell to 1,241; then by fall 1982 it rose again to 1,980. In comparison, in the fall of 1982, 1,562,789 public secondary school students were enrolled in Spanish language courses nationwide.[5] In institutions of higher education, the Modern Language Association (MLA) reports that enrollments in Chinese language courses rose from 9,809 in 1979 to 13,178 in 1983, an increase of 34 percent.[6]

Although this represents substantial growth, linguistic resources have probably fallen further behind U.S. needs, given America's increased involvement with the PRC and Chinese-speaking areas in Asia. As business, cultural, political, and other ties to Chinese-speaking areas have expanded, there has been a rapidly growing need for persons fluent in Chinese language. To exemplify the kinds of growth generating this demand for language competency: Sino-American trade expanded 90.6

percent between 1979 and 1983, and the United States now is China's third-largest trade partner, behind Japan and Hong Kong.[7]

Second, Chinese language study has not escaped a problem that afflicts virtually all foreign language study in the United States, particularly the less commonly taught languages. As the figures on secondary enrollments clearly reveal, an overwhelming percentage of students begin Chinese language instruction too late in life to really become fluent. Richard Brod, director of foreign language programs at the MLA, has said, in line with the prevailing conventional wisdom, "Unlike the Western languages, without the base of precollegiate Chinese, it's not easy to gain functional proficiency at the college level."[8] In addition, Professor Perry Link of the University of California at Los Angeles recently stated, "Those who study English and French can discuss Shakespeare or Proust and have intelligent literary discussion even as college freshmen. . . . But with the Chinese language, college students can just barely read simple stories. Most of the literary work has to be done in translation."[9]

The growing enrollments in Chinese language classes are encouraging, but they obscure the third problem: of the students who do enroll in Chinese language classes, relatively few study long enough or with sufficient intensity to become proficient. For example, Title VI East Asian Centers reported that for 1982, of all students enrolled in Chinese language courses (overwhelmingly Mandarin), 76 percent were enrolled in first- and second-year Chinese, with only 13 percent in third-year, and 10.5 percent in fourth-year and higher levels.[10]

Several structural factors have promoted this widespread practice of studying the Chinese language for short periods. One is that, particularly in the social sciences, the professional requirements of the disciplines are heavy and so students frequently treat language capability and regional concentration as peripheral concerns. Graduate students do not always see the connection between language acquisition and success either in their graduate program or subsequent academic job prospects. Compounding this, many departments measure students' progress by the speed with which they move toward completed dissertations. Concentrating on Chinese language inevitably lengthens that period, and few departments are willing to maintain financial aid for what they view as an excessive length of time. A 1983 RAND study on Foreign Language and Area Studies reported, "On average respondents [concentrating on regional studies] took slightly over 8 years to complete their Ph.D.s . . . East Asian specialists spent the longest time in graduate school (8.9 years total, 6.3 years officially enrolled), a significantly longer period than for all other world areas except Western Europe and Southeast Asia."[11]

Fourth, since Chinese language frequently is only one of several classes that a graduate student is taking at any one time, the student rarely is immersed in Chinese. Language study becomes only one brief interlude in a daily routine with many other intellectual demands.[12] This difficulty could be partially addressed if graduate students were encouraged to take intensive summer language courses both prior to their first year of graduate school and during subsequent summers. More resources should be made available for this purpose. Finally, once a person graduates and begins to teach or to undertake research, the structure of disciplinary incentives frequently works against maintaining language skills, let alone learning a new language. Those who want to pursue midcareer language study find little financial support available.

Financial constraints also are important in explaining why few Americans are truly fluent in Chinese. Looking at the Title VI fellowships (formerly referred to as National Defense Foreign Language fellowships and now described as Foreign Language and Area Studies, or FLAS, fellowships),[13] several facts emerge clearly (see Table A-33). During each of the Fiscal Years 1980 through 1984, with the exception of 1982, absolute dollar expenditures for FLAS fellowships rose. But because the cost per student is increasing, the number of awards for Chinese language study has generally remained at a rather low level, even declining by 25 percent in FY 1983. Although absolute dollar expenditures generally rose, Congress appropriated these monies in the face of executive branch desires to end such expenditures entirely.

In summary, few Americans are proficient in the Chinese language, and the proficiency levels of many students and scholars going to China are correspondingly low. To remedy this deficiency, students must start instruction earlier and be encouraged to undertake intensive language study. Chinese language study needs sustained and targeted financing for necessarily long periods, and both graduate students and faculty need professional incentives that will encourage them to make the long-term investment required to master, maintain, and enhance language skills throughout their careers.

One particularly innovative and encouraging program that takes these interlocking problems into account is the "China Initiative" of the Geraldine R. Dodge Foundation (see also Chapter 4). In 1983 the foundation initiated a program of support for Chinese language instruction *beginning in the ninth grade.* For 1983 and 1984, the foundation committed $1.4 million for Chinese language instruction in 36 high schools plus an additional $200,000 for curriculum development and teacher workshops.[14]

WHERE TO STUDY CHINESE LANGUAGE

One consequence of the 1979 "normalization" of Sino-American diplomatic and academic relations and of China's subsequent "open" policy has been the development of previously unavailable opportunities to
study Chinese language in the PRC. American and Chinese institutions
have now developed many short-term, semester, year-long, and summer language programs in China. Their very profusion and short track
records compound the difficulties inherent in judging the quality of
language instruction anywhere. In preparing this study, the authors
identified 16 American institutions that sponsor language programs in
China (see Appendix J), although there are likely to be other programs
of which the CSCPRC staff is unaware. A survey of program administrators made it clear that the limited availability of financial aid is a key
problem that keeps interested persons from applying and qualified
applicants from participating.[15]

It is of practical interest to assess how current language training
opportunities in China compare with opportunities in America, Taiwan, and elsewhere, and which choices are best for students of varying
aims and levels of fluency. These important questions provoke considerable debate, but little conclusive, comparative information is available
to answer them. For this study, a language questionnaire was sent to the
heads of Chinese language departments in 64 universities with Asian
studies programs; there were 22 responses to the language portion of the
questionnaire. Although this low response rate limits the conclusions
that may be drawn, respondents expressed sufficiently strong agreement
that the broad results would probably not change with a larger sample.
Most respondents were familiar with several of the more established
language programs in the PRC, and some respondents simply evaluated
the Chinese language programs with which their university or college
has a relationship. The respondents were not able to evaluate the many
new Chinese language programs in the PRC about which little or nothing is known in the United States.

Respondents were asked to evaluate Chinese language programs in
the PRC in general, but not to compare specific language programs in
the PRC. Thus, it is *not* possible to assess the quality of various individual programs. First, respondents were asked to rate certain aspects of
the programs and then to provide a general assessment. The rating
system was as follows: Excellent = 7, Good = 5, Only fair = 3, and
Poor = 1.

Overall, the respondents showed very substantial agreement that the
general quality of Chinese language instruction for Americans in the

PRC is not very high. The average response for each category was between "Only fair" and "Good."

Aspect of Instruction	*Average of Respondents (N=21)*
Instructional materials	4.5 ("Only fair" to "Good")
Quality of teachers	3.6 ("Only fair" to "Good")
Teaching methodology	2.5 ("Poor" to "Only fair")
General experience	4.2 ("Only fair" to "Good")
Overall	4.0 ("Only fair" to "Good")

Instructional materials were rated the best aspect of training, although the average on this rating, too, fell short of "Good." In contrast, teaching methodology was rated very low, receiving several "Poor" ratings and an average response of 2.5, or "Poor" to "Only fair." Although teaching methods undoubtedly vary from institution to institution and teacher to teacher, the overall impression is that they are not particularly good in the PRC.

Closely related to teaching methods is the quality of instruction. This was rated somewhat higher but was still not considered good. One respondent noted that the teachers have no formal training in teaching Chinese as a second language. This is a deficiency from an American perspective, since the United States generally has emphasized the importance of teaching methodology. Consequently, American students and program evaluators may react to differences in teaching style as much as to the material being taught. The Chinese, apparently, are alert to this situation; in June 1983 they established "The Association of Teaching Chinese Language to Foreigners." In 1985 the "First International Symposium on Teaching Chinese As a Foreign Language" was convened in Beijing; 260 Chinese and foreign scholars attended.[16]

Respondents to the Asian studies questionnaire also were asked to compare alternatives to studying Chinese in the PRC, including studying in the United States, Taiwan, and Hong Kong. Hong Kong was selected as an attractive choice only for persons studying Cantonese. Taiwan was the most popular alternative. Of 21 respondents, 18 said that teaching methods in the PRC were worse than those in Taiwan. Similarly, most respondents rated the quality of instruction and the general learning experience in the PRC worse than in Taiwan. One-half of the respondents believed that instructional materials in Taiwan and the PRC are the same; the other half believed that Taiwan's materials are better. Comparisons with the United States also revealed a preference for the United States over the PRC. Only in terms of the general experience did the average response favor the PRC.

In choosing the best alternative for varying levels of language instruction, the respondents favored the United States, overwhelmingly, for beginning students. Of 22 respondents, 20 expressed this preference, noting that a good foundation is important to language acquisition and that students need good teaching techniques and regimens to advance to higher levels of fluency. For the intermediate level Taiwan was preferred; only 4 respondents chose the PRC. For advanced language students Taiwan again was preferred, but less strikingly so: 10 respondents chose Taiwan, 5 chose the PRC, and 7 said that the two were equal.

Some respondents elaborated on the reasons they preferred Taiwan to the PRC. One factor was the Inter-University Program (IUP) in Taipei, administered by Stanford University. Founded in 1963, IUP is a long-established and well-respected program that strengthened interest in Taiwan considerably. Twelve of 22 respondents made positive mention of IUP. One respondent said that the "quality of teaching and teacher supervision, low teacher–student ratio, and wide range of student research and study interests that can be met there" make it an attractive choice. Others mentioned that IUP was tailored to American students' needs. An additional consideration is that students may have more extensive, informal contact with citizens in Taiwan than in the PRC; several respondents mentioned that students may live with Chinese families in Taiwan and thus increase their exposure to the language. While China is changing in this respect, at the time of the Asian studies questionnaire (late 1984), respondents still perceived only "limited opportunity to communicate with local people" in the PRC. In addition to IUP, three other language schools are operating in Taiwan for which the authors of this report have no specific evaluations: the Mandarin Training Center, the Taipei Language Institute, and the Mandarin Daily News Language School.

Two of the 22 respondents clearly favored language study in the PRC. One respondent believed that Beijing Language Institute (BLI) was improving under effective new leadership and that, given the added advantage of living in China, BLI was overtaking IUP. The other respondent felt that materials were better in China, stating, "Although one can find many things to criticize about the mainland teaching materials, they do have the definite advantage that they represent current language. For some reason materials produced abroad generally lag behind current usage by 10 or 20 years."

In sum, this limited information points up the need to know much more about the range and quality of language training alternatives in China. A standardized, widely administered measurement instrument would make it much easier to compare programs. In any event, some language training programs in China apparently are improving, and, since perceptions inevitably lag behind changing reality, they may be better than the CSCPRC survey suggests. At present, however, for American students and scholars whose principal objective is language acquisition, the basic foundation of the Chinese language can best be obtained in the United States, perhaps in an intensive program. Intermediate work is best continued in Taiwan; at the advanced level, a student should be able to profit from language training in the PRC. For many students, other scholarly pursuits may take precedence over language acquisition. In those cases the language study site must be selected according to students' needs.

ASSESSMENT OF ENGLISH LANGUAGE PREPARATION OF PRC STUDENTS AND SCHOLARS WHO COME TO THE UNITED STATES

Systematic information on the English language proficiency of Chinese students and visiting scholars who actually come to the United States is not available. Visiting Chinese scholars seldom undergo any formal application or English language evaluation process, and while students are evaluated through university procedures and examinations, there is no universally used instrument for measuring language proficiency. The best available measure is the scores of persons who listed their native country as the PRC on the Test of English as a Foreign Language (TOEFL). However, these scores do not distinguish between those who were admitted to U.S. universities after taking the test and those who were not. These scores do suggest that there has been some modest improvement in the English language capacity of PRC students since 1980, but there is still considerable room for improvement. The mean test score for the period 1980 to July 1982 was 473 out of a possible 800. For the period July 1982 through June 1984, the mean score had risen to 491. However, the average score for all foreign students was about 515 for the 1984–1985 testing year.[17]

To establish a broader base for judging English proficiency, CSCPRC staff sent a "Questionnaire for American Universities and Colleges" to 391 institutions of higher education; 216 responses were received. From these responses, two things are clear about the overall language proficiency of Chinese *students* who are accepted by American institutions. First, nearly one-half of the university and college respondents, most of whom were foreign student advisors, felt that "most" or "virtually all" of these students "require additional English training through *coursework* after arriving at the institution."[18]

Second, since 1981, the process of evaluating the English language skill of Chinese student applicants to American universities and colleges has become significantly more standardized. Of the 208 U.S. institutions that answered the question, 87 percent recognized TOEFL as one of the acceptable instruments to certify English language proficiency, and 45 percent used TOEFL as their *primary* evaluation instrument. Forty-three percent would accept other tests, such as the Michigan Test for English Language Proficiency (MTELP). TOEFL now is administered in China, although many Chinese applicants find it difficult to pay the hard-currency testing fee or to reach test centers.

In contrast to commonly held views in U.S. universities, PRC students and scholars generally do not intend to study English once they are in the United States. According to the 1983 visa application data, only 2 percent of J-1 visa holders (see Glossary) planned to study English language in America. The Chinese do take English ability into account in selecting officially sponsored students and scholars, so the language level of this group is presumed adequate by the Chinese authorities. Once in the United States, the imperative that these students and scholars obtain American financial support after one year discourages them from spending time in "peripheral" English language study.

Among F-1 visa holders (see Glossary), the situation is different. In 1983, 25 percent said that they intended to study English as well as their major field. These students are presumably self-selected, have more time to complete their studies in America, and are not subject to the one-year imperative. Since many F-1s are undergraduates and therefore subject to the language requirements of American universities and colleges, it is likely that more than 25 percent will take English courses while in the United States.

To meet the needs of the large number of foreign students studying in the United States, many universities offer English as a Second Language (ESL) courses. Usually these classes are noncredit, and students enrolled in them must reach a certain proficiency before enrolling in other classes. Universities and colleges were asked whether they offered any courses designed specifically for Chinese students and scholars to overcome their language difficulties. Two-thirds said they did not and one-third said they did. Some of those responding negatively had general ESL courses for foreign students, which were not specifically tailored to PRC students and scholars. Of those who said that they did have a specific course, more than 60 percent described a program that was actually general ESL for foreign students. Only a few universities appeared to offer PRC students anything other than general ESL— usually tutoring or intensive English courses.

Principal Findings and Recommendations

1. As the Chinese are asked to respond favorably to American requests for access to China, U.S. students and faculty must be better prepared linguistically to take full advantage of such opportunities. Indeed, many of the problems that American students and scholars encounter in China arise from poor language performance and insufficient cultural sensitivity, a sensitivity that language training could improve. The reasons for the generally poor Chinese language performance of American students are numerous; remedies will be slow in coming and expensive to carry out. Nonetheless, the United States as a nation must place importance on foreign language acquisition in general and on Chinese language acquisition in particular. This higher level of priority must be made visible in a variety of ways, such as sustaining funding at the undergraduate and graduate levels, targeting those funds on students and on institutions that perform well, and structuring disciplinary and career incentives to reward those who maintain and improve language skills. In addition, efforts should be made to determine the utility and cost effectiveness of Chinese language instruction at the secondary level.

2. Better scholarship is not the only rationale for Chinese language acquisition. With increasing economic, strategic, and cultural ties to Chinese-speaking areas in the Pacific Basin, journalists and business persons also need linguistic capabilities. Development of such skills, however, not only requires programs aimed at professionals but also that the professions be willing to devote the necessary time and resources to make such training successful. Existing exchange and language programs should take professional constituencies into greater account.[19]

3. To identify promising individuals and institutions, to target limited funds for Chinese language study, and to compare various programs, wide administration of the "Chinese Proficiency Test" of the Center for Applied Linguistics should be encouraged.

4. A systematic survey and evaluation of language study programs in China is needed. The U.S. government and professional language organizations in America should agree on the contours of such a study and then cooperate with the Chinese authorities and American institutions with programs in China to implement it. Moreover, a major study on Chinese language proficiency levels and Chinese language teaching and learning is needed.

5. There has been notable progress in standardizing evaluation of the English language capabilities of Chinese applying to American universi-

ties and colleges. Nonetheless, Chinese students, like other foreign students, still experience substantial difficulty with English. It is recommended that the Chinese government place more emphasis on language training in the United States for their students and scholars, relax the "one-year rule" that discourages English language study in the United States, and encourage students and scholars to live in English-speaking environments rather than exclusively with other speakers of Chinese. Raising official stipends would at least make this possible. It is recognized, however, that the Chinese have made a much more concerted and systematic effort to learn the English language than Americans have made to learn Chinese.

NOTES

1. "China Diversifies Its Language Craze," *Beijing Review* (July 22, 1985), p. 10.
2. "The CPT has been normed at 41 colleges and universities in the United States and abroad, and is available for administration, on a secure basis, by institutions on dates which they select. Following administration, the test is scored at CAL [the Center for Applied Linguistics] and a score report roster sent to the institution." "Newsletter," Chinese Language Teachers Association, Vol. 8 (August 1984), p. 5.
3. Richard D. Lambert et al., *Beyond Growth: The Next Stage in Language and Area Studies* (Washington, D.C.: Association of American Universities, 1984), p. 263.
4. Correspondence with Gregory Chiang, Middlebury College.
5. The figures on Chinese language enrollments, it must be realized, are deficient in at least two respects: they omit private school and extracurricular programs. Additionally, some states have not reported their possible enrollments at all. In this respect, the figures cited underestimate the secondary school Chinese language effort to some unknown extent. However, the figures cited are fall enrollment figures and therefore disregard attrition.
6. "966,000 Are Taking Foreign Languages, Up 4.5 Pct. in 4 Years," *Chronicle of Higher Education*, Vol. 34, No. 2 (Aug. 29, 1984), pp. 1 and 23.
7. *China's Economy and Foreign Trade, 1981–85* (Washington, D.C.: U.S. Department of Commerce, September 1984), p. 41.
8. Terry Hoyt, "Andover's Opening to China Studies," *New York Times*, Jan. 6, 1985, p. 61.
9. Sheppard Ranbom, "Teachers of Chinese Explore Ways to Nurture Their Difficult Subject," *Education Week* (Aug. 22, 1984).
10. Lambert et al., *Beyond Growth*, p. 320.
11. Lorraine M. McDonnell, with Cathleen Stasz and Rodger Madison, *Federal Support for Training Foreign Language and Area Specialists: The Education and Careers of FLAS Fellowship Recipients*, prepared for U.S. Department of Education (Santa Monica, Calif.: The Rand Corporation, 1983), pp. 23, 26, cited in Lambert et al., *Beyond Growth*, p. 111.
12. Lambert et al., *Beyond Growth*, pp. 76–78.
13. NDFL fellowships are also frequently referred to as either National Resource Fellowships (NRF) or Foreign Language and Area Studies (FLAS) fellowships.

14. Correspondence with Scott McVay, executive director, Geraldine R. Dodge Foundation, Oct. 31, 1984. Updated in telephone conversation with Scott McVay's office, Sept. 30, 1985.

15. Pamela Peirce, "Survey of Chinese Language Study Programs in the PRC," *China Exchange News*, Vol. 13, No. 3 (Sept. 1985), pp. 35–38.

16. For establishment of "The Association of Teaching Chinese Language to Foreigners," see *Foreign Broadcast Information Service*, Oct. 16, 1984, p. A4, from *Xinhua;* for the 1985 conference, see *Beijing Review*, No. 38 (1985), pp. 24–26.

17. Information from a telephone conversation with Vera Jones, Educational Testing Service, Aug. 13, 1985.

18. An earlier survey found that "fifty-nine percent of the 125 institutions responding to this question said that most PRC students required additional English language training. . . . " Thomas Fingar and Linda A. Reed, *Survey Summary: Students and Scholars from the People's Republic of China in the United States, August 1981* (Washington, D.C.: U.S.–China Education Clearinghouse, 1981), p. 17.

19. In 1985 the CSCPRC initiated the "Professional Language Program" component of the National Program. It offers support for individuals with the B.A. enrolled in a professional study program, or recently embarked on a nonacademic professional career, for full-time study of Chinese.

7

The Consequences of Exchange for Selected Disciplines

The effects of Sino-American academic exchanges on different fields have been varied and asymmetrical: in the United States academic exchanges with China have had the most visible effect in the field of Chinese studies; in the PRC the effects have been most evident in technical areas. However, this simple dichotomy obscures the significant effects of exchange on the social sciences in China (e.g., economics, law, and, increasingly, other social sciences) and on agriculture, seismology, cancer epidemiology, and other natural sciences in the United States.

This chapter analyzes the effects of educational exchanges in selected aspects of six broad fields: (1) Chinese studies (the study of China's past, sociology and anthropology, political science, literature, and economics), (2) American studies, (3) physics, (4) cancer epidemiology, (5) seismology, and (6) agriculture. Within the confines of this study, it was not possible to cover all fields or to provide a comprehensive assessment even of those selected for consideration. Each field was chosen either to highlight particular aspects of the exchange relationship or to present information that further elucidates trends described elsewhere in this study.

The technical nature of some of these fields necessitated the cooperation of scholars who are both eminent within their own disciplines and familiar with exchanges with China. Commissioned papers were written for this study by active scholars in physics, cancer epidemiology, seismology, economics of China, and agriculture.[1] Analyses of American studies and of selected aspects of Chinese studies were compiled from information gathered through onsite and telephone interviews, questionnaires, commissioned papers, trip reports, and published and unpublished papers.[2]

Cutting across many of these disciplines are themes and problems related to the quality of academic exchange. From the American perspective, limited access to scholarly resources in China has reduced the positive effects of the exchanges. Although the individual experiences of Americans have varied considerably, it is possible to characterize overall trends in access to these resources. In the postnormalization period of late 1978 and 1979, the Chinese opened the doors comparatively wide to American social science field research, only to restrict that access very substantially in 1981. Since 1982, the Chinese authorities have again, gradually, permitted American scholars greater access to archives, interview opportunities, and *limited* field research for scholars in both the natural and social sciences. (The field access problems of social and natural scientists have been remarkably similar. Both groups find that the principal problem remains one of moving beyond one's Chinese host unit into the larger Chinese environment, whether physical or social.)

The principal impediments to field research have changed during the 1979–1985 period. In the late 1970s and early 1980s, the Chinese resisted requests for such research for several reasons—ideological concerns about the social sciences per se, fear of letting foreigners penetrate deeply into unapproved locations, concern over the conditions in much of rural China, the chaotic state of local archives, and the opposition of local officials. Now, although some of these problems remain, they have been eased by the revival of social science in China, freer domestic travel, and new economic policies that encourage entrepreneurship. American scholars find that the obstacle to gaining access to Chinese society and archival materials is increasingly becoming the escalating and unpredictable charges for living expenses and research needs in China.

SELECTED FIELDS OF CHINESE STUDIES

Study of the Chinese Past

The long and richly documented history of China, from pre-Shang to the present, is a source of justifiable pride to the Chinese people and government. In the words of one American scholar, "China, more than any country in the world today, devotes attention, as a matter of national policy, to its premodern past."[3] For the Chinese state, throughout its long history, the study of the past has had political implications in the present, providing a standard against which to measure the current political leadership. Potentially, this may hamper the work of the many Americans to whom China's past is of enormous interest; the study of fairly contemporary periods might fall prey to current political inhibitions. The study of China's prehistory, ancient history, and imperial history is sufficiently removed from current events to make the prospects good for meaningful academic work by Americans in China. Thus far, the American scholars who have undertaken research on China's past have generally focused on four areas: archaeology, intellectual history, imperial history, and the Republican period.

Although it may be difficult to assess with precision the impact of access to China on scholarship in these fields, there is no doubt that it has been profound. The difficulty in assessing these effects stems from the fact that such effects manifest themselves slowly. Moreover, because rich source materials are also found in archives and libraries outside China, exciting new insights result from access to materials in several locations. Nonetheless, the next five years will witness a great increase in the publication of research that has benefited greatly by access to China.

American scholars are greatly interested in archaeological opportunities in China, where there is significant potential for important discoveries. In November 1982 the possibility that these scholars might participate in Chinese excavations became formalized, when "Chinese law was changed to allow foreign scholars, with the permission of relevant authorities, to engage in archaeological field work."[4] Since then a few individuals have worked on excavations, but exchanges and collaborative research in archaeology have not been numerous. Americans would like access to sites and relics that heretofore have been inaccessible, and China could benefit from Western techniques of preservation and analysis. There is some urgency to this work, for according to Professor Jack Dull, Chinese archaeologists are staying "one step ahead of the bulldozer or the shovel-and-basket brigade."[5]

Progress in archaeological cooperation has been slow for two related reasons: (1) Many Chinese feel that pre-1949 collaborative work with Americans, in the end, worked to the advantage of the Americans and not the Chinese. In the words of Harvard anthropologist K. C. Chang, "American scholars often got the better part of both fame and bounty."[6] (2) In China as in many other places in the world, an element of nationalism and commercial interest intrudes—the Chinese feel that they should be the first to tell of China's past through newly discovered and rare materials, and to profit from those discoveries. Despite these inhibitions, slow but steady progress in collaborative work has been made.

One important archaeological project has involved the collaboration of the Peabody Museum of Harvard University and the Institute of Vertebrate Paleontology and Paleoanthropology (IVPP) of the Chinese Academy of Sciences (CAS), a program funded in part by the National Science Foundation. The project deals with hominoid evolution and focuses on fossil remains from the late Miocene (7.5 to 15 million years ago). Sites in both northern Pakistan (Siwalik) and Lufeng in China's Yunnan Province are involved. Catherine Badgley, who worked in Lufeng in November 1981, sums up the importance of the site and project:

The Lufeng site is a paleontological gem. Its hominoid fossils include the only complete skulls known for Ramapithecus and Sivapithecus. . . . [T]he high concentration of fossils and the diversity of skeletal parts at Lufeng indicate that it is also a promising source of postcranial bones (e.g., arm and leg bones) of Ramapithecus and Sivapithecus. From these bones, we can infer the locomotion and body sizes of the ramapithecids. In addition, it will be possible to put together a detailed picture of the faunal and floral environment in which these hominoids lived. . . .

The two sites [Siwalik and Lufeng] are radically different records of Miocene hominoids and their environments. The Siwalik sequence contains an enormously long record with relatively little detail available at any single level. The Lufeng site represents an instant of geological time but holds as much detail as the terrestrial fossil record ever yields. Thus, comparison of these sites will be a great advance for hominoid research.[7]

Another example of cooperative Sino-American archaeological research is the 1981 and 1982 joint project of IVPP and the Smithsonian Institution, which investigated the origin of human populations in the Western hemisphere. As Dennis Stanford notes:

Competing hypotheses agree that human populations in the Western hemisphere are of Asian origin, but little data exist to confirm any hypothesis about the initial entry of people into the New World or the Old World cultural tradition from which these first peoples may have originated.[8]

To address these questions, a Chinese team came to the United States in 1981 to examine relevant North American sites and collections. The following summer, a contingent of Americans went to China and visited more than 16 Pleistocene locations in northeast China, most of which proved not to be "of primary importance for this study." In 1982 there was hope that additional Chinese sites in the northeast and west could help provide answers to the origins of New World culture.

For the strategic Neolithic and Bronze Age periods when the true character of Chinese culture was established, American researchers have greatly benefited from the opportunity to visit research institutes, museums, and an occasional dig in China. American graduate students, by taking archaeology courses in Chinese universities, have obtained invaluable insights into the training, excavation techniques, and taxonomic strategies of the authors of the published reports, both present and future, upon which understanding of the field so heavily depends. And much has been gained from the opportunity to meet with Chinese archaeologists at various international conferences held in China, the United States, and elsewhere.[9]

Attention should also be called to the considerable cultural impact of the major archaeological exhibitions from China that toured the United States in 1975–1976 and 1980–1981. There is, of course, still considerable room for improvement: many Chinese conferences are still off limits to foreigners, Americans are not able to study archaeological collections in a systematic way and only infrequently participate in digs, and the Chinese government does not give high priority to the training of its archaeologists in the United States. Nevertheless, American access to the archaeological evidence and to the scholars responsible for its excavation and for publication is now immeasurably superior to what it was only 15 years ago. China, with its wealth of Neolithic sites, is potentially the world's greatest archaeological laboratory for understanding the genesis of Chinese culture and thus of a great part of human civilization itself. Many disciplines in the United States, such as paleontology, physical anthropology, paleolinguistics, climate history, crop genetics, and cultural anthropology, stand to benefit profoundly from the continuing exchange of scholars, information, and analytical models with archaeologists in China.

To summarize, collaborative archaeological research has great potential value, but thus far progress has been slow. Exchange could be enhanced, but only with great sensitivity to and respect for Chinese concerns that grew out of previously unsatisfactory experiences with the West. From the viewpoint of Americans, progress will occur only with increased access to more localities in China and more opportunities to undertake research in more museums and research institutes.

The past six years have brought many excellent opportunities for research on imperial and Republican China and Chinese intellectual history. Two key factors have been access to Chinese archives and libraries[10] and the opportunity to conduct discussions with Chinese academics with whom personal contact has only recently been restored. One of the principal benefits to historical scholarship thus far, however, has come from the recent publication of Chinese historical documents. Chi Wang, at the Library of Congress, notes that "great emphasis is also being placed on the editing and publishing of archival historical materials."[11] The Number One Historical Archives in Beijing (with Ming and

Qing Dynasty materials), in conjunction with Nanjing's Number Two Archives (with Republican era materials), publishes *Historical Archives* (*Lishi dang'an*), a quarterly composed of selected historical documents. The Number One Archives also publishes a serial entitled *Collected Historical Materials from the Archives of the Qing Period* (*Qingdai dang'an shiliao congbian*). In addition, many other document collections that address a single theme are being published.[12]

Americans have had mixed success in gaining access to archives, libraries, and museums in China. There have been substantial successes, such as Professor Frederic Wakeman's recent archival work on law and order in Shanghai during the 1920s and 1930s, or Paul Pickowicz's studies of Chinese films. But overall, many American scholars have been continually frustrated by problems of access to archives, museums, research institutes, and libraries. Historians and other scholars frequently complain about the seemingly random imposition of the *neibu* (or internal) classification on documents, which they find particularly frustrating when materials so classified have no apparent relationship to national security or current politics. As Dull notes, "When an atlas of the Han dynasty is decreed *neibu*, it seems to be simply silly."[13] This classification also poses a more novel problem. Because of the recent proliferation of publications in China and the entrepreneurial spirit now taking hold there, it is difficult for foreign scholars to avoid coming into the possession of *neibu* materials; indeed they are freely sold in many locations. The possession of such materials does expose the foreigner to possible sanctions.

The access issue raises some basic questions that have no self-evident answers. At what point do requests for American access to materials become demands for special treatment not enjoyed by Chinese scholars? How open should archival materials be to a society's citizens and foreigners? What is embraced by the term *national security*? When is "collaborative" research a true partnership and how should credit for joint work be apportioned?

Despite the ambiguities and frustrations, scholarship dealing with China's past, in both the PRC and the United States, is experiencing a great rejuvenation. The revival is the result of recent intellectual reforms, increasing interaction between Chinese and foreign scholars, the growth in publication in China, and access to Chinese materials in China. American historians and archaeologists who have taken part in scholarly exchanges with China are virtually unanimous in their conviction that their own understanding of China was greatly enhanced by the opportunity to acquire a feel for the land and materials to which they were exposed.

Although the preceding analysis deals with only selected aspects of the study of the Chinese past, major benefits to historical research have accrued from the materials the Chinese are publishing, some of which are available abroad. While access to Chinese museums, research institutes, archives, and libraries holds great promise, not enough time has passed to permit an assessment of what all the fruits of that access will be.

Sociology and Anthropology

Although sociology and anthropology are separate fields of study, their common reliance upon ethnographic observation and shared concern with the day-to-day workings of societies present similar challenges for the Sino-American exchange relationship. Because of the similarity in the Chinese approach to the study of these two disciplines, this section considers them together. Wherever possible, the distinctive characteristics of each field are underscored.

Prior to normalization, American scholars interested in Chinese society had little choice but to rely on information gathered in interviews with refugees and émigrés who had settled in Hong Kong. Some excellent research that has withstood the test of time emerged from this work. Nonetheless, because sociology and anthropology rely on fieldwork and mass survey sampling, the opening of China held special promise for researchers in this field.

The Chinese now officially sanction and even encourage scholarship in the social sciences. Beijing's planners included provisions for social development along with economic development in the Sixth Five-Year Plan (1981–1985), with sociology specifically mentioned among the dozen key areas of research. Nevertheless, the study of sociology and particularly of anthropology is growing at only a modest pace. A delegation of American sociologists and anthropologists traveled to China in early 1984 to assess the status of these disciplines. The group noted a cautious mood among Chinese colleagues and a desire on their part to show how their disciplines could contribute to social and economic modernization.[14]

Unlike the other social sciences, which were banned during the decade of the Cultural Revolution, the study of sociology was first forbidden in 1952 and remained so until 1979. This status literally crippled the discipline for a generation. During these 27 years, U.S. social scientists made significant methodological advances and began the quantitative revolution using computer technology and statistical software packages. The Chinese have not yet made up for the long dormant period, either in terms of scope or understanding of methodology and practice. In 1984 only four Chinese universities (Beijing, Nankai, Shanghai, and Zhongshan universities) had sociology departments. A few other institutions offered sociology courses within other departments. The remainder of sociological research is undertaken by the Institute of Sociology of the Chinese Academy of Social Sciences (CASS) and the professional associations under the Chinese Sociological Association.

Anthropology enjoys even less support. As of early 1985, there were only two centers for anthropology in China: Zhongshan University and Xiamen University. The Planning Commission for Chinese Anthropology Disciplines was organized only in 1980 by CASS, and the first meeting of the Chinese Anthropological Association was held in 1981. Since the early 1980s, the development of anthropological research has been slow, and most research has focused on "the 7 percent of the population who are members of the 55 minority nationalities."[15]

The comparatively small academic infrastructure in these two fields has deeply affected the quality of Sino-American exchanges. Since the graduates of those few universities that offer relevant programs still lack the practical and linguistic experience to interact with foreign colleagues, American sociologists and anthropologists prefer to collaborate with older Chinese scholars who were active in these fields before the 1950s. Fei Xiaotong, Lei Jieqiong, Li Jinghan, Wang Kang, Wu Wenzao, and Lin Yuehua all number among these sociologists.[16] This situation, therefore, favors senior American scholars who now are reestablishing ties.

Younger American scholars without these personal ties may encounter substantial difficulty eliciting Chinese cooperation to conduct fieldwork in areas where the host institution is unfamiliar with the concepts and aims of the social sciences.[17]

That most American anthropologists and many sociologists must do fieldwork has become a point of contention and dissatisfaction for both sides. The Americans argue that "the best fieldwork can provide colorful detail, awareness of human variety, and a sensitivity to the gap between ideals and reality, features essential to any realistic picture of social life."[18] Given the opportunity to conduct field research in China, these scholars believe they could clarify or correct earlier perceptions of the culture formed from research in Taiwan or Hong Kong. Many researchers find unreasonable the Chinese reluctance to release what Americans consider innocuous documents such as local birth, death, and marital registries.

Part of this difference of opinion stems from the fundamental differences in Chinese and American perceptions and approaches to the study of culture and society. For the Chinese today, as in the past, the study of society and culture has a larger normative purpose—to make people "good" by showing them the good. For Western social scientists, "objectivity" in research has meant separating research from values as far as possible. The Chinese desire to have the foreigner study "model" units that are neither randomly selected nor representative of the larger society runs counter to the American grain. The Chinese also have resisted questionnaire research and generally preferred that interviews be conducted in groups rather than with single individuals. There is little guarantee that the responses of individuals, whether oral or written, will remain confidential between the researcher and respondents. From a methodological perspective, all of this limits the utility of sociological research in China and requires that researchers treat their subjects with a special sense of responsibility.

Beyond these differences in approach, the Chinese often are embarrassed at the backward conditions in some villages and regions, often those that American researchers view as the most interesting for research precisely because they have not yet felt the full force of modernization. The Chinese are particularly leery of anthropological (as opposed to sociological) research, possibly, as Alice Rossi suggests, because they perceive negative and condescending connotations of Westerners studying less sophisticated people.[19]

Despite these considerations, anthropologists and sociologists remain intensely interested in many facets of Chinese life and in a wide variety of topics, such as the implications of the one-child family, peasant life in the face of modernization, the changing role of women, juvenile delinquency, and labor and industrial organization. Significant research already has been undertaken on a number of important subjects: the treatment of aged persons in China's countryside;[20] the effect of economic change on village life;[21] Chinese emigration;[22] mental health in Shanghai (a collaborative study);[23] the social roles and cultural status of Chinese women;[24] and family structure.[25] Finally, China's release of its 1982 census data has provided both Chinese and foreign scholars with a very detailed look at patterns of family structure, birth, literacy, residence, and so forth. These data, together with other research, have helped to shift social scientists' perceptions of China. As Martin King Whyte puts it, "To the extent that China fieldwork has enabled . . . people to get beyond fascination with the 'Maoist model' and penetrate into actual social relationships, the result has been to reject the earlier, simpler image of China in favor of more complex portrayals."[26]

Academic exchange in sociology and anthropology is also helping to develop Chinese interest in these fields and their methodological refinement. American sociologists have had a direct impact on the revival of their discipline in China through lecture tours, minicourses, and consultations on curriculum-related matters. In the long run, the approaches of the two countries to social science may combine to produce a very worthwhile result. "If something of the American technical wizardry is blended with the Chinese subtle appreciation of the inter-connectedness of communal institutions, the explanatory power of the social sciences may undergo an exponential intellectual growth."[27]

In sum, in conducting research in China many American sociologists and anthropologists have faced very real problems, caused at least in part by the weak institutional base of their disciplines in China and by China's reluctance to provide foreigners with data on society. Nonetheless, these difficulties should not obscure the significant research that Americans have conducted in these fields. As these disciplines grow and develop, in some cases with American assistance (see Chapter 4), the opportunities for both collaborative and individual research will expand. In the future, it is probable that the trend toward charging foreigners fees for access to sites, interviews, and questionnaire respondents will become a principal issue.

Political Science

The scholar of Chinese politics immediately encounters two problems in China that make it difficult to conform to the norms of political science. In the United States the discipline has become increasingly quantitative. But in China the nature of data acquired and the limitations on the use of interview materials acquired there are highly constraining. Moreover, politics in China today, as in the past, is carried on "behind the curtain." Information that is freely published in many Western political systems is tightly held in the People's Republic.[28]

Those who are able to peer behind this curtain may find their future access curtailed if they reveal what they have seen. Many of the Americans who have the best access to political life in China are constrained by that very access, which requires that they not tear the fabric of carefully cultivated relationships by revealing too much. Taken together, studying Chinese politics, meeting the norms of the discipline and the academic standards of colleagues, assuring future access, and protecting human subjects in China are most difficult.

In addition, some American political scientists are debating whether they should devote their attention to securing access for American scholars of Chinese politics or to helping revive the PRC's political science community and assisting in its methodological and organizational development. In the latter case the hope is that a strengthened community of political scientists in China will be able and willing to deal with foreign colleagues in the future. In the authors' view, it is essential to move in *both* directions simultaneously, as indeed is occurring. The American Political Science Association is working with the recently revived Chinese Political Science Association to assist in field development, while the CSCPRC is continuing efforts to assure access for American political scientists who wish to study China.

American political scientists are dealing with their Chinese counterparts much more frequently as a result of the development of the CASS Institute on World Economics and Politics and the Institute of American Studies, the modest development of political science in China's universities, the return to China of Chinese graduate students trained abroad in political science and international relations, and the increasing interaction between foreign scholars and various international relations and policy advisory institutes. For their part, the Chinese have become increasingly attentive to interest-group politics in the United States, the process by which American foreign policy is made, and the problems of the strategic arms race.

For Americans, the study of Chinese politics has made considerable progress simply as a result of U.S. scholars' living in and coping with the Chinese system, and thus having access to Chinese officials and the growing body of printed matter in the PRC. Because of this direct exposure to the PRC, "China" can never again be the undifferentiated entity it was before the exchanges. The capacity to perceive lines of bureaucratic, regional, generational, and socioeconomic cleavage is key to political science. Americans now see more clearly the basic dividing lines in China and understand better how the Chinese manage and resolve tensions.[29] Exchanges have enhanced American knowledge of Chinese politics in three important respects: the study of the structure and operation of the Chinese policy process (for both domestic policy and, to a lesser extent, foreign policy), the study of policy implementation, and the study of political culture in today's China.

Although access to China has led to progress in the study of Chinese politics, two qualifications are important. First, an unofficial system of self-censorship means that American scholars do not propose many research subjects because they think it would be impossible to do the work in China. Topics pertaining to the public security apparatus, the military, the relations between the military and other civilian agencies, inner-Party workings, elite factionalism, and biographic research on elite political figures all have been "self-censored" by potential researchers. The issues *not* studied in the exchanges are critical, and

American political scientists must not let the limitations on research in China itself totally circumscribe their work on China's political system. Taiwan, Hong Kong, and the United States will remain the places where one can best study many critical Chinese institutions and issues for the foreseeable future; meaningful research on some important questions is not yet possible in China.

Second, increased American understanding of Chinese politics has come not only from onsite scholarly research but also from the presence of Chinese students, scholars, and officials in America, the reconstitution of the Chinese statistical system, the deluge of publications coming from localities and bureaucracies throughout China, and the generally more open environment in the PRC. In short, the availability of Chinese written materials abroad has been as important as access to China. Finally, the utility of long-term research in China depends greatly on the specific topic to be studied.

In China, American political scientists conducting research about China have had only a modest impact beyond establishing personal ties that have made subsequent interinstitutional cooperation possible. American political scientists who are lecturing about political science as a discipline there, rather than conducting research, may be encouraging the Chinese to develop the fields of comparative politics, American politics, more quantitatively oriented methods of analysis, and studies of international relations (particularly international political economy and arms control). Recently launched efforts to train Chinese students and senior scholars in international relations and political science in the United States and in China (efforts such as those of the Ford Foundation, Stanford University's U.S.–China Relations Program, and the joint Johns Hopkins University–Nanjing University Center for Chinese and American Studies) probably will have the greatest long-term impact (see Chapter 4). This impact will be increasingly evident as China builds its political analysis capability in research and policy advisory organs and in universities.

Aspects of Chinese Literature (Modern and Traditional) and the Arts *

Renewed exchange relations with China have revitalized the field of modern Chinese literature in the United States by giving scholars oppor-

---

*Many of the ideas and facts in this section have been drawn from a paper by Dr. Leo Ou-fan Lee, "Research on Chinese Literature and the Arts: A Preliminary Evaluation," forthcoming in Bullock and Oksenberg, untitled volume.

tunities to read the extensive and exciting new works of young Chinese writers and to interview Chinese authors. For instance, in recent exchanges, American scholars of the May Fourth period have used personal interviews to add substantially to biographical data on Chinese authors of the period.

The exchange relationship among literary scholars has taken many forms, from visits of individual writers and scholars to group delegations. Well-known Chinese authors such as Shen Congwen, Cao Yu, Ai Qing, Xiao Jun, and Wu Zuxiang[30] have visited various American university and college campuses. A number of joint conferences on modern literature also have been held on such themes as the following: Lu Xun, contemporary Chinese literature, comparative literature in China, and current topics in East-West comparative literature in the United States. And within China, literary journals are multiplying rapidly, restoring a long absent forum for scholarly discussion.

Nevertheless, politics and literature in China remain inextricably bound, and this too affects the climate of academic exchange. The policy of the Two Hundreds propounded by the PRC government—Let one hundred flowers bloom, let one hundred schools of thought contend—has been greeted with cautious optimism by many Chinese. At the same time, many new artists and writers of post–Cultural Revolution China are still struggling with ideological constraints while also seeking to reenter the international literary mainstream. Works produced during certain periods, such as the Sino-Japanese War, previously have been ignored because of their political sensitivity and the dearth of materials. Political constraints are being loosened, but no one is certain how long this will continue or whether the changes will endure.

In the field of traditional Chinese literature, the resumption of Sino-American educational exchanges has been less in evidence, but equally exciting for American scholars. Senior Chinese literary scholars still offer an immensely sophisticated view on the thought and theory of traditional Chinese literature. Leo Ou-fan Lee notes, however, that since much of the "rejuvenation" of the study of traditional Chinese literature has involved restoring the reputations and theories of aged and formerly venerated Chinese literary scholars, America's senior scholars are in a better position to benefit from renewed exchanges than are less established junior colleagues. (This has been the case in sociology and anthropology as well, as noted above.) Exchanges have brought about long-postponed reunions between Chinese and American experts on traditional literature. Literary debate has resumed, with new vigor and new insights from both sides, on the traditional subject of "redology" (which involves the extensive examination of the classic Chinese novel *The Dream of the Red Chamber*) and on other classics such as *Shui-hu Zhuan* and *Jin Ping Mei*.

The American scholarly community has not yet begun to examine the fascinating new works of young Chinese painters and other modern artists. The study of modern Chinese art and its relation to current societal and political trends has received little attention, and "scholarly research and field work tend to be overshadowed by media events. . . ."[31] In the performing arts, most exchange has occurred under the auspices of the Center for United States–China Arts Exchange (see Chapter 4).

Economics*

In recent years Western research on China's economy has changed both in terms of its process and substance. The research process formerly involved a considerable amount of "detective work." The economist studying China sifted through library materials trying to piece together information from diverse sources to develop an understanding of China's economy. Time-series data sets could be constructed only with difficulty. Occasionally, interviewing expatriates in Hong Kong provided valuable information. Now, although the economist must still spend considerable time perusing Chinese publications, information about China's economy is much more readily available. The increased volume of Chinese publications available in the West and the resumption of scholarly exchanges have both contributed to this change.

As a result of this influx of information, work in economics now reflects greater knowledge of economic processes and of regional and microeconomic issues. At the same time, recent research has become methodologically more sophisticated. To some extent, these developments in economic research would probably have occurred even without exchanges as economists made use of the newly available published materials. Moreover, despite their overall positive contribution, scholarly exchanges have been less productive than hoped for in some respects. This is especially true in the area of survey research and fieldwork.

Viewed in historical perspective, recent research on China's economy

---

*This section is a condensed version of the report written for this study by Professor Terry Sicular of Stanford University, entitled "Scholarly Exchange and Research on China's Economy." The full report is available from the CSCPRC.

is distinguished from earlier scholarship in four respects. First, the pace of research on China's economy has quickened in recent years. This trend reflects both the growing number of economists involved in such research and the increased productivity and shorter lead times for research projects. Many factors lie behind the growth in the numbers of economists studying China; one of them is the greater opportunity for scholarly exchange. The possibility of traveling to China has sparked the interest of general economists who do not normally study China and of some graduate students who have entered the field because of interesting dissertation possibilities.

Increased productivity and shorter lead times in research are probably due to the greater accessibility of published materials rather than to scholarly exchange. Exchange may at times speed up research in that it allows scholars to visit China to get a feel for the latest developments, discuss research already in progress, fill in information gaps, and shop for books. But those who depend on a trip to China to obtain the basic material for their work may find themselves frustrated. The considerable time and scholarly risk involved in working in China may be one reason why established economists are reluctant to go there for extended periods of in-depth research.

Second, recent research on China's economy shows greater knowledge of economic processes. Historically, economists have been interested in how China's economy functioned. Although this earlier work was superb in outlining more formal aspects of the economy, it rarely conveyed detailed knowledge about the informal mechanisms that allow the economy to function. Such knowledge is increasingly covered in recent research.[32]

Third, a rising proportion of new research looks at regional and microeconomic issues.[33] Increased research on these topics is important not only because it sheds light on how lower levels of the economy operate, but also because it dissects aggregate trends and thereby contributes to our understanding of the entire economy.

Research on regional and microeconomic issues has been boosted by the recent Chinese publication of provincial-level data in statistical yearbooks and by the publication in journals and newspapers of less systematic, but increasingly available, data for localities and lower-level economic units. These publications have important implications for research in China. With such information, scholars going to China can sharpen the focus of their research, refine their questions, and thus use the experience more productively.

Finally, the increase in information has allowed work on China's economy to become increasingly sophisticated methodologically. One can now find work that uses more advanced empirical techniques such as linear programming and econometrics. At the same time, economic scholarship on China is displaying greater theoretical sophistication.[34] Advanced empirical techniques are data-intensive, and only now are enough data available to allow their use.[35] In a few cases, economists have been able to conduct fieldwork to collect the necessary data[36] or have been able to make use of field data collected by Chinese economists or China specialists in other disciplines.[37]

Despite these welcome developments, certain gaps in the literature persist and, in general, research on China's economy remains methodologically less sophisticated than research on other developing economies. These deficiencies will persist to some extent until scholarly exchanges can arrange for economists to conduct surveys in China. American researchers currently are unable to collect systematic data to fill in gaps in published state statistical information. These, in turn, translate directly into gaps in the literature.

Exchanges are also contributing to China's knowledge about Western economics and economies. In part because of the increased scholarly exchange and in part because of improved access to Western publications within China, China's understanding of Western economics has grown considerably since the late 1970s. Evidence of this growth in understanding is widespread. Current issues of Chinese scholarly journals now often contain articles applying neoclassical economic theory or using econometric and linear programming methods. Increasingly, Western economists can find Chinese counterparts whose skills and research priorities are compatible with their own. In the long run, these developments will make scholarly exchanges more productive for both sides.

Summarizing the preceding field overviews, the impact of academic exchanges on the study of China has been very substantial, though it varies by field and by topic within fields. Exchanges have perceptibly given scholars a "feel" for China and have made it possible to differentiate and disaggregate China's society, polity, and economy in a way not possible before. Nonetheless, much of our increased understanding of China has resulted from the increased detail and availability of Chinese publications and the presence of Chinese students and scholars on American campuses. Finally, the benefits to the American scholarly community of exchanges would increase dramatically with better access to archives, museums, and research institutes, and more opportunities for survey and field research.

AMERICAN STUDIES*

In the United States, "American studies" refers to an interdisciplinary enterprise with faculty drawn from traditional departments in a cooperative exploration of themes or periods in the American experience. In China, however, with a few notable exceptions, there is no interdisciplinary study of the United States. Although there is interest in American studies in a growing number of Chinese universities, the approach is not well developed, mainly because there is a severe shortage of primary research materials and instructors with training in the West and no interdisciplinary tradition in universities and institutes. Where American studies does exist as a separate scholarly entity, it does so largely as an ideal to be realized some time in the future. In China, "American studies" generally means American subject matter—the study of the United States under the conventional rubrics of history, literature, economics, politics, and international affairs. American history is taught as a part of world history; American literature as part of world literature; and economics, politics, and American foreign policy as part of courses with an international theme.

Several key universities in China have significant teaching and research programs in American subject matter. Each university is building upon its limited material resources and faculty, many of whom were trained in the United States in the 1930s and the 1940s. Since 1979, a small but increasing number of younger faculty in history, literature, and international relations have been sent to the United States for a year or more of advanced study and research. As these students and scholars return to China in the next several years, taking up teaching positions in universities, research positions in institutes, and other posts requiring knowledge of the United States, information about American history and culture may be disseminated more widely, thereby bringing about an increase in the number of exchanges in this field.

As of 1985, there were three "centers of American studies" in the People's Republic: Beijing, Fudan, and Nanjing universities. The centers at Beijing and Fudan are loose organizations of faculty and graduate students whose primary purpose is to promote exchanges both within China and with the United States. Nanjing University is undertaking a unique effort, established jointly by the university and Johns

---

*This section has been condensed from *American Studies in China: A Report of a Delegation Visit, October 1984* (Washington, D.C.: National Academy Press, 1985).

Hopkins University, to build a Center for Chinese and American Studies. Scheduled to open in September 1986 with about 50 students from each country,[38] the program will stress the preprofessional study of economics, foreign policy, and contemporary social problems to Chinese and American students "who will someday be managing aspects of the U.S.–China relationship in both the public and private sectors."[39] Chinese students will study in English under American professors, and the Americans will study under Chinese professors teaching in Chinese.

At several key universities, notably Wuhan, Nankai, and Shandong universities, programs in American history and literature are growing steadily. Wuhan University has an Institute of American History within its Department of History, which is carrying out studies of modern American history, particularly since World War II. Nankai University's Department of History is strong in Afro-American history. Shandong University's Institute of Modern American Literature has published more than 100 articles and a dozen books on modern and contemporary American literature during the past few years.

All of these institutions are operating with inadequate collections of books, periodicals, and other materials needed to study the United States. Most university libraries have good collections of publications up to the 1960s, then very little material published until 1977–1978. Documentary collections are scarce and fragmentary. Since this situation is not likely to improve dramatically any time soon, it remains essential for Chinese universities to send their graduate students in American studies to the United States for advanced degrees. At present, relatively few Chinese are coming to the United States in American studies or allied fields, a situation that reflects both Chinese priorities and the dearth of American funding (see Chapter 3). This funding problem is one of the major factors that has led the Fulbright Program, foundations, and other private-sector organizations in the United States to emphasize the development of China's corps of American studies experts (see Chapter 4).

Several research institutes, primarily in Beijing, routinely send researchers to study in the United States. These include the Ministry of Foreign Affairs' Institute of International Relations, the State Council's Institute of Contemporary International Relations, and the Chinese Academy of Social Sciences' Institute of American Studies. Most of their research on the United States focuses on contemporary politics, economics, society, and culture. In China more material resources are available in these institutes than in the universities, but, unfortunately, few of the institute materials are available to university faculty or graduate students. Moreover, many of the research products of these institutes are policy papers written for official audiences rather than for open scholarly publication. Some of these institutes take graduate students and award M.A. degrees. All of them play important roles in studying the United States.

Academic exchanges could play an increasingly important part in improving the status of American studies in China, although the impact of those exchanges to date has been modest and difficult to assess. In the context of current economic reforms, the Chinese are seeking exchanges in this field as one way to build the foundation necessary for long-term political and economic ties to America. Some Chinese academics believe that American society, culture, and history must be understood if there is to be long-term bilateral cooperation.

Perhaps the most important component of American studies exchange has been the Fulbright Program (see Chapter 4). During the past five years, the scope of this program has been defined as American studies in the broad sense. Its principal mandate has been to help develop scholarly knowledge of the United States and to strengthen the institutional basis for this scholarship in China. American Fulbright professors teach in Chinese universities and Chinese students and senior scholars come to the United States under Fulbright auspices for periods of several months to several years.

In conclusion, like Chinese studies in America, American studies in China remains the domain of a small number of social scientists, humanities scholars, and their students. Exchanges could improve this state of affairs substantially. By expanding the exchange of books, journals, students, and scholars, the opportunities in China will also expand for personal and intellectual contact with, and deeper understanding of, the United States.

Aspects of Natural Sciences

Many observers in the United States view Sino-American exchanges in highly technical fields as largely characterized by an unbalanced flow of resources and information out of America into China. The disparate technical and economic levels of the two societies may make such an unbalanced flow inevitable. But several of the field case studies prepared for this report reveal that the benefits have been much more mutual than is generally believed. Of necessity, the overviews provided below only address selected dimensions of each of the very broad fields with which they are concerned.

*Physics**

In its "Decision on the Reform of the Science and Technology Management System" (dated March 13, 1985), China's Central Committee asserted that "modern science and technology are the most active and decisive factors in the new social productive force."[40] Whether or not this is an overassessment within science, China's development of a strong physics research and development component plays a key role in several respects. First, China needs a well-trained reserve of physicists able to conduct advanced research in high-energy and particle physics; condensed matter (solid-state) physics; plasma, atomic, and molecular physics; and nuclear physics. These specialties are important if China is to catch up and keep pace with developments in such critical areas as energy resources, materials, electronic computers, lasers, and space science and technology. Second, training in modern basic physics, including performing research recognized internationally, provides excellent background for scientific personnel who will be active in high-tech (electronics, computers, lasers, space science) developments later in their careers.

Following the death of Mao Zedong, China's scientific leadership joined other Chinese scholars in expressing alarm at the damage wrought by the Cultural Revolution to the physics research apparatus. Those leaders made plans to catch up in physics. One element of these plans was to construct a high-energy accelerator that would be used both to train Chinese scientists in modern instrumentation and to put China on the world map of experimental particle physics. Professors Robert R. Wilson (Cornell University), W. K. H. Panofsky (Stanford University), and T. D. Lee (Nobel Laureate, Columbia University) were among the leading American physicists participating in the original High Energy Plan, along with their Chinese counterparts, such as Professor Zhou Guangzhao, director of the Institute of Theoretical Physics (CAS) and a leading Chinese particle physicist who was trained in the USSR at the Dubna High Energy Physics Center and is known internationally for his original work. Financial constraints, however, forced the delay of this plan.

The attention of Chinese and American physicists then turned to alternate plans to promote cooperative Sino-American development of Chinese physics and to strengthen the research programs of Chinese

---

*This section is a condensed version of the report, commissioned for this study, by Dr. Joseph L. Birman of the City College of New York, entitled, "Case Study—Physics." The report is available from the CSCPRC.

physicists. Given China's increasing emphasis on applied science, priority naturally shifted to some important areas of basic physics that were closer to practical applications. Both sides felt that basic research in condensed-matter (solid-state) physics and in laser-related optical physics should be developed early. One plan was to set up a new, major research center to train Chinese physicists in China, specializing in condensed matter and laser-related quantum optics. This idea had the merit of putting such a laboratory close to universities and other institutes, thus enabling them to benefit from it. But because of problems in finding suitably trained leaders, obtaining and maintaining adequate equipment, and financing operations, physicists shifted their attention to activities in the United States and considered the idea of an advanced, highly selective postdoctoral scholar program in leading laboratories in America. The merit of this approach lay in the possibility of *cooperative* activities in the United States.

In this field, as in others, the practice and ideology of the Cultural Revolution prevented the emergence of scientific leaders among the scientists who were between 35 and 50 years old in 1985. The American Physical Society (APS) sponsored a Chinese-American cooperative Basic Research Program in Atomic, Molecular, and Condensed Matter Physics initiated by Professors Robert E. Marshak (Virginia Polytechnic Institute) and C. N. Yang (Nobel Laureate, State University of New York at Stony Brook). This program began in 1983 in part because leading Chinese and American physicists saw a need to train leaders in this age group for the planned expansion of basic and applied research in China. The program is designed to provide each member of a small group (about 10 individuals per year) of carefully selected, mature Chinese physicists (ages 35 to 50) with two years of advanced research training under the mentorship of a distinguished American host physicist. A total of some 15 to 20 physicists are in the United States under this program, which is supported in part by the Exxon Educational Foundation (see also Chapter 4).

China's scientific leaders hoped that by training potential scientific leaders at major American laboratories where they would work on research problems at the frontiers of knowledge, the PRC would get a group of physicists who could help move Chinese science forward. The American laboratories that sponsored the physicists would benefit from the work of these highly selected and motivated scholars, who would, after a period of adjustment, make the same contribution as a senior research associate during the two years of work. At the same time, the American hosts would be establishing strong links to China's developing physics community.

The new interest in exchange in physics also prompted development of an effective program to evaluate and place Chinese physics graduate students in American colleges and universities. In 1979 Professor T. D. Lee initiated discussions with China's leaders on a plan to train the coming generation of Chinese university graduates at the Ph.D. level in physics, chemistry, biology, and some other fields. Out of these discussions came a system to select the best Chinese university graduates and to send them to the United States for doctoral training. Each year since 1980, up to 1,000 of the top graduating seniors from Chinese universities have taken a qualifying examination in physics, which is comparable in difficulty to the American Graduate Record Examination. This program is officially called the Chinese–U.S. Physics Examination and Application (CUSPEA). Approximately 120 of the 1,000 students pass this examination each year and a subsequent English test each year, thus becoming part of that year's pool. Participating universities in the United States receive the names and test scores of the students, a precis of the students' records, and a brief statement from each student describing his or her main field of interest for graduate work. In physics, interested American departments then invite students to undertake doctoral work at their universities by enrolling in the regular Ph.D. physics program. When no university initially accepts a student, the program director works to arrange a suitable placement. About 50 American universities participate, and as of January 1985 about 340 Chinese CUSPEA students were enrolled in graduate physics programs in the United States. The CUSPEA program is a private collegial arrangement. The Chinese students generally compete for research and teaching fellowships on an equal footing with American, European, and other entering graduate students. The PRC pays the overseas travel expenses for all CUSPEA students.

Thus far these students have been excellent. They are among the top performers in Ph.D. qualifying examinations (usually second-year graduate level) in their American universities' departments. Since these students are now doing their thesis work, it is too soon to evaluate the originality and overall quality of that work. The students focusing on theoretical physics generally excel at problem solving; many Chinese experimental physics students, through hard work, compensate in part for their lack of previous hands-on experimental experience in China.

The outstanding performance of these Chinese students has had at least two major effects. First, their performance has made American universities much more receptive to candidates from China in this field, reversing a long-held belief that the years of disruption and turmoil in China had produced students who were much inferior to those trained in America or Taiwan. Second, the strong performance of these students by American and international standards reflects very well on Chinese training in basic physics. In fact, an indirect result *in China* of the CUSPEA program has been to encourage Chinese universities to apply higher standards in physics training in order to maximize the acceptance rate of their students in the program.

It is important to note that American physicists of Chinese origin have played an essential role in initiating Sino-American graduate student and postdoctoral scholar programs in physics. They provided much of the initial impetus, framework of ideas and structures, and, most importantly, the initial key contacts to senior Chinese officials. These contacts made the difference in being able to follow through on exchange plans or not.

Although the Chinese have reaped major benefits in these exchanges in physics, the United States also has achieved significant gains. For American universities, "300 excellent Chinese graduate students in physics provide a significant fraction of the total graduate student body at a time when the enrollment of American students in these programs has not recovered from the serious declines of the 1970's."[41] And for the larger American academic and governmental communities, Sino-American academic exchanges in physics have contributed to greater understanding of the Chinese bureaucracies and the financial constraints under which they operate.[42]

Cancer (Epidemiology) Research *

On November 19, 1979, the Chinese Academy of Medical Sciences (CAMS) and the National Cancer Institute (NCI) of the United States signed a Memorandum of Understanding. This agreement came shortly after the June 22 signing of a Protocol for Cooperation in the Science and Technology of Medicine and Public Health between what was then the U.S. Department of Health, Education, and Welfare (HEW) and the Chinese Ministry of Public Health (see Appendix G). These documents together provided the framework for Sino-American cooperation in the biology, prevention, diagnosis, carcinogenesis, epidemiology, and therapy of cancer.[43]

---

*Unless otherwise cited, the conclusions and information presented here were drawn from a paper written for this study by Dr. Ronald Glaser of Ohio State University. The paper, entitled "Report on Cancer Research with China: Collaborative Studies with the Chinese Cancer Institute, Beijing, and the Main Ear, Nose, and Throat Hospital, Shanghai, on Studies on Nasopharyngeal Carcinoma," is available from the CSCPRC.

Thus far, collaborative Sino-American research on cancer has been reported at a 1983 symposium, sponsored by the American Association for the Advancement of Science, on "Clues to the Etiology of Human Cancer from Studies in China" and a 1984 "Conference on Cancer in the Pacific Basin" held in Hawaii. In the words of Frederick P. Li of the National Cancer Institute, "Chinese scientists at these meetings reported impressive results from a wide range of studies, many conducted in cooperation with U.S. associates."[44]

Overall, both the United States and China have benefited from exchanges in the field of cancer research. While Chinese scientists and researchers receive advanced training and access to up-to-date instrumentation, American laboratories and universities can acquire valuable scientific specimens of cancers that are rare in the United States. Americans frequently initiate the exchanges, believing that the substantial expenditures made by American universities and funding agencies are more than compensated for by opportunities to obtain biopsies and conduct first-hand observations. The distinctive patterns of cancer incidence make the exchange especially valuable. In China, esophageal, stomach, and liver cancer are particularly prevalent among Chinese men. The most common forms of cancer among U.S. males affect the prostate, colon, and lungs.[45] Moreover, several cancers found in China are regionally localized, providing researchers the opportunity to study carcinogenic factors present in one locality and absent in another. Indeed, "one of the first collaborative efforts between NCI and CAMS scientists involved a comparison of the geographic patterns of cancer in the U.S. and China."[46]

American exchange visitors to the Chinese Cancer Institute in Beijing in 1977 discovered that an extensive survey conducted by that institute in the mid-1970s had mapped out the geographic patterns of cancer mortality throughout the nation, an accomplishment that greatly aided subsequent epidemiological studies. Henderson, Yu, and Wu report that "it was immediately obvious [in 1977] that this remarkable cancer survey would become the foundation for virtually all substantive collaborative epidemiological programs."[47] American scientists also found that while many Chinese laboratories lagged behind the United States in the sophistication and availability of equipment, their Chinese counterparts had developed innovative methods of cancer detection (for example, the friction balloon cytology test for esophageal cancer)[48] and were experimenting with traditional herbal medicines as possible cancer cures.

As in other disciplines, Americans of Chinese origin and American-educated Chinese have played key roles in making the contacts that resulted in exchanges in the cancer field. Without Chinese-American *guanxi* (connections) in the preliminary stages of negotiations, especially in situations where government agencies either could not or would not take the lead in coordinating international exchanges, many programs probably would not have been undertaken. These contacts highlight the very exclusive and personal nature of relationships within Chinese administration at all levels.

The scale of Sino-American exchange in cancer research is illustrated by the activities of the Memorial Sloan-Kettering Cancer Center. "Over the past two decades, some 65 PRC scientists have come to Memorial Sloan-Kettering as visiting investigators and research fellows for stays of up to three years."[49]

Although it is still too early to confirm the results of exchange in cancer studies, preliminary evaluations suggest that the Chinese contribution is yielding valuable results. Dr. Ronald Glaser, for instance, reports one key finding:

We found that an antibody to an enzyme made by the EB virus which we had previously described is very specific for identifying NPC (nasopharyngeal cancer) patients, particularly at the time of diagnosis. Since it is very difficult to diagnose NPC patients, any marker that can be used to identify such patients will have impact on survival rates.[50]

In conclusion, the cancer research conducted in exchanges with China has produced benefits. First, the personal contact brought about by the exchange is helping to create a durable and influential network that will facilitate future collaborative ventures. Exchange also serves the goal of gathering as much information as possible and funneling it into the collective, worldwide effort to discover a cancer cure. By providing access to the patients, specimens, and data available in China and advancing the training of Chinese scientists in the West, exchanges in the field of cancer research between the United States and China have the potential to contribute substantially to the welfare of humanity. As this collaborative relationship unfolds, it must do so with the highest standards of protection for human subjects.

Seismology*

In the field of seismology, binational cooperation and exchange have produced immediate mutual scholarly gains while simultaneously

---

*This section is a condensed version of the report, commissioned for this study, by Professor Bruce A. Bolt of the University of California at Berkeley, entitled, "The Impact of Seismological Exchanges Between the U.S.A. and the People's Republic of China, 1979–1984." The report is available from the CSCPRC.

advancing the perpetual quest for knowledge about earthquakes and the Earth's interior. The practical and political implications of seismological research—earthquake prediction in particular—convinced Chinese leaders to retain their nation's international scholarly ties in that discipline, even during the Cultural Revolution decade.[51] When Sino-American academic relations were being restored in the 1970s, exchanges in seismology and earthquake engineering were among the first to experience significant new activity. Both nations were anxious to establish cooperative research opportunities and to increase the exchange of seismological delegations. As early as 1974, when an American geophysical delegation visited the PRC, Frank Press, now president of the U.S. National Academy of Sciences, noted the unusual latitude permitted the group.

Although China has been wracked by earthquakes throughout history, it was not until 1966 that a severe tremor near Beijing prompted China's leaders to elevate seismology to its current high status. The Cultural Revolution's emphasis on mass mobilization and criticism of "bourgeois experts" paradoxically created an atmosphere conducive to an emphasis on earthquake prediction, especially using predictive methods in which mass mobilization played an important role.

On February 4, 1975, a damaging earthquake occurred near Haicheng, Liaoning Province, *following* official warnings to the populace to expect the tremor. This seemingly successful instance of earthquake prediction stirred great interest and controversy both nationally and internationally. But shortly after this apparent seismological achievement, the disastrous Tangshan earthquake in July 1976 killed more than 300,000 persons and revealed the inadequacies of China's forecasting and warning methodology.[52] It became clear that Chinese programs in seismology were based on weak scientific premises and that structural damage had been compounded by poor engineering practices. The cooperative seismological program of the United States and the PRC began in the aftermath of this earthquake, a time when tremors also ran through the political system, the most significant of which was the demise of Mao Zedong.

Exchanges in seismology were boosted dramatically in January 1980 with the signing of the protocol between the U.S. National Science Foundation, the U.S. Geological Survey (USGS), and the State Seismological Bureau (SSB) of the PRC for scientific and technical cooperation in earthquake studies (see Appendix G). The annexes to the protocol aimed at generating cooperative research in earthquake prediction, earthquake hazards evaluation, earthquake engineering, and other basic and applied studies of earthquake phenomena.

Both sides were intrigued by opportunities in the other nation. Americans were acutely interested in gathering information in China on seismic sources, active faulting, seismic zones, earthquake prediction, earthquake hazard reduction, building construction, and related topics and were equally eager to confirm Chinese claims of successful earthquake predictions. On the Chinese side, there was the hope of learning modern techniques from the United States; their first priority has been the acquisition of more technology, particularly computers and modern recording equipment. This demand for American technology complements U.S. seismological strengths, provided the cooperative arrangements include an exchange of data. Fortunately, seismology has always been an international science that recognized the necessity of free exchange of data.

The exchange program has prompted many innovations in Chinese seismology. Chinese academics and professionals bring new textbooks and lecture course materials from the United States. They also return to China with fresh formulations of problems, particularly those that deal with the importance of defining causative models based on dynamic principles. In the basic tectonic aspects of earthquake occurrence, the advanced state of plate tectonic analysis in the United States required much debate and analysis when applied to Asia.[53] Predictive models of earthquakes contrasted sharply with the largely empirical correlations previously relied upon in China.

The exchange programs also have played a role, although perhaps not a decisive one, in a change in emphasis of the PRC seismology program that goes beyond the diversification of research efforts. Recently the Chinese have redirected their efforts from earthquake forecasting to the broader questions involved in earthquake hazard mitigation. This remarkable shift parallels a similar change that took place in the United States some 10 years earlier. In both countries it became apparent that, given the lack of achievement in pure prediction, continued strong governmental support would require a more broadly based program, ranging from earthquake engineering research to economic studies of earthquake loss. In all probability, the lessons learned in the 1976 Tangshan earthquake also drove the Chinese program in this direction. Consequently, the exchange program now also involves studies of prediction of strong ground motion and intensity patterns in China. The results of this research are expected to lead to better earthquake-resistant design codes and better construction and development planning.

Sino-American seismological exchanges have had a measurable effect on research and publication in the United States, and most papers published in peer-reviewed journals are of high quality. Research results on the Tangshan earthquake precursors have been particularly noteworthy, as have work on the recurrence of slip on active faults such as the Red River fault, the study of strong-motion arrays at various sites in China, work in rock mechanics, and studies of special magnitude-moment scales that were part of a major study in earthquake prediction in Yunnan Province.

Seismological research has also served as a prototype for a new system of funding. Chinese scientific research programs have been opened up by partial adoption of NSF-type funding of research proposals. The main institutions—the SSB, the Institute of Engineering Mechanics, Harbin, and Beijing University—have been asked to work out procedures for reviewing competitive proposals on earthquake research. Delegations from the PRC already have examined the grant structure at the National Science Foundation and the USGS (see also Chapter 8).

Although generally quite successful, Sino-American seismological exchanges were hindered, especially at their outset, by obstacles related not only to cultural and political differences but also to the technological gap between the two nations. Seismologists from both nations have been frustrated at their counterparts' lack of language skill and consequent inability to study primary source material or to present complex scientific arguments. Progress has also been slowed by the dearth of computers in China and Chinese undergraduates' lack of exposure to computer facilities.[54] The quality of education in China also has been variable, and Chinese universities have had rigid academic structures. Finally, the organizational and territorial compartmentalization of various Chinese administrative units relevant to seismology and related fields also has impeded fieldwork. At times, there has been a lack of field maps, structural maps showing Quaternary faults, and associated remote-sensing data. But in most cases, both Chinese and American workers accept these difficulties as an additional challenge, and recognize that the situation is improving. Access to remote regions is becoming more common.

Most of the problems preventing both nations from reaping maximum benefits from exchange can be overcome fairly readily. In particular, such drawbacks as lack of active fault mapping and inefficient data retrieval are already being eased. As modern computers become more available, seismologists have less need for knowledge of Chinese characters. American researchers have reported difficulties in taking data out of China, but discussion and explanation help remove such hindrances. Looking ahead, however, maintenance of modern equipment, such as seismographs and data analysis systems, may present a long-term problem because of growing demand for technicians as China acquires more technologically sophisticated equipment.

Upgrading the analysis of seismological data has been a first priority in the PRC, and modern VAX-type computers will be installed at a number of provincial seismological research centers and in Beijing, paid for mainly with Chinese funds. These facilities will take advantage of a modern network of three-component digital broadband seismographs that were being linked across China in 1985. The system will be as up to date as any in the United States. A Center for Analysis and Prediction for Earthquakes will be staffed in part by returning exchange seismologists and will have the benefit of visiting American specialists.

Overall, the seismological exchange program has been successful and relatively trouble-free. Both sides agree that it should be continued and strengthened. The seismology exchange has succeeded largely because it meets the interests of both sides while also contributing to progress in seismology. Seismology, in turn, plays an important role in prospecting for oil and mineral deposits. No less important, earthquake hazard mitigation is critical in China, where a huge section of the population is housed in non-earthquake-resistant structures and where intensive construction of dams and bridges is under way. Cooperative activity is attractive to American earthquake engineers and seismologists working on strong ground-motion problems.

The exchange program is likely to expand slightly in the future. Seismologists on both sides could benefit from more sustained and regular contact in research programs; this would require additional funds for more joint U.S.–PRC seismological conferences. The program would also profit from greater involvement of international organizations, such as the International Association for Seismology and Physics of the Earth's Interior, and special Regional Assemblies; workshops at these assemblies would help to consolidate the results of the exchange program. Enhanced facilities for broad seismological research in selected Chinese universities would also strengthen exchanges in this field. The current introduction of graduate programs in China should improve the situation. At the same time, the Chinese must ensure that advanced degrees, particularly the Ph.D., are awarded by Chinese universities and not professional institutes so that the same standards as those at the best universities in the West can be maintained.

A word should be added about program costs and logistics. In seismology, accommodations are needed not only in Beijing, Harbin, Shanghai, and other cities, but in many provincial centers where earthquakes occur. Accommodations and travel have been expensive for the Chinese groups, and there are signs that local sponsors cannot indefinitely continue the past levels of local subsidy for foreign visitors. Both nations may have to work out per diem allowances for exchange visitors in each country, using a different basis than the present arrangement. In fact, many American geologists and seismologists have volunteered to live in the field under rough circumstances to reduce program costs.

Overall, it does not appear that there is urgent need to channel additional seismological cooperation through bilateral government arrangements (see Chapter 4). If Chinese society continues to open, it is very likely that the various connections that have been established in the last decade will grow stronger. As this process continues, more substantial cooperative activities should emerge in seismology and allied scientific fields. The modes of cooperation should become more diverse and relationships more reciprocal as Chinese seismologists at all levels gain further experience and training. All the evidence points to even closer collaboration in the short run between American and Chinese seismologists.

Agriculture*

Since the mid-1950s, Chinese leaders have recognized agriculture, at least rhetorically, as the linchpin in the Chinese economy, although Mao Zedong and his successors differed radically in their approaches to achieving agricultural growth. For Mao, mobilization and rural collectivization were the answers, but for his heirs, the key lies in providing peasant households with production incentives while also accelerating the transfer of science and technology to the rural sector. This latter strategy provides the context in which to view current Sino-American agricultural exchange.

Mutual interest has promoted agricultural exchange. Even before the end of the Cultural Revolution decade, the scientific communities in both nations felt they would benefit from sharing knowledge and genetic resources and exchanging scholars and students. For many in the American farm community, especially in the late 1970s and early 1980s when China was importing large quantities of grain and agricultural raw material and had ambitious plans for agricultural mechanization, such exchanges were seen as a way to promote American commercial interests. Finally, many Americans with a global perspective viewed facilitating Chinese agricultural growth as one way to minimize the likelihood that China would be chronically short of food and that it would destabilize the international food system.

---

*This section is a condensed version of the report, commissioned for this study, by Dr. Sylvan H. Wittwer of Michigan State University, entitled, "U.S.–Chinese Agricultural Exchanges—A Field Case Study." This report is available from the CSCPRC.

In 1974 the National Academy of Sciences (NAS) sent a research team on plant studies to the PRC. Other NAS-sponsored agricultural exchanges followed. After "normalization" in January 1979, many agricultural exchanges were sponsored by the U.S. Department of Agriculture (USDA) under the November 1978 U.S.–Chinese agricultural bilateral agreement entitled "Understanding on Agricultural Exchange" (See Appendix G). Beginning in 1980, many American land grant universities and related institutions established formal exchange agreements and also started sending instructors to sister agricultural research and teaching institutions in China (see Tables A-29 through A-31). For the most part, American educational institutions provide the financial support for their obligations under these agreements with little or no dependence on federal funds.

Both sides have accrued benefits from the exchanges with further potential benefits promised. The Chinese excel in waste management and by-product recycling, *Azolla* culture, methane generation, and fish production. Chinese farmers are the most efficient of the world's organic gardeners, and their advanced knowledge of soil uses has enabled them to maintain land productivity for thousands of years. Their progress in protecting plants from pests and use of integrated pest control methods are innovative and impressive. Their plant scientists are among the world's leaders in hybrid rice developments, haploid (pollen) culture of cereal grains, and new tissue-culture technologies. Chinese forestry programs involve seed exchange for trees that do not exist in the United States, though as mentioned earlier in this chapter, those who have tried to remove botanical specimens from China have encountered disquieting difficulties.

China's vast plant and crop genetic resources of both wild and cultivated species offer great potential value for the United States. The crops include wheat, Tibetan barley, sweet potato, soybeans, cowpeas, Chinese cabbage, ordinary cabbage, seven species of onions, cucurbits, medicinal herbs, and tropical, subtropical, temperate-zone, and winter-hardy fruits. China also is the place of origin for the cultivated soybean. The wild plants of China are of special international importance. With more than 30,000 species of flowering plants, gymnosperms and ferns, China's wild plants constitute one out of eight species in the world. China is a center for survival for plants that once grew across Eurasia and North America.

China's animal life also offers exotic and useful genetic resources. The black-boned chicken, used not only as a source of food but also of medicine, and the often extremely prolific native breeds of pigs that adapt to various regions of China fascinate American agricultural experts. Other exotic domesticated and wild animals, some of which are not found even in American zoos, roam the grasslands of Inner Mongolia, the Xinjiang Autonomous Region, and the Xizang (Tibet) and Qinghai plateaus where fine cashmeres and other prized natural fibers have their origin. Moreover, Chinese research efforts in animal genetics and the extensive practice of artificial insemination for cattle and pigs are of great interest to American specialists.

On the other hand, the Chinese have benefited and will continue to benefit from the knowledge and insight of American agricultural administrators, scientists, and research directors both in terms of model systems and scientific knowledge. For example, the coordinated federal, state, and county system for cooperative agricultural extension is a model that could be effective in China, especially as China is working to develop a new production responsibility system and attempting to integrate university research and economic production more closely. The Chinese also have an interest in agricultural economics, marketing economics, cell physiology, plant tissue culture, haploid culture, somatic cell fusion, integrated pest management, and biological control methods for crop and livestock pests. In the area of agricultural growth, Chinese plant scientists are eagerly seeking new fertilizer and irrigation technologies and information, developed in the United States, on the use of exotic plant growth regulators to enhance crop yields and to improve crop quality. Recent genetic engineering developments could help the Chinese improve animal health and develop disease- and weather-resistant crop varieties; new American biologically synthesized pesticides could also be of great value to China. PRC scientists are increasingly interested in protected cultivation or controlled-environment agriculture, and American, European, and Japanese scientists could contribute significantly to this movement of "climate-proofing" of crops.

Another area of great importance to China is postharvest handling of crops and food technology. For China, these problems are of enormous magnitude—it has been estimated that under certain circumstances, up to 50 percent of some of China's harvested fruits and vegetables may not reach consumers. The Chinese could benefit greatly from American expertise in this area, expertise that resides in both the public sector (e.g., USDA's Agricultural Research Service) and the private sector (in universities and food-processing and distribution companies). To merely process and preserve summer crop surpluses, primarily fruits and vegetables, for winter consumption would add greatly to China's food resources and reserves. Food conservation technologies are an important area for future collaboration.

As with many other exchange programs, the road to Sino-American cooperation in the field of agriculture remains strewn with obstacles. One constraint has been inadequate funding, particularly the very limited foundation support for agricultural exchanges (see Chapter 4) and the high cost of cooperative ventures, which usually occur in China. Deficiencies in language preparation on both sides also hinder effective collaboration. And finally, lack of communication between the various arms of the Chinese bureaucracies poses recurring problems. In 1984 the Chinese Ministry of Agriculture divested itself of university contacts, leaving the responsibility of inviting foreign lecturers and developing exchange programs with individual universities or provincial academies of agricultural science. Many of the foreign affairs officers with exchange responsibilities are inexperienced, lack knowledge of English (as their American counterparts cannot speak Chinese), and tend to confine the activities of visitors from abroad to a single university or province.

The initial American enthusiasm for agricultural exchanges is cooling for several reasons. First, the USDA has suspended all of its exchanges with China until the Chinese purchase all of the grain that they were obligated to buy for 1983 and 1984 under the long-term grain agreement. Second, many agricultural economists have encountered problems when they tried to undertake field studies in China (see Chapter 5). It is hard for faculty to win administrative and financial support for exchanges when their priority projects are not feasible through the exchanges. Finally, China's domestic agricultural policies have produced a dramatic increase in grain and cotton production (among other commodities). Thus, China's need to import some crops dropped far below levels anticipated just a few years ago, and in the case of some crops China is now an exporter to be reckoned with. This change has, in turn, led some people involved in American farm exports to fear that assisting Chinese agriculture will simply strengthen a potential competitor. American machinery, technology, and food-processing firms, however, recognize that China's agricultural growth, its land and water resources, and its favorable labor costs will open important economic opportunities for them.

Most agricultural science exchanges with China have been carried out by publicly supported research and educational institutions. But in the United States, the private sector, which does approximately two-thirds of the agricultural research and development, offers an area of great potential for future collaboration. The way is now open for American agribusiness to join hands with America's publicly supported research and educational institutions in jointly financing further exchange programs, particularly for graduate students, and other professionals in food production and processing and crop development. Such areas for cooperation, however, must be carefully selected if they are to be mutually beneficial.

CONCLUSIONS AND RECOMMENDATIONS

1. Academic exchanges with the PRC have affected China and the United States in different ways. The effects in the United States have been most apparent in Chinese studies, while in China technical areas have been most visibly affected. Nonetheless, this dichotomy obscures a significant impact on the social sciences in China (e.g., economics, law, and increasingly, other social sciences) and on the natural sciences in the United States (e.g., agriculture, seismology, and cancer epidemiology). Even in fields such as physics, where most technical information flows from the United States to China, one of the substantial benefits to America has been the infusion into U.S. physics programs of PRC Chinese students and scholars of exceptional quality.

2. In the field of Chinese studies in the United States, it is becoming essential for American students and scholars to spend significant periods in China conducting archival and field research. While acknowledging that the utility of such work depends greatly on one's topic of research and on the availability of published materials abroad, research in China has important benefits, not the least of which is building the kinds of interpersonal and institutional ties that will facilitate the scholar's own future work and that of his or her graduate students. Although many scholars in social sciences and humanities have not yet published all of the results of work done in the PRC, the experience and the materials there are providing these scholars with a deeper and more comprehensive feeling for China past and present.

Taiwan and Hong Kong, nonetheless, remain important sites in the region where certain essential topics of research on China (e.g., the Communist Party, elite conflict, the public security apparatus, the military, popular religion, and so forth) can be effectively pursued. Moreover, Taiwan and Hong Kong constitute important subjects for research in their own right.

3. Social and natural scientists have been hampered by restrictions on field research in China, and these restrictions have substantially reduced the benefits of exchanges from the American perspective. Although there has been some improvement since 1982, research opportunities and conditions must expand and improve to enhance the mutually beneficial character of academic exchanges. At the same time,

Americans must be mindful of the economic constraints in the PRC, the limits placed on China's own scholars, and the very different cultural and academic traditions in the two nations. Nonetheless, lack of field research opportunities in both the natural and social sciences has diminished the zeal with which many pursue exchange with China. Finally, as China continues the trend toward permitting more extensive field, archival, survey, and interview research, it is essential to ensure that American scholars and institutions are not subjected to unreasonable and rapidly escalating fees for such access.

4. Access to Chinese archives, museums, and research institutes is critical from an American perspective, and to date this also has been a problem. It would enhance the mutually beneficial character of the exchanges if the Chinese authorities at central, regional, and local levels made the archives under their control increasingly accessible to foreign scholars.

5. American scholars have had a variety of experiences in China, and the quality of those experiences does not necessarily reflect central Chinese government policy in all respects. A number of factors influence the character of any particular researcher's experience in the PRC: the researcher's ties ("connections") with relevant Chinese academics and officials, the researcher's interpersonal skills, domestic politics in China, the state of Sino-American bilateral relations, the topic of research, the social, political, and/or professional status of the American scholar, ties between the scholar's home organization and the Chinese host unit, the specific financial arrangements covering the scholar's stay in China, and the personality and cooperativeness of key Chinese officials in local organizations.

6. Increasing attention should be given to long-term and large-scale cooperative research in China in both the social and natural sciences, as a vital supplement to ongoing individual research. Many social and natural processes (e.g., economic and environmental change) can only be examined through careful longitudinal measurement. Work in cancer epidemiology is a good example of how observations of localities and regions over time, in a cooperative project, can produce mutual scholarly benefits. The Committee on Scholarly Communication with the People's Republic of China can play an important role in developing frameworks for such cooperative activity in China.

Cooperative and long-term research must be built upon strong intellectual and interpersonal foundations. Fields in which academic exchange has been most extensive and productive have developed through a long process that began with delegation trips and briefings, which were followed by individual research and conferences. Moreover, there must be a critical mass of Chinese scholarly interest if cooperative research is to be feasible. In retrospect, the problems that emerged in some social science exchanges in the early 1980s occurred in part because an adequate foundation was not built.

7. Chinese graduate students in the American physics community (and more generally in some natural sciences) are an important element in American graduate education. They are high-quality students, and it is expected that a high percentage of them will return to the PRC to play significant roles. All of this, however, raises two broader questions. First, is the United States underinvesting in training its own citizens in many scientific and technical fields and, therefore, depending on students from abroad to fill the gap? Nationally, in 1983, 54 percent of all engineering doctorates earned in the United States were awarded to non-U.S. citizens; in mathematics the proportion was 37 percent, and in agricultural sciences, 35 percent.[55] In some respects, the United States has some interest in highly trained foreign citizens choosing to remain here. This raises the question of whether and to what degree the interests of the United States run counter to the hopes of the PRC in sending its students abroad in the sciences—namely, that they will return to assist China in its modernization drive. As of 1985, it seems most likely that a large percentage of PRC officially sponsored students will return home, but the lure of the scientific infrastructure and economic level in the United States will be strong. These cross-cutting interests, therefore, are likely to be a source of debate in the United States itself, and between China and America.

NOTES

1. A list of these authors and their institutional affiliations is provided in Appendix K. Copies of these studies are on file and available from CSCPRC.
2. Mary B. Bullock and Michel C. Oksenberg, untitled volume, forthcoming from Westview Press.
3. Jack L. Dull, "Premodern Chinese History: A Personal Assessment" (unpublished), p. 1 (forthcoming, in Bullock and Oksenberg, untitled volume).
4. Ibid., pp. 4–5.
5. Ibid., p. 3.
6. K. C. Chang, "A Decade of US–China Relations in Archaeology," *China Exchange News* (hereafter referred to as *CEN*), Vol. 11, No. 1 (March 1983), p. 1.
7. Catherine Badgley, "Collaborative Research on a Remarkable Fossil Site in Yunnan," *CEN*, Vol. 11, No. 1 (March 1983), p. 4.
8. Dennis Stanford, "Pleistocene Studies in Northeast China and the Rocky Mountains of Colorado: A Joint US–China Research Program on New World Cultural Origins," *CEN*, Vol. 11, No. 1 (March 1983), p. 6.

9. Workshop on the Mawangdui Manuscripts (Berkeley, Calif., June 1979); The Great Bronze Age of China (New York, April 1980); Fourth Annual Conference of the Chinese Paleography Association (Taiyuan, Shanxi, September 1981); The International Conference on Shang Civilization (Hawaii, September 1982); La Civlita Cinese Antica (Venice, April 1985); Ancient China and Social Science Generalizations (Airlie House, Virginia, June 1986). See David N. Keightley, University of California at Berkeley, correspondence, Oct. 12, 1985, p. 3.

10. In 1982 there were reportedly 29 provincial historical archives, 305 regional archives, and 2,337 county-level archives.

11. Chi Wang, "An Overview of Libraries in the People's Republic of China," CEN, Vol. 12, No. 3 (September 1984), p. 5.

12. Yeh-chien Wang, "Working at the First Historical Archives in Beijing," CEN, Vol. 12, No. 3 (September 1984), p. 9.

13. Dull, "Premodern Chinese History," p. 18.

14. Alice Rossi, ed., Sociology and Anthropology in the People's Republic of China: Report of a Delegation Visit, February–March 1984, (Washington, D.C.: National Academy Press, 1985), p. 130.

15. Ibid., p. 49.

16. Ibid., p. 3.

17. For example, see Patricia Beaver, "Social Anthropological Research on Women in China," CEN, Vol. 12, No. 4 (December 1984), pp. 12–14.

18. Martin King Whyte, "Research on Chinese Society: A Preliminary Evaluation," unpublished, 1983, pp. 21–22 (forthcoming, in Bullock and Oksenberg, untitled volume).

19. Rossi, Sociology and Anthropology in the PRC, pp. 6–7.

20. Deborah Davis-Friedmann, Long Lives: Chinese Elderly and the Communist Revolution (Cambridge, Mass.: Harvard University Press, 1983).

21. "Victor Nee of the University of California, Santa Barbara . . . traveled to Wuping County to conduct fieldwork in Yangbei village. . . . Nee spent three weeks in the village both to obtain an independent check on the data he had collected in the U.S. and to collect additional data on subsequent developments in the village following the departure of the educated youths. Nee conducted household surveys in four production teams; interviewed peasants, cadres and technical personnel; and had free access to all brigade and team statistical records on population trends and economic performance." In Lucie Cheng, "Chinese American Collaboration with Chinese Scholars on Social Science Research: The UCLA-Zhongshan Joint Research Project on Chinese Emigration," CEN, Vol. 12, No. 4 (December 1984), p. 11.

22. Ibid., pp. 7–11.

23. "William Liu initiated a collaborative study on mental health in January 1983 between the Pacific/Asian American Mental Health Research Center (PAAMHRC) in Chicago and the Shanghai Psychiatric Hospital. The study is the largest undertaking by an American sociologist. It is a longitudinal, multi-wave project involving a psychiatric epidemiological survey of 3,120 households in the Xuhui Health District of Shanghai and a case-control study that calls for intensive interviews of samples of individuals who scored positive or negative on the latest version of the Diagnostic Interview Schedule developed by the National Institute of Mental Health in 1981. . . . 'Major objectives of the study are to estimate the prevalence rate of psychiatric disorders for the adult population aged 18 to 64, and to assess various socio-economic, cultural, psychological and environmental factors associated with psychiatric disorders.'" in Cheng, CEN, p. 11.

24. Beaver, CEN, pp. 12–14, and the work of Margery Wolf.

25. Tamara K. Hareven, "Chinese Families Close Up," *CEN*, Vol. 12, No. 4 (December 1984), pp. 14–16.

26. Whyte, "Research on Chinese Society," p. 22.

27. Rossi, *Sociology and Anthropology in the PRC*, p. 132.

28. Information of interest to the political scientist is frequently classified *neibu* (for internal use only).

29. Information on this subject will appear in a forthcoming volume edited by David M. Lampton: *Policy Implementation in Post-Mao China* (to be published by the University of California Press in 1987). The papers for this volume were prepared for the workshop on "Policy Implementation in Post-Mao China," cosponsored by the Joint Committee on Chinese Studies of the American Council of Learned Societies and the Social Science Research Council, and the Mershon Center of the Ohio State University; Columbus, Ohio, June 20–24, 1983.

30. Leo Ou-fan Lee, "Research on Chinese Literature and the Arts: A Preliminary Evaluation," forthcoming in Bullock and Oksenberg, untitled volume, p. 5.

31. Ibid., p. 22.

32. Such knowledge is reflected in the work of Christine Wong, "Ownership and Control in Chinese Industry: The Maoist Legacy and Prospects for the 1980s," forthcoming in Joint Economic Committee of the U.S. Congress, *The Chinese Economy in the 1980s* (Washington, D.C.: U.S. Government Printing Office); and that of Barry Naughton, "Economic Reforms and Decentralization: China's Problematic Materials Allocation System," paper prepared for the Regional Seminar in Chinese Studies, University of California at Berkeley, April 6, 1984. These papers examine not simply the formal structure of planning and the materials allocation system in industry, but also analyze who actually makes economic decisions and how enterprises are able to operate under the complex web of controls and inconsistent plans. Similarly, a recent article by Susan Shirk ("Recent Chinese Labour Policies and the Transformation of Industrial Organization in China," *China Quarterly*, No. 88 (December 1981), pp. 575–593) explains not just the form of new industrial labor policies, but the way in which the new policies were received by enterprises and workers and how they ultimately affected hiring, wage, and bonus practices. Another recent article by Anita Chan and Jonathan Unger ("Grey and Black: The Hidden Economy of Rural China," *Pacific Affairs*, Vol. 55, No. 3 (Fall 1982), pp. 452–471) describes the numerous, informal economic arrangements that arise in rural areas. All of these authors have spent extended periods of time in China.

33. New work that treats provincial-level economics includes Kenneth R. Walker's *Food Grain Procurement and Consumption in China* (New York: Cambridge University Press, 1984) and A. S. Bhalla's *Economic Transition in Hunan and Southern China* (Hong Kong: Macmillan, 1984). Works examining county or lower-level microeconomic units include Tom Wiens's study of triple-cropping in production teams in Suzhou Prefecture ("The Limits to Agricultural Intensification: The Suzhou Experience," in *China Under the Four Modernizations, Part 1*, Joint Economic Committee of the U.S. Congress [Washington, D.C.: U.S. Government Printing Office, 1982], pp. 462–474). See also Y. Y. Kueh's article on county-level economic reform: "Economic Reform at the Xian Level," *China Quarterly*, No. 96 (December 1983), pp. 665–688.

34. See, for example, Terry Sicular, "Using a Farm-Household Model to Analyze Labor Allocation in a Chinese Collective Farm," in J. Strauss, I. Singh, and L. Squire, eds., *Agricultural Household Models: Extensions, Applications and Policy* (Baltimore: Johns Hopkins, forthcoming).

35. The works of Gregory C. Chow (*The Chinese Economy* (New York: Harper and Row,

1985)) and Loren Brandt ("A Note on Rural Incomes and Productivity Differences in Chinese Agriculture," unpublished manuscript, 1984), for example, rely heavily on information newly available in statistical yearbooks. Nicholas R. Lardy, in *Agriculture in China's Modern Economic Development* (New York: Cambridge University Press, 1983), used information culled from Chinese newspapers and journal articles.

36. For example, the works of Sicular and Wiens, cited above.

37. For example, Jushan Bai, Teh-wei Hu, and Suzhong Shi, "Household Expenditure Patterns in a Large Chinese City," unpublished manuscript, 1984.

38. William M. Speidel, "An Experiment in International Relations," *China Business Review*, Vol. 12, No. 3 (May–June 1985), pp. 42–43.

39. Ibid., p. 42.

40. FBIS, March 21, 1985, p. K1, from *Xinhua*.

41. Joseph L. Birman, "Case Study-Physics," pp. 2–3.

42. Ibid., p. 3.

43. J. Wesley Simmons, "US-PRC Health Protocol: Cooperation in Cancer," in *CEN*, Vol. 13, No. 1 (March 1985), p. 3.

44. Frederick P. Li, "US–Chinese Cooperation in Cancer Research," in *CEN*, Vol. 13, No. 1 (March 1985), p. 3.

45. Ibid., p. 2.

46. Simmons, "US-PRC Health Protocol," p. 4.

47. Brian Henderson, Mimi C. Yu, and Anna H. Wu, "University of Southern California Cancer Epidemiology Programs with China," *CEN*, Vol. 13, No. 1 (March 1985), p. 6.

48. Gerry S. de Harven, "The American Cancer Society and the Development of Cancer Control in China," *CEN*, Vol. 13, No. 1 (March 1985), p. 17.

49. "Memorial Sloan-Kettering Cancer Center Work with China," *CEN*, Vol. 13, No. 1 (March 1985), p. 15.

50. Glaser, p. 9.

51. Frank Press et al., "Earthquake Research in China," *EOS Trans. AGU*, Vol. 56, No. 11 (1975), pp. 838–881; and Frank Press, "Plate Tectonics and Earthquake Prediction: Contrasting Approaches in China and the United States," Bulletin, American Academy of Arts and Sciences, Vol. 28, No. 8 (1975), pp. 14–27.

52. Lester Ross, "Earthquake Policy in China," *Asian Survey*, Vol. 24, No. 7 (1984), pp. 773–787.

53. Peter Molnar and P. Tapponier, "Relation of the Tectonics of Eastern China to the India-Eurasian Collision: Application of Slip-line Field Theory to Large-Scale Continental Tectonics," *Geology*, Vol. 5 (1977), pp. 212–216.

54. T. A. D'Auria, ed., "ACM's Visit of the People's Republic of China," Special Report, Communications of the ACM, Vol. 27, No. 3 (1984).

55. Compare these figures to those in 1973, when 35 percent of all engineering doctorates earned in the United States were earned by foreign citizens; 21 percent in mathematics, and 37 percent in agricultural sciences. Figures in *Higher Education & National Affairs*, Vol. 34, No. 6 (Apr. 8, 1985), p. 3; and compiled by the National Research Council, "Doctorate Recipients from United States Universities," 1973 and 1983 Summary Reports.

8

Future Issues and Opportunities

By virtue of its immense size, its strategic location, its character as a developing nation and a nuclear power, the creativity of its people, and the grandeur of its civilization, the People's Republic of China presents special issues and opportunities to other nations, most particularly to the United States. This chapter addresses the broader effects of Sino-American academic exchanges to date, the issues they raise in both societies, and the challenges that lie ahead.

INSTITUTIONAL CHANGES

One principal consequence of Sino-American academic exchanges has been to provide China's elite with alternative institutional models as it strives to modernize the country. Since the mid-nineteenth century, China's leaders and intellectuals have frequently looked abroad for models that could promote internal order, economic growth, and national security. Although the PRC's leaders adamantly oppose uncritical institutional borrowing from abroad, they are intensely interested in systems and institutions that might be useful in China. Although it is not certain to what extent *any* American systems are in fact relevant to China, the Chinese have been particularly attracted to American educational and scientific institutions.

For example, on March 19, 1985, China's Communist Party Central Committee announced:

171

The system of science foundations will be gradually introduced on a trial basis to support basic and some applied research projects, and the funds will primarily come from state appropriations. A national natural science foundation and other science and technology foundations will be established, opened to the public, and will accept fund applications from all sectors, organize the appraisal of the applications by people in the given field, and select the most feasible projects for support, in accordance with the national science and technology development plan.[1]

Presumably, the U.S. National Science Foundation and the American private foundation community inspired the Chinese to shift to peer review and remove some research monies from China's traditional budgetary mechanisms.[2] Similarly, Chinese interest in policy advisory "think tanks" and contract research has been given focus and direction as Beijing's leaders have interacted with such organizations in America, elsewhere in the West, and in the USSR.[3] Both in the pre-1949 era and today, the concept of comprehensive research universities, the extension functions of American land grant universities, the close ties between some American universities and high-tech industries, and internal American university organization, financing, and personnel policies and practices have all piqued Chinese interest.

This is not to say that China is copying, or should copy, American (or other) institutional patterns. Nonetheless, as China's leaders are moving forward, they are looking abroad at a wide range of options, and many American institutional forms have attracted particular notice. It behooves Americans not to oversell the U.S. system. China, for its part, should and will continue to cast its net very wide. Beijing's consideration of foreign approaches to major institutional problems may be one of the most enduring legacies of academic exchanges.

RETURNED PRC STUDENTS AND SCHOLARS: "REABSORPTION"

The "reabsorption" of PRC students and scholars who have studied and worked abroad is a major concern in both nations. The Chinese government wants to protect its investment in this training by avoiding socially disruptive consequences that occur if returnees are not successfully reintegrated into their work units and Chinese society. Some PRC students and scholars abroad are uncertain what their role will be on returning to China. These anxieties influence their decision about whether to return home or to stay abroad. American educational and research institutions are interested in the experiences of returnees because they want to provide training appropriate to China's needs and conditions.

China has problems in putting the skill and training of returned students and scholars to best use despite the fact that Beijing is making an earnest effort to alleviate this difficulty. From November 23 to 29, 1984, China's State Council convened a national conference at which State Councillor Zhang Jingfu was reported to have "called for a change in work conditions for the 14,000 people who have returned from overseas study. *Seventy percent* of them were not being fully used because of a shortage of advanced facilities and unsuitable work assignments"[4] (emphasis added). Although both officially sponsored and self-paying students and scholars have encountered difficulties being "reabsorbed," the "self-paying" students apparently experience somewhat greater problems. In his speech, Zhang Jingfu took particular pains to note that "students studying abroad at their own expense must be treated equally and given the necessary assistance as are those studying abroad at the state's expense."[5]

The variations in the experiences of exchange participants upon returning depend upon their previous status and their circumstances in China. Those sent abroad by the Chinese government are dispatched by a particular "unit" or organization. Those who are "research scholars" frequently have considerable seniority in their unit, and, therefore, an organizational niche usually awaits them on their return. In contrast, "self-paying" students, who generally go abroad under ad hoc personal arrangements, are less likely to have an organizational home awaiting them. Most self-paying students are young, with little or no seniority, and the skills they acquire abroad might not fit any particular Chinese organization's needs at home. Because China has virtually no labor market or mobility (though this may gradually change), those who are not in an organization's personnel plan find it very difficult to locate a good job. In many cases, these students are gambling, hoping that if there is not a suitable position in China they will find one in the United States.

Even those individuals who have an organizational base could find their effectiveness reduced by a number of factors. The unit's senior leaders might not choose to facilitate the returned individual's work, depending upon whether his or her skills are viewed as an opportunity or a threat. Similarly, seniority frequently conflicts with considerations of merit in promotion decisions; more deserving workers who have studied abroad can still be passed over in favor of a more senior colleague.[6] Even when individuals trained abroad are appropriately placed in an organization, insufficient funds, equipment, and supplies frequently retard their work.[7] Ever present, too, is the possibility that the research an individual undertook abroad simply is not a high prior-

ity for the unit upon return. At least one Chinese report suggests that
this has been a problem:

The research projects in which they were engaged while overseas should be
basically linked up with the work they did before going abroad. . . . After their
return from abroad, their professional directions can be adjusted slightly in
light of China's specific realities and conditions, merging each person's aspirations and characteristics and rationally arranging his or her work.[8]

The present heavy emphasis on applied research could create some
friction with returned students and scholars whose work in the United
States was more "basic" in character.

How well China succeeds in reintegrating students and scholars who
return from abroad will greatly affect the rate at which PRC students
and scholars return to China in the future. As noted in Chapter 3, the
return rate for J-1 students and scholars is likely to be higher than for
F-1s. Nonetheless, action by the Chinese government could affect the
potentially unstable rate at which J-1s return to China. If more J-1s stay
in the United States, the resulting "brain drain" would become a political issue in China. In the United States, it would become part of the
larger immigration issue.

Through policy pronouncements and institutional changes, the Chinese have tackled the reabsorption issue directly and promptly, and
China's top leaders have resolved publicly to make effective use of
returned students and scholars. The 1984 conference mentioned earlier
was one forum for airing this issue. Before that, in late 1983, a video-
tape of senior Chinese leaders was played to Chinese students and
scholars studying in the United States. A principal purpose of this tape,
brought to the United States by a group "entrusted by the Central
Committee of the Chinese Communist Party and the State Council,"
was to reassure the students and scholars that "when you have finished
your study and come home, you should be a fresh crack force for China's cause of socialist modernization and pillars of the state by the first
years of the 21st century."[9]

China has also made a financial commitment toward helping the
returnees. In late 1984, the government announced that the State would
allocate 20 million yuan (U.S. $8 million) to "set up 10 places through-
out the country where returned students would have equipment to work
with while they spent two years seeking suitable jobs."[10] Furthermore,
from 1982 through 1986, China's Ministry of Education (MOE) used
$150 million U.S. dollars in World Bank loan funds to purchase teach-
ing and research equipment for 28 major universities. According to
senior Chinese scientists and officials interviewed by University of

Southern California Professor Otto Schnepp, returning exchange scholars have benefited from this investment in instrumentation.[11]

If the science reforms promulgated in March 1985 take full effect,[12] they will enhance the prospects of returning scholars. These scholars presumably would benefit from China's efforts to move toward a peer review and competitive grant system, freer labor mobility for technical personnel, and more opportunities for consultancy and contract research. The reforms are still in the early stages and progress is uncertain, but the direction is promising. Three questions are paramount. Will these policies be effectively implemented? Will they be sustained long enough for wary scientists and intellectuals to become more confident? Will a perception of favored treatment for returning scholars become a serious domestic political problem in China? Nonetheless, PRC students and scholars in the United States demonstrate a great sense of obligation to their homeland, which will almost certainly keep their return rate higher than has been the case for many other student groups from developing countries in the United States.

TECHNOLOGY TRANSFER: ISSUES FOR THE FUTURE

Though the 1982 National Research Council study entitled *Scientific Communication and National Security* was principally concerned with the Soviet Union, its recommendations are a fitting starting point for U.S. policies on China and technology control in the university setting. The key recommendation of that study is as follows:

No restriction of any kind limiting access or communication should be applied to any area of university research, be it basic or applied, unless it involves a technology meeting *all* the following criteria:
• The technology is developing rapidly, and the time from basic science to application is short;
• The technology has identifiable direct military applications; or it is dual-use and involves process or production-related techniques;
• Transfer of the technology would give the U.S.S.R. [China] a significant near-term military benefit; and
• The U.S. is the only source of information about the technology, or other friendly nations that could also be the source have control systems as secure as ours.[13]

Technology transfer issues in the Sino-American academic relationship are complex and of far-reaching importance. Four points are clear. First, the Chinese turned toward the West, and particularly to the United States in the 1970s, in part because they wanted to acquire a broad range of high technology. Second, the United States must protect its security and proprietary interests. Third, American national security concerns have caused friction with the PRC. On at least two occasions in 1984, Chinese officials expressed concern that Chinese students and scholars had been "restricted to [a] certain number of courses or specialties, and the extent of such restriction exceeds that for the students and scholars from other countries or regions."[14] PRC officials have raised similar concerns about limitations on attendance of Chinese at some academic and professional association meetings in the United States. Fourth, the complexity of the American monitoring and regulatory mechanisms makes it difficult for both Americans and Chinese to know what our technology transfer policy really is and who is responsible for its enforcement, since the mechanisms are fragmented among the intelligence community, the Departments of Defense, State, Commerce, Energy, and Justice, and the Customs Service.

In the American system, a distinction should be drawn between universities, which should remain as open as possible, and government and private research laboratories that quite appropriately seek to protect national security and proprietary information. We believe that, on balance, America is best served by its universities when they pursue a policy of continual innovation and openness. Given the importance of foreign graduate students in basic science research at universities, any restraints placed on the access of foreign nationals to technical information and nonclassified research equipment[15] will greatly slow important research progress on American campuses.

American universities have given Chinese students and scholars the same reception accorded all other foreign students and overall have been very open in their dealings. Nonetheless, a very few American universities have restricted enrollment in some classes to United States citizens (see Appendix L). Several professional association meetings, or parts of these meetings, have been closed to non-U.S. citizens even though participants were discussing *unclassified* technology subject to export control. One recent example was the January 1985 conference of the Society of Manufacturing Engineers (SME) on "Composites in Manufacturing 4." The program announcement reportedly said, "This conference is open to U.S. citizens only. You must prove citizenship in order to be admitted."[16] In speaking of the effects on academic freedom of new export control regulations, Harvard Vice-President John Shattuck said that they

are dramatically illustrated by a course on Metal Matrix Composites offered recently at U.C.L.A., that was advertised in the course catalogue as restricted to "U.S. Citizens Only." The restriction was required because the course material involved unclassified technical data appearing on the [U.S. government's] Munitions Control List (I.T.A.R.) and thus subject to export control.[17]

It must be noted, however, that this action was not aimed solely at PRC students and that UCLA has since refused to participate in programs restricted to U.S. citizens.[18] In short, the Chinese are now affected by the same restrictions that also affect our allies in Japan and Western Europe.[19] It must also be observed that the Chinese have closed many of their conferences to foreigners. It is hoped that in a spirit of responsiveness, this trend will be reversed so that Americans and other foreigners will be able to attend more conferences in China.

FUTURE OPPORTUNITIES FOR CUMULATIVE AND COOPERATIVE RESEARCH

In the immediate wake of diplomatic "normalization," both the Chinese and American sides, appropriately, focused their attention on the exchange of individual students and scholars. It now is time to think about longer-term, group, and collaborative research to supplement—not replace—the individual research and study in the PRC that remains critically important.

As increasing numbers of PRC students and scholars return from study and research in the West, they do so with personal ties, improved foreign language command, greater commonality of intellectual frameworks, and more compatible research objectives that will make long-term collaborative research feasible. Sustained, systematic, and interdisciplinary projects could focus on such varied topics as the following: monitoring changes in the global distribution of toxic substances; charting ecological or societal change on the Tibetan Plateau; looking at demographic processes during economic change; following disease patterns as internal mobility, urbanization, industrialization, and foreign contact all increase; or charting socioeconomic change. Any such studies of physical and social change require systematic observation over time.

The United States is now, it may be hoped, near a point in its relationship with China that such undertakings are possible, with research occurring in both the United States and the PRC. The challenge for scholars is to define the priority areas for inquiry and to identify participants from both sides. Rich possibilities exist in both the social and natural sciences.

INVOLVEMENT IN SCIENTIFIC, ECONOMIC, AND
TECHNICAL CHANGE IN CHINA

American government and private-sector organizations are becoming involved in helping to build or revitalize some fields of study in China. At the same time, some American institutional forms have impressed the Chinese as they seek promising directions for economic and social reform. In addition, a few American foundations have supported the physical expansion and modernization of Chinese academic and scientific institutions. American government initiatives, such as the Dalian Center for Industrial Science and Technology Management Development (see Chapter 4), contribute to Chinese manpower training. And, in the case of Johns Hopkins University and its joint project with Nanjing University, an American university has made a long-term commitment to institutional development in the PRC.

In essence, academic exchanges now are beginning to address issues of structural reform in China, and American academics and industrial scientists are, for better or worse, becoming involved in Chinese institutional change. To prevent disillusionment in both societies, the United States' challenge is to make it plain that American institutions have limits even in America, let alone in the far different circumstances of a China that is socialist, 80 percent peasant, and still deeply ambivalent about what Westerners almost gleefully call "interdependence." Moreover, American financial resources are small in comparison to Chinese needs.

This opportunity for involvement in China's economic and scientific development raises profound questions that are not easily answered. Is it wise to fuel Chinese expectations about American technical and financial capacities? Can the United States, and should it ever, be more than a marginal influence on the course of Chinese development? What would be the costs of standing on the sidelines compared to the costs of disillusionment in both China and the West if China's current efforts do not produce the desired results? What are the United States' security interests? If China imports products and commodities from abroad, it must also export, and that means that some American and Western industries will face unwelcome competition. Is it in the U.S. interest to help potential competitors develop? As American universities become involved in China's economic development, what is the "proper" relationship between institutions of higher education and the entrepreneurial activities of both Chinese and American businesses? For business, knowledge is a saleable commodity—for the university, it traditionally has been a free good.

This study concludes as it began—with questions. However, the new questions confronting educational and scientific leaders in both countries document how far the Sino-American exchange relationship has progressed in the short span of six years.

NOTES

1. Foreign Broadcast Information Service Daily Report: China (hereafter referred to as *FBIS*), March 21, 1985, p. K2, from *Xinhua*.
2. Marjorie Sun, "China's Science Academy Revamps Funding Process," *Science*, Vol. 227, No. 4687 (1985), p. 615.
3. *Joint Publications Research Service* (hereafter referred to as *JPRS*), CST-85-003, Jan. 28, 1985, Science and Technology, pp. 27–36, from *Guangming Ribao* and *Keyan Guanli (Scientific Research Management)*; also, *JPRS*, CPS-84-054, Aug. 10, 1984, Political, Sociological, and Military Affairs, pp. 17–19.
4. *China Daily*, Nov. 30, 1984, p. 1.
5. *FBIS*, Nov. 30, 1984, p. K9, from *Xinhua*.
6. *Wall Street Journal*, July 6, 1984, p. 1.
7. Otto Schnepp, "The Chinese Visiting Scholar Program in Science and Engineering," unpublished manuscript prepared for National Science Foundation, July 1985, pp. 20–29.
8. *JPRS*, CPS-85-003, Jan. 28, 1985, pp. 23–24, from *Guangming Ribao* [*Bright Daily*], Aug. 29, 1984, p. 1.
9. *FBIS*, Dec. 30, 1983, p. B1, from *Xinhua*.
10. *China Daily*, Nov. 30, 1984. It should be noted that some PRC students and scholars in the United States view these centers with apprehension, fearing that they also are intended to control returned students rather than facilitate their work.
11. Schnepp, "The Chinese Visiting Scholar Program," pp. 35–36.
12. *FBIS*, March 21, 1985, pp. K1–K10, from *Xinhua*; also, *FBIS*, March 8, 1985, pp. K1–K3, from *Xinhua*.
13. *Scientific Communication and National Security: A Report Prepared by the Panel on Scientific Communication and National Security and the Committee on Science, Engineering, and Public Policy* (Washington, D.C.: National Academy Press, 1982), p. 5.
14. Correspondence, August 1984.
15. "Curb on Campus Computers: Pentagon vs. Academia," *New York Times*, Aug. 17, 1985, p. L-7; also, "NSF Backs Off Rules Restricting Access to Supercomputers," *Chronicle of Higher Education* (July 24, 1985), p. 1.
16. Robert L. Park, "Intimidation Leads to Self-Censorship in Science," *Bulletin of the Atomic Scientists* (March 1985), p. 22.
17. *Chronicle of Higher Education* (Jan. 9, 1985), pp. 15–16.
18. Park, p. 23.
19. *Wall Street Journal*, Jan. 25, 1985.

TABLE A-1 Native Provinces of Chinese Students in the United States, for Selected Years, 1903 Through 1945 (percent)

	1903[a]	1909	1910	1911	1914	1918	1921[b]	1943	1945
Kwangtung	58.0	38.1	38.0	51.2	47.2	43.0	24.2	36.9	33.6
Kiangsu	4.0	28.5	23.2	22.0	13.9	13.4	21.9	20.9	22.3
Chekiang	6.0	11.3	11.6	9.2	8.3	9.2	10.8	8.4	7.5
Fukien	2.0	4.6	5.1	3.7	5.3	8.8	7.8	6.4	5.5
Hunan	—	0.4	2.1	1.0	8.0	4.7	5.2	2.6	3.0
Hupeh	12.0	1.7	3.1	1.6	2.4	3.7	2.8	1.9	3.2
Hopeh	—	8.4	8.2	4.3	2.2	3.7	9.7	10.6	10.9
Anhwei	16.0	3.4	4.1	2.0	—	2.8	2.3	2.0	1.6
Kiangsi	—	1.3	1.4	0.4	4.1	2.6	2.4	1.5	1.7
Szechuan	—	—	—	1.0	—	1.6	1.8	1.5	2.2
Shantung	—	—	0.4	2.1	2.7	1.4	2.2	2.2	2.5
Honan	—	0.4	0.4	—	—	0.8	3.8	1.2	1.5
Shansi	—	0.4	0.7	—	—	0.5	0.9	0.8	1.1
Liaoning	—	—	—	—	—	0.1	0.9	1.3	1.3
Kirin	—	—	—	—	—	0.8	0.1	—	0.4
Heilungkiang	—	—	—	—	—	—	—	—	—
Others	2.0	1.5	1.7	1.5	5.9	2.9	3.3	1.8	1.7
Total (%)	100.0	100.0	100.0	100.0	100.0	100.0	100.0	100.0	100.0
Total (no.)	50	239	292	490	830	990	679	1,191	1,972
Including unknown	50		292	650	847	1,124	805	1,295	3,066

[a]The information is not complete, only 50 out of "some two hundred students" being listed. The sample seems, however, fairly representative.

[b]After 1921 the native origin of a student is no longer listed in directories of Chinese students, except during the years from 1943 to 1945 when a great expansion of the activities of the China Institute caused it to issue directories much more comprehensive in scope than was customarily the case.

SOURCE: Adapted, with permission, from Y. C. Wang, *Chinese Intellectuals and the West: 1872-1949* (Chapel Hill, University of North Carolina Press, 1966).

TABLE A-2   Fields of Chinese Students in America, for Selected Years, 1905 Through 1952–1953 (percent)

	1905	1906–1907	1909	1914	1918	1920–1921	1924	1927	1931–1932	1934–1935
Humanities	—	—	16.4	2.1	11.9	8.6	10.2	10.7	20.8	13.4
Literature	—	—	—	—	0.5	—	0.2	2.6	5.4	—
History	—	—	—	0.3	0.5	0.9	2.1	1.6	1.0	1.6
Philosophy	—	—	0.6	0.1	1.0	1.0	—	1.7	0.8	—
Library science	—	—	—	—	0.3	0.2	—	0.2	6.5	0.8
Journalism	—	—	—	—	0.2	—	0.7	0.2	0.4	1.6
Fine arts	—	—	—	0.1	0.3	1.0	2.3	0.2	0.1	—
General	—	—	15.8	1.6	9.1	5.5	4.9	4.2	6.6	9.4
Social Science	5.4	5.6	19.7	10.2	12.3	15.1	10.1	19.3	12.5	14.1
Law	1.5	—	8.2	1.7	2.6	1.5	5.5	2.3	1.7	1.6
Political science	1.6	5.6	7.7	2.8	3.1	4.6		7.3	4.2	5.9
Economics	2.3	—	3.8	4.7	5.9	6.8	4.6	7.6	4.4	2.7
Sociology	—	—	—	1.0	0.7	2.2	—	2.1	2.2	3.9
Business	5.4	8.6	9.3	4.0	10.5	10.1	14.0	14.1	10.8	12.4
Education	4.6	—	4.4	4.7	8.9	7.1	8.7	9.0	9.2	11.4
Education	4.6	—	2.2	3.5	5.8	5.6	7.5	6.0	6.5	7.2
Home economics	—	—	—	—	0.7	0.2	0.1	0.1	0.6	2.7
Religion	—	—	—	1.0	1.6	1.2	1.1	1.1	1.5	1.5
Music	—	—	2.2	—	0.8	0.1	—	1.8	0.6	—
Social work	—	—	—	0.2	—	—	—	—	—	—
Engineering	23.8	27.2	33.9	30.8	28.2	38.3	36.3	23.7	22.4	30.1
Sciences	4.6	—	9.8	7.5	9.3	9.3	10.2	11.1	11.7	5.1
Medicine	4.6	—	2.2	4.8	7.9	6.0	6.8	7.6	7.8	9.5
Agriculture	4.6	—	4.3	6.0	4.3	5.2	3.5	3.3	4.2	3.9
Military Sciences	0.8	—	—	0.4	0.5	0.3	0.2	1.2	0.6	0.1
Preparatory	46.2	58.6	—	29.5	6.2	—	—	—	—	—
Total	100.0	100.0	100.0	100.0	100.0	100.0	100.0	100.0	100.0	100.0
Subtotal:										
no. students	130	162	183	747	1,058	862	1,225	1,272	933	931
Unknown	—	55	—	100	66	55	412	141	323	573
Total no. students	130	217	183	847	1,124	917	1,637	1,413	1,256	1,504

SOURCE: Adapted, with permission, from Y. C. Wang, *Chinese Intellectuals and the West: 1872–1949* (Chapel Hill, University of North Carolina Press, 1966).

1935–1936	1936–1937	1937–1938	1941–1942	Nov. 1942	1943	1945	1949–1950	1950–1951	1951–1952	1952–1953	Total %	Total No.
22.8	12.4	15.0	6.5	5.8	6.8	7.0	14.3	13.2	11.9	10.5	11.7	3,690
0.1	—	—	0.4	1.4	3.1	2.2	2.3	2.7	3.0	3.2	3.5	1,112
—	—	—	0.8	0.8	1.5	1.3	1.3	1.2	1.2	1.7	1.0	314
0.4	—	—	0.6	—	0.7	0.7	0.7	0.8	1.0	0.5	0.6	181
0.6	—	0.5	0.1	—	—	0.3	0.4	0.5	0.4	0.7	0.5	160
2.3	1.8	1.5	3.1	1.9	0.3	0.8	0.7	0.6	0.3	0.9	1.0	300
—	—	—	1.5	1.7	1.1	1.2	0.3	0.4	0.6	0.6	0.6	182
19.4	10.6	13.0	—	—	—	0.5	8.6	7.0	5.4	2.9	4.5	1,441
13.3	13.8	11.9	14.5	15.3	18.6	15.9	11.9	14.0	13.4	11.4	13.6	4,270
1.7	1.5	0.6	1.0	1.3	2.1	1.8	0.9	1.3	0.9	1.5	1.5	461
3.4	3.9	3.3	4.5	4.3	5.6	5.1	4.4	3.9	4.7	3.8	4.3	1,348
4.9	5.6	5.2	4.3	4.8	7.1	6.0	4.9	5.9	5.1	3.8	5.2	1,636
3.3	2.8	2.8	4.7	4.9	3.8	3.0	1.8	3.0	2.7	2.3	2.6	825
7.0	8.6	7.8	8.6	7.9	6.5	6.9	7.5	8.5	7.7	8.6	8.6	2,708
16.1	17.8	17.8	13.1	8.0	8.3	7.2	15.7	14.7	12.9	11.3	12.2	3,840
11.5	12.6	12.3	6.5	4.6	5.0	4.7	6.2	6.2	5.4	4.3	6.8	2,137
2.7	2.1	2.5	2.3	2.0	0.4	0.6	2.8	1.9	1.4	1.6	1.6	493
1.5	2.2	1.9	2.3	—	0.6	—	3.4	3.1	2.8	2.8	1.9	605
0.4	0.9	1.1	2.0	1.4	1.6	1.3	2.4	2.6	2.2	1.8	1.5	464
—	—	—	—	—	0.7	0.6	0.9	1.0	1.1	0.8	0.4	141
23.0	22.4	25.5	28.4	39.1	34.8	41.1	27.5	25.8	25.5	26.9	28.7	9,023
6.6	10.4	6.3	13.6	15.7	14.5	10.9	14.8	15.0	17.4	18.6	12.3	3,872
7.3	11.1	11.0	13.1	5.2	6.5	7.6	5.1	5.9	8.4	10.2	7.8	2,455
3.6	3.4	4.6	2.1	2.9	2.8	2.4	3.2	2.9	2.8	2.5	3.3	1,045
0.3	0.1	0.1	0.1	0.1	1.2	1.0	—	—	—	—	0.3	87
—	—	—	—	—	—	—	—	—	—	—	1.5	442
100.0	100.0	100.0	100.0	100.0	100.0	100.0	100.0	100.0	100.0	100.0	100.0	—
1,585	1,909	2,221	1,545	1,042	1,259	2,372	3,634	3,351	2,773	2,238	—	31,432
299	253	117	204	15	38	650	290	274	224	410	—	4,499
1,884	2,162	2,338	1,749	1,057	1,297	3,022	3,924	3,625	2,997	2,648	—	35,931

TABLE A-3 Number of Faculty Members Trained Abroad and to Be Sent Abroad Under China University Development Project, Between September 1982 and April 1984

No.	Institution[a]	Total	M	F	Age 56 & over	51-55	41-50	31-40	21-30	20 & under	Title Prof.	Assoc. Prof.	Lect.	Ass't.	Grad.	U.G.
1	Beijing U.	39	34	5	5	22	12	—	—	—	2	36	1	—	—	—
2	Fudan U.	38	35	3	—	2	9	15	11	1	—	3	7	—	4	24
3	Nanjing U.	59	54	5	—	8	31	4	16	—	—	10	31	18	—	—
4	Nankai U.	35	28	9	—	7	5	10	10	3	—	2	1	9	7	16
5	Wuhan U.	39	36	3	1	—	10	11	17	—	1	10	8	4	1	15
6	Zhongshan U.	44	37	7	—	2	6	13	23	—	—	2	13	9	5	15
7	Xiamen U.	34	34	—	—	—	2	7	24	1	—	2	—	15	1	16
8	Shandong U.	31	31	—	—	1	3	4	23	—	—	1	1	11	5	13
9	Jilin U.	52	41	11	3	8	20	8	13	—	2	15	19	2	6	8
10	Lanzhou U.	33	30	3	—	3	14	1	13	2	—	7	11	2	—	13
11	Sichuan U.	19	15	4	—	—	3	6	10	—	—	—	5	6	1	7
12	Qinghua U.	109	96	13	—	9	66	18	16	—	—	24	66	5	—	14
13	Xian Jiaotong U.	61	57	4	—	7	21	12	21	—	—	12	17	11	2	19
14	Chinese U. of Sci. & Tech.	53	46	7	—	—	22	20	11	—	—	4	32	5	—	12
15	Shanghai Jiaotong U.	42	42	—	—	—	—	15	27	—	—	—	—	16	—	26
16	Zhejiang U.	51	49	2	—	5	3	3	39	1	2	4	3	—	1	41
17	Tianjin U.	35	33	2	—	5	2	7	20	1	—	6	11	25	6	20
18	Dalian I.T.	64	58	6	1	3	18	9	33	—	—	3	10	14	8	5
19	Huanan I.T.	47	42	5	—	2	7	12	26	—	—	2	9	5	7	24
20	Nanjing I.T.	45	42	3	—	5	3	5	32	—	—	6	2	2	3	32
21	Huazhong I.T.	59	55	4	—	3	9	25	22	—	1	10	12	16	—	20
22	Chongqing U.	30	22	8	—	—	1	5	21	3	—	—	3	2	2	23
23	Beijing A.U.	41	30	11	4	19	7	3	8	—	—	22	5	9	2	3
24	Beijing M.C.	46	37	9	—	18	18	9	1	—	—	16	21	9	—	—
25	Beijing N.U.	42	20	22	—	1	18	8	15	—	—	9	15	8	1	9
26	Huadong N.U.	28	25	3	—	2	1	12	13	—	—	—	4	9	3	12
27	Tongji U.	5	5	—	—	—	2	3	—	—	—	—	2	1	—	2
28	SFEI	—	—	—	—	—	—	—	—	—	—	—	—	—	—	—
	Total	1,182	1,034	148	14	132	320	245	467	12	8	205	209	204	65	390

[a]U. = University; I.T. = Institute of Technology; A.U. = Agricultural University; M.C. = Medical College; N.U. = Normal University; SFEI = Shanghai Institute of Finance and Economics.

[b]These figures were supplied by China's Ministry of Education. There are several errors of arithmetic and inconsistencies.

[c]These figures report the number of individuals awarded grants to study in various countries. This is *not* a report of actual grantee activities.

SOURCE: China University Development Project, World Bank.

TABLE A-3 (Continued)

Country[b]										Training[c]			
U.S.	Can.	Jpn.	Austral.	Fr.	FRG	U.K.	Belg.	Neth.	Other	1 yr	2 yr	Ph.D.	M.
34	—	2	—	—	1	—	—	—	—	39	—	—	—
22	4	—	—	1	1	8	—	—	2	9	2	4	23
37	5	5	3	1	2	3	—	1	2	42	—	4	13
24	7	1	—	—	1	2	—	—	—	4	1	7	23
20	4	1	1	1	5	—	—	—	—	12	7	1	19
31	5	1	—	—	2	5	—	—	—	3	14	8	19
18	10	1	—	1	1	3	—	—	—	2	—	1	31
20	3	1	1	1	4	—	—	—	1	1	5	1	20
26	5	13	1	1	3	1	—	—	2	35	1	6	10
13	14	1	—	1	1	2	—	—	1	18	—	—	15
9	4	3	—	—	—	1	—	—	2	—	6	—	13
51	16	7	—	2	12	14	—	1	6	89	2	—	18
34	8	2	—	1	2	9	—	3	2	27	—	13	21
35	4	1	2	—	3	8	—	—	—	31	8	2	12
33	2	1	—	—	4	1	—	—	1	—	—	12	30
35	2	3	—	—	2	—	—	—	9	9	—	—	42
25	4	—	—	—	2	3	—	1	—	7	—	7	21
33	4	10	—	—	1	7	4	2	3	17	12	9	26
31	12	—	—	—	1	2	—	—	1	3	14	7	23
25	3	1	2	1	—	13	—	—	—	8	—	3	34
49	3	4	—	—	3	6	—	1	—	20	—	14	25
18	4	2	—	—	—	2	2	1	1	5	1	2	22
21	4	1	2	1	—	6	4	1	1	25	5	1	10
29	2	4	1	2	—	1	—	1	6	40	3	2	1
24	5	2	2	—	1	4	—	—	4	25	—	1	16
16	6	1	2	—	—	2	—	1	—	3	—	3	22
2	—	—	—	—	2	1	—	—	—	3	—	2	—
—	—	—	—	—	—	—	—	—	—	—	—	—	—
709	140	68	17	14	54	106	10	13	43	447	81	114	510

TABLE A-4   PRC-Government-Sponsored Students Sent to Japan

	1979	1980	1981	1982	1983[a]	Total	Current[b]
Undergraduate students	—	103	115	117	50	385	364 (17)
Jinxiusheng	131	238	224	266	47	906	526 (108)
Graduate students	—	—	—	148	—	148	148 (50)
Total	131	341	339	531	97	1,439	1,038 (175)

[a]As of April 1983.
[b]Current = in Japan as of April 1983. Figures in parentheses: number of Chinese students sponsored by the Japanese government.
SOURCE: Data from Ministry of Education, Japan.

TABLE A-5   Percentage Distribution of J-1 and F-1 Visa Holders by Sex and Marital Status, 1983

Sex and Marital Status	J-1	F-1	J-1 and F-1
Men	81	63	77
Single	21	40	26
Married	59	22	51
Previously married	0	0	0
Women	19	37	23
Single	5	29	11
Married	14	8	12
Previously married	0	0	0
Total	100	100	100
N =	(3,183)	(949)	(4,132)

NOTE: Percentage of missing data excluded from totals is less than 1 percent.
SOURCE: Records of visas issued in 1983.

TABLE A-6 Percentage Distribution of PRC J-1 Students and
Scholars by Field of Study and Category, 1979 Through 1984

Field of Study	Category of Scholar						
	Student	Trainee	Teacher	Professor	Research Scholar	Int'l. Visitor	Professional Trainee
Agriculture	2	33	0	3	3	5	3
American studies	—	1	2	0	—	—	0
Architecture	—	—	0	1	—	—	0
Business management	2	6	2	1	1	3	2
Computer science	4	4	1	7	3	2	5
Education	3	2	21	4	1	5	—
Engineering	23	27	23	20	34	10	18
English as a second language	1	1	3	1	—	—	0
Health sciences	3	6	5	16	13	29	47
Humanities	5	—	15	4	2	5	1
Law	1	3	1	2	—	1	4
Library and archival science	—	1	1	—	—	1	1
Life sciences	8	4	3	8	10	9	5
Mathematics	7	0	4	5	4	1	—
Physical sciences	31	4	9	15	24	9	5
Social sciences	6	1	4	9	3	8	3
Other	3	8	9	6	1	10	5
Total	100	100	100	100	100	100	100
N =	(7,897)	(579)	(182)	(1,021)	(15,669)	(606)	(312)

NOTE: Individuals are counted in this table for each year they study a given field. Some persons are counted more than once. The symbol "—" indicates a value less than 0.5 percent. Missing data account for less than 1 percent for all years.
SOURCE: USIA data tape.

TABLE A-7   Percentage Distribution of Female PRC
J-1 Students and Scholars by Field, 1979 Through 1984

Field	Percent	Female[a]
Agriculture	16	(536)
American studies	48	(23)
Architecture	16	(45)
Business management	14	(220)
Computer, information science	11	(448)
Education	30	(341)
Engineering	8	(3,450)
ESL[b]	31	(108)
Health sciences	33	(1,372)
Humanities	31	(409)
Law	15	(121)
Library and archival science	40	(53)
Life sciences	26	(1,133)
Mathematics	9	(546)
Physical sciences	14	(2,965)
Social sciences	19	(653)
Other	36	(11)
Total J-1 visa holders beginning new programs	17	(12,434)

[a]The figures in parentheses indicate the total number of all J-1 visa holders from which the percentages were derived.
[b]English as a second language.
SOURCE: USIA data tape.

TABLE A-8   Percentage Distribution of PRC F-1 Visa
Holders by Sex and Educational Background, 1983

Highest Level of Education Completed	Male	Female	Total
Middle school or less	14	17	15
Technical school	12	17	14
College/university—no degree	13	13	13
College/university—degree	59	50	56
Graduate study	2	3	3
Total	100	100	100
N =	(532)[a]	(318)[b]	(850)[a]

[a]Percentage of missing data excluded from total is 11 percent.
[b]Percentage of missing data excluded from total is 9 percent.
SOURCE: Records of visas issued in 1983.

TABLE A-9 Percentage Distribution of J-1 Students and Scholars Beginning New Programs in the United States, by Age, 1979 Through 1983

Age	1979	1980	1981	1982	1983
Below 30	5	6	9	21	34
30–39	33	22	21	21	20
40–49	55	55	57	42	31
50–59	5	13	11	14	12
60 and above	2	3	2	2	2
Total	100	100	100	100	100
N =	(884)	(1,844)	(2,989)	(2,945)	(3,088)

SOURCE: USIA data tape.

TABLE A-10 Estimated Financial Support for All PRC Students and Scholars, by Visa Category, 1979 Through 1983

Visa Type	1979	1980	1981	1982	1983	Total
F-1 students						
Number	523	2,840	4,972	5,407	5,190	
Average amount spent per person	$7,203	$7,084	$7,509	$7,841	$8,597	
Total amount spent per year (in thousands)	$3,769	$20,119	$37,335	$42,396	$44,618	$148,237
J-1 students						
Number	184	497	1,163	2,027	3,147	
Average amount spent per person	$7,415	$7,935	$8,399	$9,653	$10,873	
Total amount spent per year (in thousands)	$1,364	$3,944	$9,768	$19,567	$34,217	$68,860
J-1 scholars						
Number	707	1,839	3,704	4,253	3,990	
Average amount spent per person	$6,776	$6,821	$7,086	$6,994	$6,846	
Total amount spent per year (in thousands)	$4,791	$12,544	$26,247	$29,745	$27,316	$100,643
J-1 other						
Number	134	384	701	691	603	
Average amount spent per person	$8,534	$7,038	$8,122	$7,516	$8,134	
Total amount spent per year (in thousands)	$1,144	$2,703	$5,694	$5,194	$4,905	$19,640
Total J-1 and F-1 (in thousands)	$11,068	$39,310	$79,044	$96,902	$111,056	$337,380

NOTE: Compare these figures with similar figures for American students, compiled in the American Council on Education's (ACE) data on average undergraduate costs for 1 year of higher education in the United States: total cost (including tuition, room, board, and fees) for academic year 1979–1980 was $3,935; $4,340 for academic year 1980–1981; $4,823 for academic year 1981–1982; estimated $5,245 for academic year 1982–1983; and estimated $5,656 for academic year 1983–1984.

SOURCES: Tables 3-6 and 3-15 in this report and USIA data tape.

TABLE A-11   CIES American Fulbright Lecturers to the PRC, 1980 Through 1984

Year	Lecturers
1980	13
1981	12
1982	13
1983	18
1984	17
Total	73

NOTE: Total numbers include eight renewals.
SOURCE: Data set provided by the Council for International Exchange of Scholars (CIES).

TABLE A-12   Field Distribution of CIES American Fulbright Lecturers in the PRC, 1980 Through 1984

Field of Study	1980	1981	1982	1983	1984	Total
ESL[a]	8	3	2	1	0	14
Linguistics	1	2	0	0	0	3
American literature	2	4	2	4	6	18
American studies	2	1	0	0	1	4
American history	0	1	5	4	2	12
Education	0	0	1	0	0	1
Law	0	0	2	3	2	7
Economics	0	0	1	2	2	5
Political science	0	0	0	2	0	2
Business	0	0	0	1	1	2
Library resources	0	0	0	0	1	1
Other	0	1	0	1	2	4
Total	13	12	13	18	17	73

NOTE: Data include eight renewals.
[a]English as a second language.
SOURCE: Data set provided by the Council for International Exchange of Scholars (CIES).

TABLE A-13   Percentage Distribution of CIES
American Fulbright Lecturers in the PRC, by
City, 1980 Through 1984

City	Lecturers
Beijing	34
Guangzhou	5
Shanghai	25
Tianjin	14
Nanjing	10
Wuhan	5
Jinan	5
Dalian	1
Total	100[a]

NOTE: Data include eight renewals.
[a]Percentages have been rounded to the nearest percentage point.
SOURCE: Data set provided by the Council for International Exchange of Scholars (CIES).

TABLE A-14   Field Distribution of CIES Chinese
Fulbright Lecturers in the United States, 1980
Through 1984

Field of Study	Lecturers
Chinese geography	4
Chinese literature	3
Chinese law	2
Economics	5
Linguistics	1
Chinese history	2
Business	1
Arts	2
China studies	2
Total	22

NOTE: Data include two renewals.
SOURCE: Data set provided by the Council for International Exchange of Scholars (CIES).

TABLE A-15   Field Distribution of CIES Chinese Fulbright Researchers in the United States, 1980 Through 1984

Field of Study	Researchers
American studies	1
American political science	5
History	8
American law	2
American literature	10
U.S. economics	8
Urban planning	2
Business management	1
Chinese language	1
English as a second language	3
Other	3
Not stated	1
Total	45

NOTE: Data include eight renewals.
SOURCE: Data set provided by the Council for International Exchange of Scholars (CIES).

TABLE A-16   CIES Chinese Fulbright Lecturers and Researchers in the United States, by Year, 1980 Through 1984

Year	Lecturers	Researchers	Total
1980	5	2	7
1981	7	7	14
1982	3	9	12
1983	3	13	16
1984	4	14	18
Total	22	45	67

NOTE: Data include 10 renewals.
SOURCE: Data set provided by the Council for International Exchange of Scholars (CIES).

TABLE A-17 CSCPRC National Program Grantees in Anthropology, Economics, Political Science, and Sociology, by Program Year, 1978–1979 Through 1984–1985

Program Year	Anthropology	Economics	Political Science	Sociology
1978–1979	2	0	1	2
1979–1980	4	2	4	0
1980–1981	3	3	2	1
1981–1982	1	1	1	0
1982–1983	4	1	2	1
1983–1984	2	2	3	0
1984–1985	3	0	5	1
Total	19	9	18	5

NOTES: Figures were determined by counting the field of study indicated by the grantee on his or her application. Grantees who indicated two fields were counted twice.

Program year 1978–1979 began January 1, 1979. All other program years begin on July 1.

SOURCE: Committee on Scholarly Communication with the People's Republic of China (CSCPRC) National Program files.

TABLE A-18 The 12 U.S. Universities with the Most CSCPRC National Program Grantees, 1978–1979 Through 1984–1985

University	National Program Grantees
Stanford University	23
University of Michigan	19
Harvard University	14
University of California, Berkeley	13
Columbia University	11
University of Washington	11
University of Chicago	9
Princeton University	9
Yale University	8
Ohio State University	6
Cornell University	6
University of Hawaii, Manoa/Honolulu	6
Total	135

NOTE: Program year 1978–1979 began January 1, 1979. All other program years begin on July 1.

SOURCE: CSCPRC National Program files.

TABLE A-19   Geographic Distribution of Principal Hosts of CSCPRC National Program Grantees by Province/Municipality in China, 1978–1979 Through 1984–1985

Province/Municipality	No. of Grantees
Anhui	2
Beijing	152
Fujian	2
Gansu	2
Guangdong	8
Guangxi Autonomous Region	0
Guizhou	2
Hebei	1
Heilongjiang	0
Henan	0
Hubei	6
Hunan	1
Jiangsu	24
Jiangxi	0
Jilin	4
Liaoning	2
Nei Mongol	2
Ningxia[a]	0
Qinghai	2
Shaanxi	4
Shandong	7
Shanghai	23
Shanxi	0
Sichuan	4
Tianjin	5
Xinjiang Autonomous Region	0
Xizang Autonomous Region	0
Yunnan	1
Zhejiang	4
Total	258

NOTES: Program year 1978–1979 began January 1, 1979. All other program years begin on July 1.

A total of eight province-level units have received *no* National Program Grantees, 1978–1979 through 1984–1985. This tabulation includes only principal host location in China, not *all* sites at which research may have been undertaken.

[a]One scholar received a grant extension that enabled him to spend a substantial amount of time in Ningxia although his initial principal host was located in Beijing.

SOURCE: CSCPRC National Program files.

TABLE A-20   Chinese DSEP Grantees by Sex, 1979–1980 Through 1984–1985

Sex	Grantees
Male	115
Female	14
Total	129

NOTE: Program years begin on July 1.
SOURCE: CSCPRC Distinguished Scholar Exchange Program (DSEP) files.

TABLE A-21   American DSEP Grantees by Sex, 1979–1980 Through 1984–1985

Sex	Grantees
Male	155
Female	9
Total	164

NOTE: Program years begin on July 1.
SOURCE: CSCPRC Distinguished Scholar Exchange Program (DSEP) files.

TABLE A-22   Chinese and American DSEP Grantees by Program Year, 1979–1980 Through 1984–1985

Program Year	Chinese Grantees	American Grantees
1979–1980	16	35
1980–1981	13	13
1981–1982	25	25
1982–1983	14	29
1983–1984	32	33
1984–1985	29	29
Total	129	164

NOTE: Program years begin on July 1.
SOURCE: CSCPRC Distinguished Scholar Exchange Program (DSEP) files.

TABLE A-23 (Part I) Number of Faculty Members Trained Abroad and to Be Sent Abroad for Degrees from 10 Project[a] Universities in Beijing and Shanghai, as of June 30, 1985

	Beijing					Shanghai				
Category	Qinghua University	Beijing University	Beijing Normal	Beijing Medical	Beijing Agricultural	Fudan University	Shanghai Jiaotong	Tongji University	Huadong[b] Normal	Shanghai Institute of Economics & Finance
Total faculty members in plan	157	125	98	106	78	—	—	—	—	10
Visiting scholars	137	122	57	64	54	26	13	6	23	—
Professor	—	6	1	—	—	—	—	—	—	—
Associate Professor	38	62	17	24	25	6	5	—	12	—
Lecturer	96	37	35	35	18	12	6	—	8	—
Assistant	3	17	4	5	11	8	2	—	3	—
Graduate students	20	3	29	6	24	24	41	3	60	—
Faculty members sent abroad	124	94	86	70	64	50	54	—	83	1
Number of faculty members returned	32	26	3	27	16	9	—	—	—	—
Theses and works published abroad by participants	32	33	7	49	—	—	1	—	—	—
Theses and works published by participants after returning	—	12	3	13	—	—	—	—	—	—
Established new courses	20	15	—	27	18	5	—	—	—	—
Renewed courses	—	14	—	—	35	—	—	—	—	—

[a]World Bank Chinese University Development Project.
[b]Includes those sent to Honeywell training.

TABLE A-23 (Part II) Number of Students Abroad Under the World Bank China University Development Project (from beginning of project to March 31, 1985)

Country	Teachers for Advanced Study		Postgraduates		Total	
	No. Abroad	No. Returned	No. Abroad	No. Returned	No. Abroad	No. Returned
U.S.A.	461	96	435	2	896	98
Canada	128	10	92	—	220	10
U.K.	87	11	66	—	153	11
Japan	85	13	11	—	96	13
Federal Republic of Germany	48	8	11	—	59	8
France	24	4	5	—	29	4
Australia	14	—	10	—	24	—
Sweden	9	4	2	—	11	4
Switzerland	10	2	1	—	11	2
Belgium	5	—	4	—	9	—
Holland	9	1	1	—	10	1
Denmark	5	2	—	—	5	2
Austria	2	—	—	—	2	—
Italy	3	—	—	—	3	—
Norway	2	—	—	—	2	—
New Zealand	1	—	—	—	1	—
Spain	1	—	—	—	1	—
Total	894	151	638	2	1,532	153

NOTE: From the beginning of the project to March 31, 1985, there were altogether 1,532 students and visiting scholars sent abroad by the World Bank project. Among them, 894 went for further study and 638 for degrees; 153 have returned after training.

SOURCE: World Bank Chinese University Development Project.

TABLE A-24 Percentage Distribution of PRC J-1 and F-1 Visa Holders by Intended Region of Residence in the United States, 1983

Region in United States	Resident Population 1982	Institutions of Higher Education 1982	Number of New Students and Scholars J-1	F-1
Northeast				
New England	5	8	9	7
Middle Atlantic	16	17	23	24
North Central				
East North Central	18	16	20	16
West North Central	8	10	7	7
South				
South Atlantic	17	16	11	7
East South Central	6	7	2	1
West South Central	11	8	5	7
West				
Mountain	5	5	5	5
Pacific	14	12	17	27
Total	100	100	100	100
N =		(3,269)	(3,040)[a]	(938)[b]

NOTE: Regions include the following states: **New England**—Connecticut, Maine, Massacusetts, New Hampshire, Rhode Island, Vermont; **Middle Atlantic**—New Jersey, New York, Pennsylvania; **East North Central**—Illinois, Indiana, Michigan, Ohio, Wisconsin; **West North Central**—Iowa, Kansas, Minnesota, Missouri, Nebraska, North Dakota, South Dakota; **South Atlantic**—Delaware, Washington, D.C., Florida, Georgia, Maryland, North Carolina, South Carolina, Virginia, West Virginia; **East South Central**—Alabama, Kentucky, Mississippi, Tennessee; **West South Central**—Arkansas, Louisiana, Oklahoma, Texas; **Mountain**—Arizona, Colorado, Idaho, Montana, Nevada, New Mexico, Utah, Wyoming; **Pacific**—Alaska, California, Hawaii, Oregon, Washington.
[a]Percentage of missing data excluded from total is 5 percent.
[b]Percentage of missing data excluded from total is 1 percent.
SOURCES: Population—*Statistical Abstract of the United States*, 1984, p. 10; higher education—*Statistical Abstract of the United States*, 1984, p. 136; students and scholars—records of visas issued in 1983.

TABLE A-25 Percentage Distribution of PRC J-1 and F-1 Visa Holders in California and New York, 1983

State	F-1 Visa Holders	J-1 Visa Holders
California	24	13
New York	18	15
Total	42	28

SOURCE: Records of visas issued in 1983.

TABLE A-26 U.S. Colleges and Universities with the Largest
Numbers of PRC J-1 and F-1 Visa Holders Issued Visas in 1983

College or University	Number of New Students and Scholars in 1983
Both J-1 and F-1	
Columbia University	98
University of Wisconsin, Madison	90
University of California, Berkeley	87
University of California, Los Angeles	78
University of Michigan	71
Stanford University	67
University of Minnesota	65
Michigan State University	60
Purdue University	58
University of Illinois, Champaign-Urbana	58
Cornell University	57
University of Maryland, College Park	54
University of Pittsburgh	53
City University of New York, The City College	52
Massachusetts Institute of Technology	51
J-1 visa only	
University of Wisconsin, Madison	83
University of California, Berkeley	77
Columbia University	66
University of Michigan	66
University of California, Los Angeles	61
Stanford University	58
University of Minnesota	58
University of Illinois, Champaign-Urbana	55
Cornell University	54
University of Pittsburgh	52
Michigan State University	52
F-1 visa only	
Columbia University	31
La Guardia Community College, N.Y.	19
The Loop College, Ill.	19
City University of New York, The City College	17
Hunter College	17
University of California, Los Angeles	17
University of Wisconsin, Madison	17
Rutgers University	13
University of Houston	12
San Francisco State University	11

NOTE: Since these data were compiled from 1983 visa application files, the U.S. colleges
and universities listed are the ones that the Chinese students and scholars *intended* to
attend.
SOURCE: 1983 visa data.

TABLE A-27   Ten U.S. Universities/Colleges and States with Largest
PRC Student Populations, Academic Year 1984–1985

Universities/Colleges[a] and States[b]	No. of PRC Students
CUNY Queens College	135
University of Michigan, Ann Arbor	129
SUNY at Stony Brook	122
University of California, Los Angeles	105
City College of Chicago, Loop College (2-year)	102
University of Wisconsin, Madison	99
University of Texas, Austin	90
New York University	83
SUNY at Buffalo	80
University of Washington	78
New York	890
California	690
Illinois	310
Michigan	284
Massachusetts	254
Texas	250
Pennsylvania	186
Ohio	167
Indiana	127
Wisconsin	123

[a]PRC students are enrolled in at least 390 U.S. colleges and universities.
[b]PRC students are enrolled in universities in all 50 states, the District of Columbia, and Guam.
SOURCE: Data provided by Jay Henderson, Institute of International Education.

TABLE A-28   Percentage Distribution of PRC J-1 and F-1 Visa
Holders by Type of American University Affiliation, in 1983

Type of Institution	Type of Visa	
	J-1	F-1
Private research universities[a]	23	11
Public research universities[a]	53	27
Other private institutions	9	24
Other public institutions	16	38
Total	100	100
N =	(2,758)[b]	(861)[c]

[a]Among the top 100 research universities in the United States.
[b]Percentage of missing data excluded from total is 14 percent.
[c]Percentage of missing data excluded from total is 9 percent.
SOURCES: Records of visas issued in 1983; National Science Foundation, "Early Release of Summary Statistics on Academic Science/Engineering Resources," November 1984; and data supplied by the National Center for Education Statistics.

TABLE A-29 University-to-University Exchanges, by Agreement Type and Number of Students and Scholars Exchanged Through 1983–1984

U.S. Institution	PRC Institution	Type of Agreement		Number of Students and Scholars	
		Sister	Other	Received from China	Sent to China
University of Alabama, Huntsville	University of Science and Technology, Hefei	X	—	10	1
Appalachian State University	Northeast University of Technology	X	—	—	—
Boston University	Huazhong Institute of Technology	X	X	6	—
Bowling Green State University	Xian Foreign Language Institute	X	—	3	3
Brigham Young University, Hawaii Campus	Jilin University	—	X	—	—
Brown University	Nanjing University	X	—	—	—
University of California, Davis	Huazhong Agricultural College	X	(Lapsed, but may be renewed)		
	Beijing Medical College	X	—	—	—
	Henan Medical College	—	—	—	—
University of California, Los Angeles	Chinese University of Science and Technology, Graduate School, Beijing	X	—	12	5
	Zhongshan University	X	—	11	8
	English Language Center, Zhongshan University	X	—	10	6
	Beijing Institute of Foreign Trade, Institute of International Management	X	—	8	—
University of California, San Diego	Chongqing University	X	—	—	—
	Huazhong University of Science and Technology	X	—	3	48
	Shanghai Jiaotong University	X	—	—	—
	Fudan University	X	—	—	—
University of California, San Francisco	Shanghai Second Medical College	—	X	—	—
University of California, Santa Barbara	Chinese Academy of Sciences	—	—	—	—

US Institution	Chinese Institution				
University of California, Santa Cruz	Beijing Language Institute	X	—	9	9
California Polytechnic University, Pomona	Yunnan University	X	—	2	1
	Heilongjiang University	—	—	—	—
California State University, Northridge	Beijing Institute of Technology	X	—	—	—
	Harbin Institute of Technology	X	—	—	—
	Jinan University	X	—	—	—
	Shaanxi Normal University	X	—	—	—
	South China Normal University	X	—	—	—
	Zhejiang University	—	—	—	—
Carnegie-Mellon University	Ministry of Education	—	—	—	—
	Academia Sinica	—	—	—	—
University of Chicago	Beijing University	X	—	2	3
City University of New York, City College	Nanjing Institute of Technology	—	—	—	—
	Shandong University	—	—	—	—
	Xibei University	—	—	—	—
	Zhongshan University	—	—	—	—
Colorado State University	East China Institute of Hydraulic Engineering	X	—	3	1
	Chinese Academy of Sciences, Gansu Province	X	—	3	—
	Gansu Grassland Ecological Institute & Gansu Agricultural University	X	—	—	—
University of Colorado Health Sciences Center	Hunan Medical College	—	X	—	—
Cornell University	Chinese Academy of Sciences	X	—	12	2
	Beijing University	X	—	6	—
	Fudan University	X	—	5	1
	Xian Jiaotong University	X	—	1	—
	Shanghai Jiaotong University	X	—	2	—
	Southwest Jiaotong University	X	—	—	4
	Nanjing Agricultural College	—	X	4	2
Eastern Illinois University	Northwest Polytechnic University	—	—	16	—
Eastern Michigan University	Chengdu Institute of Science and Technology	X	—	—	—
Emory University	Beijing University	X	—	—	2

(Continued)

TABLE A-29 (Continued)

U.S. Institution	PRC Institution	Sister	Other	Received from China	Sent to China
Georgetown University	East China Normal University	(pending)		1	1
Hamline University	Beijing University		X	10	5
University of Houston, University Park	Beijing Institute of Foreign Trade		X	—	—
University of Idaho	Ministry of Forestry		X	—	—
	University of Inner Mongolia	X	—	—	—
	Beijing Forestry College		X	—	—
	Northwest College of Agriculture		X	—	—
	Ministry of Agriculture		X	—	—
	Wuhan Geological College		X	—	—
	Changchun College of Geology		X	—	—
	Forestry College of Inner Mongolia		X	—	—
	Shanxi Agricultural College, Taiyuan		X	—	—
	Shaanxi Forest Research Institute		X	—	—
	Fujian College Forestry		—	—	—
University of Illinois, Chicago Circle	Jilin University of Technology	X		—	1
University of Illinois, Urbana	Fudan University	X		14	12
	Beijing University	X		7	10
	Chinese Academy of Sciences	X		—	—
Indiana University	Hangzhou University	X		—	—
	Shandong University	X		—	3
	Nankai University		—	—	—
Indiana University of Pennsylvania	Shanghai Foreign Languages Institute	X		4	5
University of Iowa	East China Technical University of Water Resources	X		2	2
	Wuhan Institute of Hydraulic & Electrical Engineering	X		1	—

Iowa State University	Shenyang Agricultural College	X	—	—	—
University of Massachusetts, Amherst	Beijing Institute of Agricultural Mechanization	—	—	—	—
	Beijing Normal University	X	—	21	70
	Shaanxi Teacher's College	X	—	13	16
	Fudan University	X	—	14	9
	Beijing Institute of Foreign Language	X	—	5	4
	Chinese Academy of Sciences, Institute of Systems Science	X	—	3	3
	Beijing Teacher's College	—	X	3	8
	Foreign Language Press	X	—	4	3
	Central Translation Bureau	X	—	1	1
	Zhejiang University	X	—	2	—
	Tianjin University	—	X	2	—
Michigan State University	Beijing University	X	—	6	—
	Sichuan University	X	—	65	3
	Nankai University	X	—	4	—
	Guangxi University	X	—	1	—
	Xibei University	X	—	1	—
	Jiangsu Academy of Agricultural Sciences	X	—	24	—
	Heilongjiang Academy of Agricultural Sciences	—	X	4	—
	Northeast Agricultural College	—	X	3	—
	Chinese Academy of Sciences, Institute of Botany	—	X	1	—
University of Minnesota	East China Normal University	—	X	1	—
	Chinese Academy of Sciences	—	—	—	—
	Jilin University of Technology	—	—	—	—
	Beijing Agricultural University	—	—	—	—
	Academy of Agricultural Science and Agricultural Engineering	—	—	—	—

(Continued)

TABLE A-29 (Continued)

U.S. Institution	PRC Institution	Type of Agreement		Number of Students and Scholars	
		Sister	Other	Received from China	Sent to China
	Nankai University	—	—	—	1
	Xian Jiaotong University	—	—	—	—
	Jilin University	—	—	—	—
	Fudan University	—	—	—	—
	Central South Institute of Mining and Metallurgy	—	—	—	—
	Changchun Institute of Geography	—	—	—	—
	Chongqing Architectural Engineering Institute	—	—	—	—
	Huazhong Institute of Technology	—	—	—	—
	Zhejiang University	—	—	2	—
	Beijing University	—	—	2	2
	Qinghua University	—	—	—	—
University of Missouri, Columbia	Anhui University	X	—	4	1
	Lanzhou University	X	—	4	1
	Zhengzhou University	X	—	1	1
	Xinhua News Agency	—	X	6	2
	Radio Beijing	—	X	6	—
	Foreign Language Publication and Distribution Bureau	—	X	4	1
	China Daily	—	X	—	—
University of Missouri, Kansas City	Shanghai Second Medical College	X	—	5	8
	Wuhan University	X	—	2	1
	Harbin Medical University	X	—	2	7

U.S. University	Chinese Institution				
University of Nebraska	South China Normal University	—	—	—	—
	Xibei University	—	—	—	—
	Sichuan University	—	—	—	7
	Beijing University	—	—	—	—
	East China Normal University	—	—	—	—
University of New Mexico	Zhongshan University	—	X	—	—
Northeastern University	Shanxi Teacher's College	—	X	—	—
	Beijing Polytechnic University	—	X	—	—
	Hunan University	—	X	—	—
	Shanghai University of Science and Technology	—	X	16	—
	Qinghua University	—	X	—	—
North Texas State University	Beijing Institute of Foreign Trade	—	X	1	1
Northwestern University	Fudan University	—	X	17	8
University of Notre Dame	Tongji University, Shanghai	—	X	23	—
Oberlin College	Taiyuan Institute of Technology	X	—	4	4
	Shanxi Agricultural University	X	—	4	4
	Beijing University of Iron and Steel Technology	—	X	—	—
Ohio State University	Hubei Bureau of Education	—	X	8	2
	Wuhan University	—	X	4	9
	Beijing Language Institute	—	—	—	—
Oregon State University	Shandong College of Oceanography	—	X	8	2
	Zhejiang Agricultural Institute	X	—	8	2
	Northeast Forestry Institute	X	—	3	1
Pace University	Beijing Institute of Foreign Trade	X	—	—	—
Pennsylvania State University	South China Agriculture College	—	X	5	8
University of Pittsburgh	Tianjin University	—	—	—	—
	Northeast Institute of Technology	—	—	—	—
	Shandong University	—	—	—	—
	Xian Jiaotong University	—	—	—	—
	Zhongshan University	—	—	—	—
	Xinjiang University	—	—	—	—

(Continued)

TABLE A-29 (Continued)

U.S. Institution	PRC Institution	Type of Agreement		Number of Students and Scholars	
		Sister	Other	Received from China	Sent to China
	Shanghai Institute of Foreign Language	—	—	—	—
	East China Normal University	—	—	—	—
	South China Institute of Technology	—	—	—	—
	Xian Foreign Language Institute	—	—	—	—
	Hubei Medical College	—	—	—	—
Pomona College	Nanjing University	X	—	5	1
Portland State University	Zhengzhou University	X	—	—	—
	Beijing Institute of Foreign Language	X	—	—	—
Princeton University	Fudan University	—	—	13	3
Rochester Institute of Technology	Shanghai University of Technology	X	—	45	—
	Zhejiang University in Hangzhou	X	—	—	—
Rutgers University	Jilin University	X	—	21	29
St. Mary's College of Maryland	Fudan University	—	—	5	8
San Francisco State University	Shandong Teacher's University	X	—	1	1
Seton Hall University	Beijing Institute of Foreign Trade	X	—	—	—
	Hangzhou School of Nursing	X	—	—	6
	Wuhan University	X	—	8	5
Siena Heights College	Jilin University	—	—	—	—
Simmons College	Wuhan University	—	X	7	—
South Dakota School of Mines and Technology	Kunming Institute of Technology	X	—	40	—
Southern Illinois University	Northeast Normal University	X	—	—	—
	Sichuan University	X	—	—	—
	Liaoning University	X	—	—	—
Stanford University	Beijing University Department of Chinese Language	—	X	—	2

US Institution	Chinese Institution				
State University of New York, Albany	Beijing Language Institute	X	—	—	1
	Beijing Normal University	X	—	2	2
	Fudan University	X	—	20	14
	Nanjing University	X	—	23	12
	Nankai University	X	—	—	2
	Beijing University	X	—	17	19
State University of New York, Cortland	Beijing Teacher's College	X	(1-to-1 exchange)		—
	Beijing Institute of Physical Education	X			
	Chengdu Institute of Physical Culture	X			
State University of New York, New Paltz	Beijing University	X	—	—	1
	Nankai University	X	—	—	—
Temple University	Tianjin Normal College	—	X	6	8
	Lanzhou University	—	X	—	2
University of Tennessee	Chongqing Institute of Architecture and English	—	X		—
	Qinghua University	—	X	—	—
University of Texas, Dallas	Beijing Second Medical College	—	—	46	8
University of Texas, Health Science Center, Houston					
Thunderbird Graduate School of International Business	Beijing Institute of Foreign Trade	X	—	17	39
University of Utah	Zhejiang University	X	—	5	—
Wake Forest-Bowman School of Medicine	Zhongshan Medical College	—	X	—	—
University of Washington	Shandong University	X	—	5	—
	Nanjing Technical College Forest Production	X	—	—	—
	Chongqing Institute, Architecture and English	—	X	—	—
	Sichuan Medical College and Chongqing Medical College	—	X	—	—
Washington State University	Sichuan Foreign Language Institute	X	—	—	—
	Sichuan Agricultural College	X	—	—	—
	Chengdu University of Science and Technology	X	—	31	2
Washington University, St. Louis	Shanghai Jiaotong University	X	—	5	—

(Continued)

TABLE A-29 (Continued)

U.S. Institution	PRC Institution	Type of Agreement		Number of Students and Scholars	
		Sister	Other	Received from China	Sent to China
Wayne State University	Chinese Academy of Sciences	X	—	—	—
	Zhejiang University	X	—	—	—
	Chinese University of Science and Technology	X	—	—	—
	Shanghai Jiaotong University	X	—	—	4
Western Illinois University	Shandong College of Oceanography	—	X	4	4
	Yunnan Province	—	X	4	3
	Southwest Teacher's College	—	X	3	1
Western Michigan University	Guangxi University	X	—	7	2
	Xibei University	X	—	2	—
	Nankai University	X	—	8	6
Yeshiva University	Beijing Medical College	X	—	6	—
Total				838	506

NOTE: See also Table A-30 in this report.
SOURCE: University questionnaire.

TABLE A-30 Additional Interinstitutional Agreements Between U.S. and PRC Institutions

U.S. Institution	PRC Institutions
University of Arizona (under negotiation)	Beijing University Nanjing University Southwestern Jiaotong University Xinjiang University
University of California at Berkeley	Beijing University Fudan University Nanjing University
Columbia University	Beijing University Shanghai Jiaotong University
Harvard University	Beijing University Chinese Academy of Social Sciences Fudan University Nanjing University Shandong University Zhongshan University
Johns Hopkins University	Beijing Medical Institute Chinese Academy of Medical Sciences Nanjing University Shanghai First Medical College
University of Michigan	Beijing University Chinese Academy of Social Sciences Qinghua University Shanghai Jiaotong University
University of Pennsylvania	Beijing University of Iron and Steel Technology (with Penn's School of Engineering) Northwest Telecommunications Institute Shanghai Jiaotong University (with the Wharton and Engineering Schools)
University of Wisconsin at Madison	Harbin Medical College Harbin Teachers University Heilongjiang University Nankai University Harbin Institute of Technology (pending) Northeast Agricultural College (pending) Nanjing University (pending) Qinghua University (pending) Shanghai Jiaotong University (pending) Tianjin University (pending)
Yale University	Wuhan University

NOTE: This table complements the information in Table A-29.
SOURCE: Telephone interviews conducted by CSCPRC staff.

TABLE A-31   PRC Institutions Known to Have One or More
Exchanges with a U.S. University

Institution	No. of Agreements (If greater than 1)
COLLEGES AND UNIVERSITIES	
Anhui University	
Beijing Agricultural University	
Beijing Forestry College	
Beijing Institute of Agricultural Mechanization	
Beijing Institute of Foreign Trade (now called The University of International Business and Economics)	6
Beijing Institute of Foreign Language-Branch (Agent, China Educational Tours)	2
Beijing Institute of Physical Education	
Beijing Institute of Technology	
Beijing Language Institute	2
Beijing Medical College	2
Beijing Normal University	2
Beijing Polytechnic University	
Beijing Second Medical College	
Beijing Teacher's College	2
Beijing University of Iron and Steel Technology	
Beijing University	9
Beijing University—Department of Chinese Language	
Central-South Institute of Mining and Metallurgy	
Changchun Institute of Geography	
Chengdu Institute of Physical Culture	
Chengdu University of Science and Technology	2
Chinese Academy of Agricultural Sciences and Agricultural Engineering	
Chinese University of Sciences and Technology (Beijing)	2
Chongqing Architectural Engineering Institute	3
Chongqing University	
College of Geology, Changchun	
East China Institute of Hydraulic Engineering	
East China Normal University, Shanghai	4
East China Normal University	
East China Technical University of Water Resources	
Forestry College of Inner Mongolia	
Fudan University	10
Fujian College of Forestry	
Gansu Agricultural University	
Gansu Grassland Ecological Institute	
Guangxi University	2
Hangzhou School of Nursing	
Hangzhou University	
Harbin Institute of Technology	
Harbin Medical University	

TABLE A-31   (Continued)

Institution	No. of Agreements (If greater than 1)
Heilongjiang University	
Henan Medical College	
Huazhong Agricultural College	
Huazhong Institute of Technology	2
Hubei Medical College	
Hunan Medical College	
Hunan University	
Jiaotong University, Shanghai.	4
Jiaotong University, Xian	3
Jilin University of Technology	2
Jilin University	3
Jinan University	
Kunming Institute of Technology	
Lanzhou University	2
Liaoning University	
Nanjing Agricultural College	
Nanjing Institute of Technology	
Nanjing Technological College of Forest Products	
Nanjing University.	4
Nankai University	6
Northeast Agricultural College, Harbin	
Northeast Normal University	
Northeast University of Technology, Shenyang	2
Northeastern Forestry Institute	
Northwest College of Agriculture	
Northwestern Polytechnic University	
Qinghua University	3
Shaanxi Forest Research Institute	
Shaanxi Normal University	
Shaanxi Teacher's University	
Shandong College of Oceanography	2
Shandong Teacher's University	
Shandong University	4
Shanghai Institute of Foreign Languages	2
Shanghai Second Medical College	2
Shanxi Agricultural College	
Shanxi Agricultural University	
Shenyang Agricultural College	
Sichuan Agricultural College	
Sichuan Foreign Language Institute	
Sichuan Medical College and Chongqing Medical College	
Sichuan University.	3
South China Agricultural College	
South China Institute of Technology	
South China Normal University	2
Southwest Teacher's College	

(Continued)

TABLE A-31　(Continued)

Institution	No. of Agreements (If greater than 1)
Southwestern Jiaotong University	
Taiyuan Institute of Technology	
Tianjin Normal College	
Tongji University, Shanghai	
University of Inner Mongolia	
University of Science and Technology of China (Hefei)	2
Wuhan Geological College	
Wuhan Institute of Hydraulic and Electrical Engineering	
Wuhan University	4
Xian Foreign Language Institute	
Xibei University	4
Yunnan University	
Zhejiang Agricultural University	
Zhejiang University	5
Zhengzhou University	2
Zhongshan Medical College	
Zhongshan University English Language Center	
Zhongshan University	5

OTHER

Beijing Language Institute	2
Central Translation Bureau	
China Daily	
Chinese Academy of Agricultural Science and Agricultural Engineering	
Chinese Academy of Sciences	6
Chinese Academy of Sciences, Gansu Province	
Chinese Academy of Sciences, Institute of Systems Science	
Chinese Academy of Sciences, Institute of Botany	
Foreign Languages Press	
Foreign Language Publications and Distribution Bureau	
Heilongjiang Academy of Agricultural Sciences	
Hubei Bureau of Education	
Jiangsu Academy of Agricultural Sciences	
Ministry of Agriculture	
Ministry of Education	
Ministry of Forestry	2
Radio Beijing	
Xinhua News Agency	
Yunnan Province	

SOURCE:　University questionnaires.

TABLE A-32   Number of American Scholars Supported by University Funds for Travel to the PRC, 1983 Through 1985

Scholars Supported (No.)	Institutions Supporting Scholars (No.)					
	Undergraduate		Graduate		Faculty	
	1983–84	1984–85	1983–84	1984–85	1983–84	1984–85
0	10	13	15	14	10	12
1	4	2	1	1	5	3
2	2	3	2	3	2	3
3	3	—	—	—	1	—
4	—	—	1	1	1	1
More than 4	—	1	—	—	—	—
Number of universities responding to question	19	19	19	19	19	19

NOTE: The symbol "—" indicates a value of less than 0.5 percent.
SOURCE: Asian studies questionnaires.

TABLE A-33   Title VI Fellowship[a] Expenditures and Grants Awarded, by Year, Fiscal Years 1980 Through 1984

Fiscal[b] Year	Total Program Expenditures	Expenditures for East Asia	Awards to East Asia	Awards to China
1980	4,799,500[c]	1,166,278	190	110
1981	6,099,996[c]	1,423,290[c]	187	111
1982	5,924,700[c]	1,370,174[c]	178	117
1983	6,000,000[c]	1,376,450[c]	151[c]	87[c]
1984	7,200,000[c]	1,626,518[c]	—[d]	—[d]

NOTE: These figures on numbers of awards do *not* include numbers of summer grants which started in FY 1981, although the dollar figures do include summer allocations.
[a](National Defense Foreign Language fellowships—also known as either Foreign Language and Area Studies fellowships [FLAS] or National Resource Fellowships [NRF].) Title VI of the Higher Education Act was formerly Title VI of the National Defense Education Act; hence the former National Defense Foreign Language fellowships (NDFL) are now referred to as Foreign Language and Area Studies fellowships (FLAS).
[b]Fiscal year 1980 refers to funding awarded during academic year 1980–1981; this is the same for all years.
[c]These figures were provided by Ann I. Schneider of the U.S. Department of Education. All other figures were calculated by CSCPRC staff from Department of Education data.
[d]Data for these years were not yet available.
SOURCE: Dr. Ann I. Schneider, U.S. Department of Education.

Institutions Responding to University Questionnaire

In 1984, the CSCPRC staff sent a questionnaire to 391 American universities and colleges that were identified as having five or more Chinese students and scholars. (The questionnaire requested information about how universities handle students from the PRC, including admissions policies, student adjustment, problems in health and housing, and financing.) About 60 percent of the questionnaires were returned. Following is a complete list of responding institutions.

Alabama
University of Alabama, Birmingham
University of Alabama, Huntsville
Auburn University
University of South Alabama
Alaska
University of Alaska
Arizona
American Graduate School of International Management (Thunderbird)
Arizona State University
Arkansas
University of Arkansas
California
Armstrong College
California Institute of Technology
California State College
California State Polytechnic University, Pomona
California State University, Chico
California State University, Dominguez Hills
California State University, Hayward
California State University, Los Angeles
California State University, Northridge
California State University, Sacramento
Canada College

Claremont Graduate School
ESL Language Center*
El Camino College
Evergreen Valley College
Foothill College
Harvey Mudd College*
Mills College*
Pasadena City College
Pomona College
San Francisco Conservatory of Music
San Francisco State University
San Jose State University
Santa Monica College
Stanford University
University of Southern California
University of California, Berkeley
University of California, Davis
University of California, Irvine
University of California, Los Angeles
University of California, Riverside
University of California, San Diego
University of California, San Francisco
University of California, Santa Barbara
University of California, Santa Cruz
University of La Verne
West Coast University
William Carey International University*
Woodbury University
Colorado
Colorado School of Mines
Colorado State University
University of Colorado*
University of North Colorado*
Connecticut
Wesleyan University
Delaware
Delaware Technical and Community College*
University of Delaware
District of Columbia
Gallaudet College
George Washington University
Georgetown University
Southeastern University
University of the District of Columbia

*Indicates that the questionnaire was unusable.

Florida
  Florida State University
  Miami-Dade Community College
  University of Miami
Georgia
  Dekalb Community College
  Emory University
  Georgia State University
  Savannah State College
  University of Georgia
Hawaii
  Brigham Young University, Hawaii Campus
  Hawaii Pacific College
  University of Hawaii, Hilo*
  University of Hawaii, Honolulu
  East-West Center
Idaho
  Idaho State University
  University of Idaho
Illinois
  City Colleges of Chicago, The Loop College
  City Colleges of Chicago, Truman College
  Eastern Illinois University
  Loyola University of Chicago
  Northeastern Illinois University
  Northwestern University
  Roosevelt University
  Southern Illinois University
  University of Chicago
  University of Illinois, Champaign-Urbana
  University of Illinois at Chicago Circle
  Western Illinois University
Indiana
  Ball State University
  Indiana Institute of Technology*
  Indiana State University
  Indiana University
  University of Notre Dame
Iowa
  Iowa State University
  University of Iowa
Kansas
  Donelly College
  Fort Hays State University*
  Kansas State University
  Pittsburgh State University
  University of Kansas

  Wichita State University
Kentucky
  Berea College
  Kentucky Wesleyan College*
  Midway College
  University of Louisville
Louisiana
  University of Louisiana
  Louisiana State University
  University of Southwest Louisiana
Maryland
  Bowie State College*
  Johns Hopkins University
  Prince Georges Community College
  St. Mary's College of Maryland
Massachusetts
  Boston College
  Brandeis University
  Harvard University
  Massachusetts Institute of Technology
  Mount Holyoke College
  Northeastern University
  Pine Manor College*
  Radcliffe College
  Simmons College
  Slater International Center
  Southeastern Massachusetts University*
  Tufts University
  University of Massachusetts, Amherst
  Woods Hole Oceanographic Institute
Michigan
  Andrews University
  Eastern Michigan University
  Michigan State University
  Michigan Technological University
  Oakland University
  Saginaw Valley State College
  Siena State College
  University of Michigan
  Wayne State University
  Western Michigan University
Minnesota
  Carleton College
  Hamline University

---

*Indicates that the questionnaire was unusable.

Minnesota, *continued*
  Macalester College
  Mankato State University
  Moorhead State University*
  University of Minnesota
Mississippi
  Mississippi State University
  University of Mississippi
Missouri
  University of Missouri, Columbia
  University of Missouri, Kansas City
  Washington University
Montana
  Montana State University
  University of Montana
Nebraska
  University of Nebraska
  Union College
Nevada
  University of Nevada, Las Vegas*
  University of Nevada, Reno
New Jersey
  Bergen Community College
  Glassboro State College
  Middlesex County College
  New Jersey Institute of Technology*
  Princeton University
  Rutgers State University
  Seton Hall University
  Stevens Institute of Technology
New Mexico
  University of New Mexico
  New Mexico Institute of Mining and Technology
New York
  American Language/Cultural Institute
  CUNY College of Staten Island
  CUNY La Guardia Community College*
  CUNY City College
  Columbia University
  Cornell University
  Gloucester County College
  Hunter College*
  Mohawk Valley Community College
  New York University
  Pace University
  Rensselaer Polytechnic Institute
  Rochester Institute of Technology

Rockefeller University
Rockland Community College
SUNY College at Albany
SUNY College at Binghamton
SUNY College at Cortland
SUNY College at New Paltz
SUNY College at Stony Brook
SUNY Upstate Medical Center
University of Rochester
Vassar College
Yeshiva University
North Carolina
Appalachian State University
Bowman Gray School of Medicine
Duke University
North Carolina State University
Ohio
Bowling Green State University
Cuyahoga Community College
Oberlin College
Ohio State University
University of Dayton
University of Toledo*
Wright State University
Oklahoma
University of Oklahoma, Norman Campus
University of Tulsa
Oregon
Oregon Graduate Center, Beaverton
Oregon State University
Portland State University
University of Oregon
Pennsylvania
American Language Institute (Center for International Languages)
Bryn Mawr College
Bucknell University*
Carnegie-Mellon University
Edinboro University
Lehigh County Community College
Pennsylvania State University
Philadelphia College of Art
Point Park College
Temple University
University of Pittsburgh

---

*Indicates that the questionnaire was unusable.

Rhode Island
  Brown University
South Carolina
  Clemson University
South Dakota
  South Dakota School of Mines and Technology
Tennessee
  University of Tennessee
Texas
  Baylor College of Medicine
  Baylor University*
  Lamar University
  North Texas State University
  Rice University
  Texas A & M University
  Texas Christian University
  University of Houston, University Park
  Health Science Center, University of Texas, Houston
  University of Texas, Austin
  University of Texas, Dallas
Utah
  Brigham Young University
  University of Utah
  Utah State University
Vermont
  School for International Training, Brattleboro
  University of Vermont
Virginia
  Old Dominion University
Washington
  Institute for Intercultural Learning, Seattle
  Lower Columbia College
  North Seattle Community College
  Shoreline Community College
  University of Washington
  Walla Walla College*
  Washington State University
West Virginia
  Marshall University*
Wisconsin
  Medical College of Wisconsin, Milwaukee
  University of Wisconsin, Madison
  University of Wisconsin, Oshkosh

---

*Indicates that the questionnaire was unusable.

Institutions Responding to
Asian Studies Questionnaire

To obtain information about students and scholars traveling to China, the CSCPRC staff sent a survey in mid-1984 to 64 universities with Asian studies programs. Although only 50 percent of these questionnaires were returned, this survey is one of the few sources available on Americans visiting China for scholarly purposes. Following is a complete list of institutions that responded to the Asian studies questionnaire.

California
    California State University, Chico
    University of California, Berkeley
Connecticut
    Connecticut College
District of Columbia
    George Washington University
    School of Advanced International Studies,
        Johns Hopkins University
Hawaii
    Center for Asian and Pacific Studies
    University of Hawaii, Manoa
Iowa
    University of Iowa
Illinois
    University of Chicago
Kansas
    University of Kansas
Massachusetts
    Amherst College
Michigan
    Michigan State University
    Wayne State University
Missouri
    Washington University

Responding Institutions (*continued*)
New Hampshire
   Dartmouth College
New Jersey
   Princeton University
New York
   CUNY Hunter College
   Cornell University
   St. Johns University
   SUNY College at New Paltz
North Carolina
   Duke University
Ohio
   Oberlin College
   Wittenberg University
Pennsylvania
   University of Pennsylvania
Rhode Island
   Brown University
Tennessee
   Vanderbilt University
Texas
   University of Texas, Austin
Virginia
   University of Virginia
   Washington and Lee University
Washington
   University of Puget Sound
   University of Washington
Wisconsin
   University of Wisconsin

APPENDIX *D*

National Key Institutions

A significant percentage of Chinese students and scholars who were issued J-1 visas in 1983 (see Chapter 3 in this report) came from "key schools" in China—that is, from institutions that receive more money and better personnel from Chinese educational authorities and that have high priority in China's development scheme. Following is a list of those key institutions. *

Beijing Agricultural University
Beijing College of Aeronautics
Beijing College of Chemical
 Engineering
Beijing College of Chinese Medicine
Beijing College of Iron and Steel
 Technology
Beijing Foreign Language Institute
Beijing Institute of Foreign Trade
Beijing Institute of Forestry
Beijing Institute of Post and Telecom-
 munications
Beijing Institute of Technology
Beijing Medical College
Beijing Normal University
Beijing Physical Culture Institute
Beijing University
Central Academy of Fine Arts
Central China Agricultural Institute
Central China Institute of Technology
Central Institute for Nationalities

Central Music Conservatory
Central-South College of Mining and
 Metallurgy
Changchun College of Geology
Chengdu Institute of Telecommunica-
 tion Engineering
Chengdu University of Science and
 Technology
China Mining Institute
China University of Science and
 Technology
Chongqing Architectural Engineering
 Institute
Chongqing University
Dalian Institute of Technology
Dalian Merchant Marine Academy
Daqing Petroleum Institute
East China College of Chemical
 Engineering
East China Institute of Engineering

---

*This list is from Thomas Fingar, *Higher Education and Research in the People's Republic of China: Institutional Profiles*, U.S.–China Education Clearinghouse (Washington, D.C.: Committee on Scholarly Communication with the People's Republic of China and the National Association for Foreign Student Affairs, 1981), App. E, pp. 261–262.

National Key Institutions *(continued)*
East China Institute of Water
 Conservancy
East China Normal University
East China Petroleum Institute
Fudan University
Fuxin College of Mining
Harbin College of Shipbuilding
Harbin Institute of Technology
Hefei Polytechnical University
Hunan University
Inner Mongolia University
Jiangxi Agricultural University
Jilin Polytechnical University
Jilin University
Lanzhou University
Nanjing College of Aeronautics
Nanjing Institute of Meteorology
Nanjing Institute of Technology
Nanjing University
Nankai University
North China Institute of Agricultural
 Machinery
North China Institute of Electrical
 Power
North China Jiaotong University
Northeast College of Heavy
 Machinery
Northeast Institute of Technology
Northwest Agricultural College
Northwest China College of Light
 Industry
Northwest China Institute of Tele-
 communication Engineering
Northwest China Polytechnical
 University
Northwest China University
People's University of China
Qinghua University

Shandong College of Oceanology
Shandong University
Shanghai First Medical College
Shanghai Institute of Foreign
 Languages
Shanghai Jiaotong University
Shanghai Textile College
Shanxi Agricultural University
Shenyang Agricultural Institute
Shenyang Institute of Technology
Sichuan Medical College
Sichuan University
South China Agricultural College
South China College of Engineering
Southwest Agricultural College
Southwest China Jiaotong University
Southwest Institute of Law and
 Politics
Tianjin University
Tongji University
Wuhan Institute of Building Materials
Wuhan Institute of Geodesy, Photo-
 grammetry and Cartography
Wuhan Institute of Geology
Wuhan Institute of Water Conser-
 vancy and Electric Power
Wuhan University
Xiamen University
Xi'an Jiaotong University
Xiangtan University
Xinjiang University
Yunnan Forestry Institute
Yunnan University
Zhejiang University
Zhenjiang Institute of Agricultural
 Machinery
Zhongshan Medical College
Zhongshan University

Multivariate Analysis of the Determinants of Financial Aid Given to J-1 Visa Holders by the Chinese Government and American Universities

Tables E-1 and E-2 give the results of the multivariate analyses of the determinants of financial aid from American universities and the Chinese government for J-1 visa holders. The first column in each table lists the factors found to be significant determinants of the amount of money given each visa holder. The second column indicates the weight given to each factor. Because the dependent variable is the number of dollars provided per year, the "B" (Beta) coefficients in this column can be interpreted as the dollar amounts that should be added to or subtracted from the intercept given at the bottom of the table in order to derive an estimate of the amount of money a student with certain characteristics would be expected to receive. The third column shows t-statistics that indicate whether the coefficient in column 2 is significant. T-statistics larger than 1.96 indicate that the probability of obtaining a coefficient that large by chance is less than 5 percent. Since all the t-statistics shown are greater than 1.96, all factors listed are highly significant. When a sample is very large, as in the case $N = 19,859$, statistical significance is more frequently obtained.

The R^2 shown at the bottom of the table indicates the proportion of the variation in the amount of money received that could be explained by the available factors. For the analysis of the financial aid from the Chinese government, this was 13 percent; for the universities, it was 17 percent. This leaves a significant portion of the variation unexplained. However, given that the unit of analysis frequently was zero, and given the limited number of independent variables, these are quite satisfactory results.

Following are two specific examples of how characteristics of individuals would affect the amount of money each would have been expected to receive from an American university or the Chinese government.

These examples are intended to show how the same individual would have been evaluated differently for funding by the Chinese government and a U.S. university based on the data available to CSCPRC staff for 1979 to 1983.

Example 1:   *A new research scholar came to the United States to study engineering in 1981. He is 25 years old and has just graduated from a university in China.*

The intercept is given, followed by addition or subtraction of amounts based on the applicant's characteristics. As shown below, the applicant is expected to receive more money from the Chinese government than from the U.S. university.

	Chinese Government	*U.S. University*
Intercept	$2,981.67	$224.73
1981	−895.94	1,540.82
Age	−833.74	—
Research scholar	1,973.28	1,130.42
Engineering	2,313.86	−461.04
Expected level of funding	5,539.12	2,454.93

Example 2:   *A female university professor in China is a continuing student studying law on a J-1 visa. She is 38 years old, and is applying for funding in 1980.*

As shown below, this student would be expected to receive some support from a U.S. university, but nothing from the Chinese government. In fact, the predicted amount from the PRC is negative. (Anyone who would receive a negative estimated amount of funding would be very unlikely to have received any support from that particular source of funds.)

	Chinese Government	*U.S. University*
Intercept	$2,981.67	$224.73
1980	−775.88	996.73
Continuing	−631.09	287.50
Age	−1,267.30	—
Female	−637.49	209.27
Student	1,357.37	3,239.27
Law	−1,053.18	1,280.97
University professor	—	−1,243.15
Expected level of funding	−25.90	4,995.32

TABLE E-1   Determinants of the Yearly Amount of Money Given to a J-1 Student or Scholar by a U.S. University, 1979 Through 1983

Independent Variable	Estimate of B	t-statistic
Year		
1980	996.73	5.17
1981	1,540.82	8.80
1982	1,754.02	10.10
1983	1,703.61	9.83
Continuing student or scholar	287.50	4.29
Female	209.27	2.38
Category		
Student	3,239.27	20.24
Professor	2,610.27	12.14
Teacher	1,420.59	3.49
Research scholar	1,130.42	7.63
Field of study		
Agriculture	−967.61	−4.61
Architecture	−1,631.91	−3.17
Computer science	−879.72	−4.50
Engineering	−461.04	−3.72
Health sciences	1,508.57	10.17
Law	1,280.97	3.36
Life sciences	2,017.43	13.55
Mathematics	1,415.81	7.56
Physical sciences	2,208.23	17.64
Social sciences	643.89	3.49
Occupation		
Government official	−1,434.54	−9.92
University professor	−1,243.15	−11.37
Secondary teacher	−1,756.63	−4.98
Media	−1,323.87	−2.82
Business management	−1,705.98	−6.09
Other organization	−1,607.84	−10.89
Intercept	224.73	0.52
$R^2 = .167$		
Adjusted $R^2 = .166$, N = 19,859		

NOTE: Variables not found to be significant are not included.
SOURCE: USIA data tape.

TABLE E-2   Determinants of the Yearly Amount of Money Given to a J-1 Student or Scholar by the Chinese Government, 1979 Through 1983

Independent Variable	Estimate of B	t-statistic
Year		
1980	−775.88	−5.35
1981	−895.94	−6.60
1982	−1,086.54	−8.08
1983	−792.19	−5.90
Continuing student or scholar	−631.09	−12.17
Age in years	−33.35	−12.07
Female	−637.49	−9.49
Category		
Student	1,357.37	10.88
Professor	1,247.59	7.46
Teacher	1,957.77	6.26
Research scholar	1,973.28	17.07
Field of study		
Agriculture	1,569.54	9.69
American studies	−1,537.77	−2.27
Architecture	2,275.32	5.80
Computer science	1,721.11	13.05
Engineering	2,313.86	39.88
Humanities	343.68	2.29
Law	−1,053.18	−3.69
Library science	981.48	2.17
Occupation		
Agricultural worker	−2,205.72	−6.98
Intercept	2,981.67	14.90
$R^2 = .126$		
Adjusted $R^2 = .125$, N = 19,859		

NOTE: Variables not found to be significant are not included.
SOURCE: USIA data tape.

Responding American Philanthropic Organizations, Professional Associations, and Other Exchange Organizations

The CSCPRC staff sent requests for information on contributions to Sino-American educational exchanges to 51 foundations and 54 professional associations. Responses were received from the foundations and professional and other associations listed below.

RESPONDING PHILANTHROPIC AND OTHER EXCHANGE ORGANIZATIONS

The Ahmanson Foundation*
American Field Service
Asia Foundation
Asian Cultural Council
Atlantic Richfield Foundation
Center for U.S.–China Arts Exchange
China Medical Board of New York
Council on International Educational Exchange
The Cowles Foundation*
Geraldine R. Dodge Foundation
Exxon Education Foundation
The Ford Foundation
Foundation for Child Development
The Institute of International Education
International Foundation for Cancer Research*
The Kettering Foundation
The Luce Foundation
The Macy Foundation*
Mayo Foundation
The Mellon Foundation
Mennonite Central Committee (China Educational Exchange)
Merck Company Foundation*
National Committee on United States–China Relations, Inc.

---

*Not involved in Sino-American exchanges.

National Science Foundation (U.S.–China Program)
People-to-People Health Foundation (Project Hope Health Sciences)
The Rockefeller Brothers Fund
The Rockefeller Foundation
Arthur Sackler Foundation (Foundation for Nutritional Advancement)
The Sloan Foundation*
The Spencer Foundation
The Stanley Foundation*
Wang Institute of Graduate Studies
World Ministries Commission (Brethren Service Exchange Programs)
Yale–China Association

RESPONDING PROFESSIONAL ASSOCIATIONS

American Association for the Advancement of Science
American Association of Colleges for Teacher Education
American Association of State Colleges and Universities
American Bar Association
American Cancer Society
American Council on Education
American Institute of Chemists
American Library Association
American Physical Society
American Phytopathological Society
American Political Science Association
American Psychological Association
American Society for Engineering Education
American Society for Metals
American Society for Microbiology
IEEE (Computer Society)

OTHER RESPONDING ASSOCIATIONS

American Association of University Professors*
American Educational Research Association*
American Society of Agricultural Engineers*
American Society of Animal Science*
American Society of Parasitologists*
American Sociological Association*
The Ecological Society of America*
Entomological Society of America*
The Wildlife Society*

---

*Not involved in Sino-American exchanges.

Protocols and Memoranda of Understanding Under the U.S.–PRC Agreement on Cooperation in Science and Technology

The following list of U.S.–Chinese government protocols and memorandums of understanding is based on information provided by the U.S. Department of State in November 1984. This information was updated when this report was written. (Abbreviation key follows listings.)

Agreement:	Understanding on Exchange of Students and Scholars
Date signed:	October 1978, Exchange Letter of January 1979
Date extended:	Unlimited
U.S. agency:	USIA, DOE, NSF, NAS, NEH
Chinese unit:	MOE, CASS, SSTC

Agreement:	Understanding on Agricultural Exchange
Date signed:	November 1978
Date extended:	Unlimited
U.S. agency:	USDA, USGS, and DOI/Fish and Wildlife Service
Chinese unit:	Ministry of Agriculture, Animal Husbandry and Fisheries

Agreement:	Understanding on Space Technology (overall protocol on Space Science Application and Technology currently under negotiation)
Date signed	January 31, 1979
Date extended:	Unlimited
U.S. agency:	NASA
Chinese unit:	Chinese Academy of Space Technology (under the Ministry of Astronautics) and CAS

Agreement:	Implementing Accord on Cooperation in the Field of High Energy Physics
Date signed:	January 31, 1979
Date extended:	February 1984
Date expires:	February 1989
Annexes and dates:	Annex June 12, 1979, Joint Committee Reports 1979–1980, 1980–1981, 1982–1983
U.S. agency:	DOE
Chinese unit:	CAS (formerly signed with SSTC)

Agreement: Protocol on Cooperation in the Field of Metrology and
                  Standards
Date signed: May 8, 1979
Date extended: May 8, 1984
Date expires: May 8, 1989
Annexes and dates: Annex (1), May 8, 1979; Annex (2), May 5, 1981
                  (supersedes Annex (1)). (Annexes do not apply to
                  extension.)
U.S. agency: DOC (National Bureau of Standards)
Chinese unit: State Bureau of Metrology and State Bureau of
                  Standardization

Agreement: Protocol on Cooperation in the Field of Atmospheric
                  Science and Technology
Date signed: May 8, 1979
Date extended: May 1984
Date expires: May 1989
Annexes and dates: Annex (1), May 1979; Annex (2), May 1979; Annex
                  (3), September 1980; Annex (4), September 1980;
                  Annex (5), November 1981; Annex (6), November
                  1981
U.S. agency: NOAA, NSF, NASA, USDA
Chinese unit: State Meteorological Administration

Agreement: Protocol on the Field of Marine and Fishery Science
                  and Technology
Date signed: May 8, 1979
Date extended: May 1984
Date expires: May 1989
Annexes and dates: Annex (1), May 1979; Annex (2), Working Group
                  Meeting 1980; Annex (3), Working Group Meeting
                  1982; Annex (4), Working Group Meeting 1984
U.S. agency: NOAA, NSF
Chinese unit: National Bureau of Oceanography and Ministry of
                  Agriculture, Animal Husbandry and Fisheries

Agreement: Protocol on Cooperation in the Sciences and
                  Technology of Medicine and Public Health
Date signed: June 22, 1979
Date extended: Extension under negotiation
Date expired: June 22, 1984
Annexes and dates: Annex (1), November 1980; Annex (2), November
                  1980; Annex (3), January 1982
U.S. agency: HHS (NIH)
Chinese unit: Ministry of Public Health

Agreement: Protocol on Cooperation in Hydroelectric Power and Related Water Resource Management

Date signed: August 28, 1979

Date extended: Expired; no plans for extension

Date expired: August 28, 1984

Annexes and dates: Annex (1), March 1980; Annex (2), September 1982

U.S. agency: DOC, DOI (Bureau of Reclamation, Corps of Engineers, Tennessee Valley Authority)

Chinese unit: Chinese Ministry of Water Resources and Electric Power

Agreement: Protocol for Scientific and Technical Cooperation in the Earth Sciences

Date signed: January 24, 1980

Date extended: January 24, 1985

Date expires: January 24, 1990

Annexes and dates: Annex (1), Patents, November 1981; Annex (2); Annex (3); Annex (4), Copyrights; Annex (5); Annex (6) Working Group Meeting 1984

U.S. agency: DOI (USGS) and NSF

Chinese unit: Chinese Academy of Geological Sciences

Agreement: Protocol for Scientific and Technical Cooperation in Earthquake Studies

Date signed: January 24, 1980

Date extended: January 24, 1985

Date expires: January 23, 1990

Annexes and dates: Annexes (1–8)

U.S. agency: USGS and NSF

Chinese unit: Chinese State Seismological Bureau

Agreement: Protocol for Scientific and Technical Cooperation in the Field of Environmental Protection

Date signed: February 5, 1980

Date extended: February 1985

Date expires: February 1989

Annexes and dates: Annexes (1–3)

U.S. agency: Environmental Protection Agency

Chinese unit: Office of the Environmental Protection Leading Group

Agreement: Protocol on Cooperation in the Basic Sciences

Date signed: December 10, 1980

Date expired: December 1985

Annexes and dates: Annex (1), Patents and Copyrights, March 1981

U.S. agency: NSF

Chinese unit: CAS and CASS

Agreement: Protocol on Cooperation in the Field of Building
                        Construction and Urban Planning Science and
                        Technology
Date signed: October 17, 1981
Date expires: October 1986
Annexes and dates: Annex (1)
U.S. agency: Department of Housing and Urban Development
Chinese unit: Ministry of Urban and Rural Construction and
                        Environmental Protection

Agreement: Protocol on Cooperation in Nuclear Safety Matters
Date signed: October 17, 1981
Date expires: October 1986
U.S. agency: NRC
Chinese unit: National Nuclear Safety Administration (formerly
                        SSTC)

Agreement: Protocol on Scientific and Technical Cooperation in
                        the Study of Surface Water Hydrology
Date signed: October 17, 1981
Date expires: October 1986
Annexes and dates: Annexes (1–4), 1983; Annexes (5–6), 1985
U.S. agency: DOI (USGS)
Chinese unit: Bureau of Hydrology (under the Ministry of Water
                        Conservancy)

Agreement: Cooperation in the Fields of Nuclear Physics and
                        Controlled Magnetic Fusion Research
Date signed: May 11, 1983
Date expires: May 1988
Annexes and dates: Annexes (1–5), 1985
U.S. agency: DOE
Chinese unit: SSTC

Agreement: Cooperation in Aeronautical Science and Technology
Date signed: May 11, 1983
Date expires: May 1988
Annexes and dates: Annex (1), Copyrights, April 5, 1985; Annex (2), April
                        5, 1985
U.S. agency: NASA
Chinese unit: Chinese Aeronautical Establishment (under the
                        Ministry of Aeronautics)

Agreement:	Protocol on Cooperation in Science and Technology of Transportation
Date signed:	May 11, 1983
Date expires:	May 1988
U.S. agency:	Department of Transportation
Chinese unit:	Ministry of Communications
Agreement:	Protocol on Cooperation in the Field of Scientific and Technical Information
Date signed:	May 8, 1979
Date extended:	April 30, 1984
Date expires:	April 1989
Annexes and dates:	Annex (1); Annexes (2–4), February 8, 1982
U.S. agency:	DOC (NTIS)
Chinese unit:	ISTIC (under SSTC)
Agreement:	Cooperation in the Field of Management of Industrial Science and Technology
Date signed:	May 1979
Date extended:	April 1984
Date expires:	April 1989
U.S. agency:	DOC
Chinese unit:	State Economic Commission, SSTC, MOE
Agreement:	Protocol on Cooperation in Statistics
Date signed:	July 24, 1984
Date expires:	July 1989
U.S. agency:	DOC (Bureau of the Census)
Chinese unit:	State Statistical Bureau
Agreement:	Memorandum of Understanding on Cooperation in the Basic Biomedical Sciences
Date signed:	May 11, 1983
Date extended:	Automatic extension (Article 8)
Date expires:	May 1988
U.S. agency:	NIH
Chinese unit:	CAS
Agreement:	Protocol for Scientific and Technical Cooperation in Surveying and Mapping Studies
Date signed:	April 16, 1985
Annexes and dates:	Annex (1), 1985
U.S. agency:	USGS/Defense Mapping Agency
Chinese unit:	National Bureau of Surveying and Mapping (under SSTC)

Agreement: Protocol on Cooperation in the Field of Fossil Energy
                         Research and Development
Date signed: April 16, 1985
Annexes and dates: Annex (1), 1985
U.S. agency: DOE
Chinese unit: Ministry of Coal Industry

Under Negotiation

Agreement: Landsat Ground Station Memorandum of
                         Understanding
U.S. agency: DOC (NOAA/NESDIS)
Chinese unit: CAS

Agreement: Telecommunications
U.S. agency: DOC
Chinese unit: Ministry of Post and Telecommunications

Agreement: Health Memorandum of Understanding between the
                         Center for Disease Control and the China National
                         Center for Preventative Medicine
U.S. agency: HHS (PHS and CDC)
Chinese unit: China National Center for Preventative Medicine

ABBREVIATION KEY

U.S. agencies: **CDC**—Centers for Disease Control; **DOC**—Department of
Commerce; **DOE**—Department of Energy; **DOI**—Department of the Interior;
HHS—Department of Health and Human Services; **NAS**—National Academy
of Sciences; **NASA**—National Aeronautics and Space Administration; **NBS**—
National Bureau of Standards; **NEH**—National Endowment for the Humani-
ties; **NESDIS**—National Environmental Satellite Data and Information
Service; **NIH**—National Institutes of Health; **NOAA**—National Oceanic and
Atmospheric Administration; **NRC**—Nuclear Regulatory Commission; **NSF**—
National Science Foundation; **NTIS**—National Technical Information Service;
PHS—Public Health Service; **USDA**—U.S. Department of Agriculture;
USGS—U.S. Geological Survey; **USIA**—U.S. Information Agency.

Chinese units: **CAS**—Chinese Academy of Sciences; **CASS**—Chinese Academy
of Social Sciences; **ISTIC**—Institute of Science and Technology Information of
China; **MOE**—Ministry of Education; **SSTC**—State Science and Technology
Commission.

CSCPRC Programs, 1972–1985

Programs of the Committee on Scholarly Communication with the People's Republic of China, 1972 Through 1985

Year	To China	From China
DELEGATIONS (BY SUBJECT AREA, 1972–1979)		
1972	None	Medicine Science (interdisciplinary)
1973	CSCPRC (interdisciplinary) Medicine (interdisciplinary) Art and Archaeology Early Childhood Education	Hydrotechnology High Energy Physics Insect Hormones Library Science Computer Science Biomedical Engineering and Physiology of Pain Language Teaching
1974	Acupuncture Anesthesia Herbal Pharmacology Plant Studies Seismology Linguistics	Seismology Laser Research Agriculture Pharmacology Plant Photosynthesis
1975	Schistosomiasis Paleoanthropology Rural Small-Scale Industry Insect Control Solid State Physics	Solid State Physics Molecular Biology Communications Techniques Petrochemical Industry Scientific and Technical Association Industrial Automation
1976	Pure and Applied Mathematics Wheat Studies Liaoning Earthquake Prediction Steroid Chemistry and Biochemistry	Earthquake Engineering Tumor Immunology Agricultural Mechanization Environmental Science Astronomy

(Continued)

Year	To China	From China
1977	Vegetable Farming Systems	Chemistry
	CSCPRC (interdisciplinary)	Hematite Ore Beneficiation
	Cancer	Metrology
	Astronomy	Geological Drilling Equipment and
	Applied Linguistics	Techniques
	Chinese Painting	Tunnel Boring
		Citrus
1978	Pure and Applied Chemistry	Marine Sciences
	Rural Health Systems	Fertilizer Development Centers
	Earthquake Engineering and Hazards	Nuclear and Plasma Physics
	Reduction	Animal Feedstuffs
	Engineering Education	Light Construction Materials
	Han Dynasty Culture	Science and Technology
	Oceanography	
1979	Nuclear Physics	Chinese Academy of Social Sciences
	Ming-Qing History	Remote Sensing
	Animal Sciences	New Energy Sources
	Plate Tectonics	Theoretical and Applied Mechanics
	Economics	Materials Science

SYMPOSIA AND DELEGATIONS, 1979–1985

Year	To China	From China
1979	Polymer Chemistry and Polymer Physics Symposium	Pharmacology Symposium
1980	Chinese Social and Economic History Symposium	Chinese Academy of Sciences Delegation
	Partial Differential Equations and Differential Geometry Symposium	Chinese Academy of Social Sciences Graduate Studies Delegation
	NAE Delegation	Mathematics
		Alternative Strategies for Economic Development Conference
		CAST Delegation
1981	Social Science/Humanities Planning Commission	Surface Science Symposium
	Development Strategy Workshop	CAST Delegation
	Partial Differential Equations and Differential Geometry Symposium	
	Phycology Symposium	
1982	Science Policy Study Group	Nitrogen Fixation Symposium
	Mountain Meteorology Symposium	International Conference on Shang Civilization
	Biocontrol of Insects Symposium	
	Biomass Conversion Technologies Symposium	

Year	To China	From China
1983	Comparative Literature Symposium	Science Policy Conference
		American Studies Conference
		CAST Delegation
		Psychology Conference
		Geochemistry Delegation
1984	Sociology/Anthropology Delegation	Economics Delegation
	American Studies Delegation	Renewable Resources Symposium
	CAS-NAS Presidential	
	Visit/Biotechnology Delegation	
1985	Science Policy Workshop	Computer Recognition of Chinese
	Sedimentary Basins Workshop	Characters Conference
		American Studies Conference
		Sociology/Anthropology Workshop

World Bank Group Education Projects in China

Summarized on the following page are the first 11 projects related to education in China, current as of February 1, 1985; 4 were effective, 2 others had been approved by the Bank's Board of Directors, 1 more had been negotiated, another appraised, and the final 3 were in various stages of the project cycle. The loan/credit amounts total over $1 billion and total project costs over $3.5 billion.

World Bank Group Education Projects in China

Project Name	Numbers Loan/Credit	Amounts in U.S.$ (millions)			Total Cost (U.S. $ millions)	Years	Ministry[a]
		Loan	Credit	Total			
Active							
1. University Development I	2,021/1,167	100	100	200	295	1981–86	MOE
2. Agricultural Education and Research I	1,297	—	75	75	201	1982–88	MAAF
3. Polytechnic/TV University	1,411	—	85	85	206	1983–89	MOE
4. Agricultural Education II	2,444/1,500	45	24	69	175	1984–89	MAAF
5. Rural Health and Medical Education	1,472	—	85[b]	85	290	1984–89	MOPH
6. Agricultural Research II	1,516	—	25	25	59	1984–89	MAAF
Soon to Start							
7. University Development II		—		145	1,385[c]	1985–90	MOE
Future							
8. Provincial Universities		—	150	150	400	1986–90	MOE
9. Technical Education		—	130	130	230	1987–91	MOE/MOLP
10. Instructional Materials Curriculum Design and Production and Computer Education		—	60	60	180	1987–92	MOE
11. Innovative Graduate Curricula		—	140	140	300	1988–92	MOE

[a]MOE = Ministry of Education; MAAF = Ministry of Agriculture, Animal Husbandry, and Fisheries; MOPH = Ministry of Public Health; MOLP = Ministry of Labor and Personnel.
[b]Of which $43 million is for medical education.
[c]Total higher education investment plan.

APPENDIX *J*

Chinese Language Study Programs in the PRC

The CSCPRC/staff identified 16 American institutions that sponsor language programs in China. (This list may not be all-inclusive.) Part I (below) lists these institutions together with the Chinese institution at which the programs are located. Part II indicates which of these have summer-semester programs and which have fall and winter/spring programs.

PART I

American Institute for Foreign Study	Beijing Language Institute
	Beijing University
CET	Beijing Foreign Language Institute
Council on International Educational Exchange (CIEE)	Beijing University
	Nanjing University
	Fudan University
Duke University	Beijing Normal College
	Nanjing University
Foundation for American-Chinese Cultural Exchanges	East China Normal University
	Shanghai Jiaotong University
Hofstra University	East China University
Institute of China Studies	Shanghai University
Michigan State University	Northwest University
Pomona College	Nanjing University
Rosemont College	East China Normal University
Rutgers University	Jilin University
St. Mary's College of Maryland	Fudan University
State University of New York, Albany	Beijing Language Institute
	Beijing Normal College
	Beijing University
	Fudan University
	Nankai University
	Nanjing University

244

University of California, Los Angeles	Beijing Language Institute
	Zhongshan University
University of Massachusetts	Beijing Foreign Language Institute
	Beijing Normal College
	Fudan University
	Shaanxi Normal University
University of Minnesota	Nankai University

PART II

Summer-Semester Programs

American Institute for Foreign Study	Beijing Language Institute
CET	Beijing Foreign Language Institute
CIEE	Beijing University
	Fudan University
Duke University	Beijing Normal College
Foundation for American-Chinese	East China Normal College
Cultural Exchanges	Shanghai Jiaotong University
Hofstra University	East China University
Institute of China Studies	Shanghai University
Michigan State University	Northwest University
Rosemont College	East China Normal College
Rutgers University	Jilin University
University of Minnesota	Nankai University

Fall- and Winter/Spring-Semester Programs

American Institute for Foreign Study	Beijing University (fall only)
CET	Beijing Foreign Language Institute
CIEE	Beijing University
	Nanjing University (fall only)
Duke University	Nanjing University (fall only)
Hofstra University	East China University
Pomona College	Nanjing University (winter/spring only)
St. Mary's College of Maryland	Fudan University
State University of New York, Albany	Beijing University
	Beijing Language Institute
	Beijing Normal College
	Nankai University
	Nanjing University
	Fudan University

(Continued)

University of California, Los Angeles	Beijing Language Institute
	Zhongshan University
University of Massachusetts	Beijing Normal College
	Beijing Foreign Language Institute
	Fudan University
	Shaanxi Normal College

Authors of Commissioned Papers

Agriculture:

SYLVAN H. WITTWER, Director Emeritus
Agricultural Experiment Station
Michigan State University

Cancer (Epidemiology) Research:

RONALD GLASER
Department of Medical Microbiology and Immunology
Ohio State University Medical Center

Economics:

TERRY SICULAR
Food Research Institute
Stanford University

Physics:

JOSEPH BIRMAN
Department of Physics, City College of New York
Chairman, American Coordinating Committee
American Physical Society

Seismology:

BRUCE BOLT
Seismographic Station
University of California at Berkeley

APPENDIX *L*

Restricted Classes and Conferences

Following is a list of classes and conferences held in the United States between August 1982 and January 1986 at which attendance was closed to non-U.S. citizens.* The list is not necessarily comprehensive, but does include instances of which CSCPRC staff is aware.

Date	Class or Conference
January 1986	Society of Manufacturing Engineers Annual Conference Will have some closed sessions
March 1985	Society for the Advancement of Material and Process Engineering Anaheim, California Advancing technology in materials; 4 of 39 sessions will be open only to U.S. citizens
January 1985	Society of Manufacturing Engineers Anaheim, California "Composites in Manufacturing" Attended by over 500, and all required to submit proof of U.S. citizenship
November 1984	Government Microcircuit Applications Conference Las Vegas, Nevada Attendance restricted
October 1984	Society for the Advancement of Material and Process Engineering Albuquerque, New Mexico 4 of 20 sessions restricted to U.S. citizens (carbon carbon and metal matrix)
October 1984	American Astronautical Society Palo Alto, California 31st National Conference Space Propulsion for the 90s Secret session on SDI, restricted to U.S. citizens with security clearance

*Source of list: Robert Park, Public Affairs, American Physical Society.

Date	*Class or Conference*
June 1984	University of California, Los Angeles
	Short Course on Metal Matrix Composites
	Restricted to U.S. citizens
May 1984	American Institute of Aeronautics and Astronautics
	Palm Spings, California
	"Structural Dynamics and Materials"
	Closed to foreigners
January 1984	American Ceramics Society
	Florida
	Composite Materials Conference
	Sponsored by the Department of Defense and NASA
	Restricted to U.S. citizens
March 1983	University of Maryland
	Short Course on Metal Matrix Composites
	U.S. citizenship required
August 1982	Society of Photo-Optical Instrumentation Engineers
	San Diego, California
	26th Annual Technical Symposium
	100 of 700 papers withdrawn, first major incident

Glossary

F-1 VISA. The type of visa issued to foreign citizens who want to study in the United States at any level of school from precollege to graduate study. To qualify, a person must receive an I-20 form from an American institution that shows that they intend to pursue a full course of study in a field for which they qualify. Students with F-1 visas have usually developed their plan to study on their own or with the help of overseas relatives. In China, most persons who are sponsored by the PRC government receive J-1 visas, which denote a higher level of scholarship than the F-1 visas. The U.S. Department of State defines an F-1 visa as one issued to

an alien having a residence in a foreign country which he has no intention of abandoning, who is a bona fide student qualified to pursue a full course of study and who seeks to enter the United States temporarily and solely for the purpose of pursuing such a course of study at an established institution of learning or other recognized place of study in the United States, particularly designated by him and approved by the Attorney General after consultation with the Office of Education of the United States, which institution or place of study shall have agreed to report to the Attorney General the termination of attendance of each nonimmigrant student, and if any such institution of learning or place of study fails to make reports promptly the approval shall be withdrawn. . . .

F-2 VISA. The type of visa issued to family members of a person holding an F-1 visa.

I-20. A form issued to applicants for F-1 visas, which documents that they have been accepted into a program offering a full course of study. This form is issued by the school administering the program and must be presented when applying for an F-1 visa.

IAP-66. A form issued to applicants for J-1 visas, which documents that they qualify under one of the programs designated by the United States Information Agency (USIA). This form is issued by the school or other institution, such as a hospital, and must be presented when applying for a J-1 visa.

J-1 VISA. The type of visa issued to persons who qualify under a program designated by USIA. Unlike the F-1 visas, the J-1 visas are not issued only to students, but also to several other categories of visitors, including research scholars, teachers, trainees, and international visitors. To receive a J-1 visa, an applicant must possess a valid IAP-66 form. Persons issued a J-1 visa are considered to possess a higher level of scholarship than those issued an F-1 visa, and they generally are subject to the "two-year rule" (q.v.). The U.S. Department of State defines a J-1 visa as one issued to

> an alien having a residence in a foreign country which he has no intention of abandoning who is a bona fide student, scholar, trainee, teacher, professor, research assistant, specialist, or leader in a field of specialized knowledge or skill, or other person of similar description, who is coming temporarily to the United States as a participant in a program designated by the Secretary of State, for the purpose of teaching, instructing or lecturing, studying, observing, conducting research, consulting, demonstrating special skills, or receiving training and who, if he is coming to the United States to participate in a program under which he will receive graduate medical education or training, also meets the requirements of section 212(j) [the two-year rule]. . . .

J-2 VISA. The type of visa issued to family members of a person holding a J-1 visa.

NATIONAL KEY INSTITUTION. A designation used in China identifying the institutions of higher learning considered most vital to the modernization of China. Key institutions receive more money and preference in acquiring personnel and high-quality students.

OFFICIALLY SPONSORED. Refers to those PRC students and scholars who have been chosen to come to the United States by the Chinese government and/or subordinate organizations. Most J-1 visa holders are officially sponsored, but some are not. And while most F-1 visa holders are *not* officially sponsored, there are also a few exceptions. Official sponsorship does not necessarily mean that the Chinese government is paying the expenses of the student or scholar; many of them have fellowships and scholarships from American sources.

RESEARCH OR VISITING SCHOLAR. A category of J-1 visa holder who comes to the United States to study and do research but who does not enroll in a degree program. Research or visiting scholars may go to research institutions rather than to universities. They tend to be older than "students."

SELF-SUPPORTING. Students and scholars who come to the United States from China without being chosen by the Chinese government. They are most commonly F-1 visa holders, although some J-1 students and scholars have also made their own arrangements. The money for their support usually comes from overseas relatives, although they also may qualify for scholarships and fellowships from American institutions.

TWO-YEAR RULE. An American legal regulation that applies to some persons issued J-1 visas, which requires that the person reside outside of the United States for two years following the time in which they held a J-1 visa in the United States before they are eligible to apply for an immigrant visa or certain categories of nonimmigrant visas. The consular officer who issues the J-1 visa makes a determination at the time of visa issuance as to whether the person has received aid from the United States government or the Chinese government. If they have received such aid, they are subject to the two-year rule.

Index

255

WITH GENTLENESS, HUMOR AND LOVE

A 12-Step Guide For Adult Children
In Recovery

Kathleen W. and Jewell E.

Health Communications, Inc.
Deerfield Beach, Florida

Kathleen W.
Jewell E.
Eureka, California

©1989 Kathleen W. and Jewell E.
ISBN 0-932194-77-X

Publisher: Health Communications, Inc.
          3201 S.W. 15th Street
          Deerfield Beach, Florida 33442